Algorithmic Harm

Algorithmic Harm

Protecting People in the Age of Artificial Intelligence

OREN BAR-GILL
AND
CASS R. SUNSTEIN

OXFORD
UNIVERSITY PRESS

Oxford University Press is a department of the University of Oxford. It furthers the University's objective of excellence in research, scholarship, and education by publishing worldwide. Oxford is a registered trade mark of Oxford University Press in the UK and in certain other countries.

Published in the United States of America by Oxford University Press
198 Madison Avenue, New York, NY 10016, United States of America.

CIP data is on file at the Library of Congress

ISBN 9780197778203
ISBN 9780197778197 (hbk.)

DOI: 10.1093/oso/9780197778197.001.0001

Paperback printed by Integrated Books International, United States of America

Hardback printed by Bridgeport National Bindery, Inc., United States of America

The manufacturer's authorised representative in the EU for product safety is Oxford University Press España S.A. of El Parque Empresarial San Fernando de Henares, Avenida de Castilla, 2 – 28830 Madrid (www.oup.es/en or product.safety@oup.com). OUP España S.A. also acts as importer into Spain of products made by the manufacturer.

Oren dedicates this book to Sigal, Noam, Guy, and Elrond

Cass dedicates this book to the memory of Daniel Kahneman

I can stroke your body and relieve your pain
And charm the whistle off an evening train

—Bob Dylan, "Silvio"

There's a sucker born every minute.

—Attributed (falsely) to P. T. Barnum

Contents

Acknowledgments

We have many people to thank. This book grew out of an article co-authored with the computer scientist Inbal Talgam-Cohen: Oren Bar-Gill, Cass R. Sunstein, & Inbal Talgam-Cohen. 2023. "Algorithmic Harm in Consumer Markets." *Journal of Legal Analysis*, 15(1): 1–47. We are grateful to Inbal for teaching us about AI-powered algorithms. For helpful comments and conversations, we thank Jennifer Arlen, Ian Ayres, Scott Baker, Todd Baker, Sagit Bar-Gill, Omri Ben-Shahar, Ryan Bubb, Emiliano Catan, Kevin Davis, Ben Eidelson, Merritt Fox, Jens Frankenreiter, Meirav Furth, Brian Galle, Talia Gillis, Shafi Goldwasser, Zohar Goshen, Moshe Halbertal, Assaf Hamdani, Sharon Hannes, Scott Hemphill, Rebecca Hollander-Blumoff, Sam Issacharoff, Howell Jackson, Marcel Kahan, Louis Kaplow, Avery Katz, Pauline Kim, Jon Kleinberg, Lewis Kornhauser, Tamar Kricheli-Katz, Claire Lazar Reich, Daryl Levinson, Jens Ludwig, Florencia Marotta-Wurgler, Sendhil Mullainathan, Aileen Nielsen, Julian Nyarko, Gal Oestreicher-Singer, Mitch Polinsky, Haggai Porat, Lucia Reisch, Ricky Revesz, Ed Rock, Sarath Sanga, Alan Schwartz, Steve Shavell, Yonadav Shavit, Holger Spamann, Jeff Strnad, Neel Sukhatme, Eric Talley, Josh Teitelbaum, Andrew Tuch, Rory Van Loo, Abe Wickelgren, Inbal Yahav Shenberger, Eyal Zamir, and workshop and conference participants at Columbia, Georgetown, Harvard, NYU, Stanford, Tel Aviv University, Washington University in St. Louis, the 2022 Annual Meeting of the American Law and Economics Association, the 2024 Annual Meeting of the Spanish Law and Economics Association, the 2024 Mapping and Governing the Online World conference, and the 2024 Annual Meeting of the Berlin Center for Consumer Policies. Andy Gu, Ethan Judd, Rachel Neuburger, Davy Perlman, and Cecilia Wu provided excellent research assistance.

We are also grateful to the Harvard Law School Initiative on Artificial Intelligence and the Law, based at the Berkman Klein Center. Dean (and now Provost) John Manning and Dean John Goldberg provided valuable support.

Introduction

We are in the midst of an explosion in the use of artificial intelligence (AI).[1] Sellers and service providers are increasingly using AI-powered algorithms to promote the sale of goods and services. On your Facebook page you can likely find advertisements that have been selected specifically for you, given what the relevant algorithm knows about you. For example, one of us (Sunstein) is finding advertisements for a Men's Micro Fleece Pullover and for DoorDash ("fried or die chicken"). On the basis of what it knows about Sunstein, the algorithm thinks that he is likely to be interested in both items.

This particular algorithm did not get Sunstein's tastes quite right (he doesn't like the idea of "fried or die chicken"), but many such uses of algorithms should greatly benefit consumers. Suppose that algorithms can accurately predict what goods and services people will buy and at what price. If algorithms give people information about beneficial healthcare products that are ideally suited to their particular situations (say, diabetes or heart disease), consumers should be able to gain a great deal.[2] With respect to health problems, people often lack relevant information, and if an algorithm can steer them toward products that will help, they will be better off (bracketing privacy issues).

But other uses of algorithms should not be welcomed. Suppose that the seller's AI exploits a lack of information on the part of identifiable people so as to induce them to buy ineffective baldness cures or dietary supplements or pointless insurance policies, or to overpay for valuable goods and services. Or suppose that the seller's AI is aware that certain people suffer from specific behavioral biases. Perhaps they are unrealistically optimistic (and hence suffer from "optimism bias"); perhaps they focus on the short term (and hence suffer from "present bias"); and perhaps these biases lead them to overestimate the benefit from a product or service. If an algorithm can exploit behavioral biases, it will essentially take people's money and engage in what might be seen as a form of theft.

We use the term "algorithmic harm" to capture this kind of injury. We catalog the different ways in which AI algorithms are being or may be used in consumer markets and identify the market conditions under which these uses harm consumers. We then identify legal responses that can

Algorithmic Harm. Oren Bar-Gill and Cass R. Sunstein, Oxford University Press. © Oren Bar-Gill and Cass R. Sunstein (2025). DOI: 10.1093/oso/9780197778197.003.0001

reduce algorithmic harm. Our primary focus is on consumer markets. But much of the analysis—including the descriptive, normative, and prescriptive components—applies also to labor markets, where employers use AI in making hiring and wage-setting decisions. We will explore that problem. A less direct but equally important application is to political markets, where AI is used to influence demand for certain candidates, parties, or policies. AI can have horrific effects on the political process; it can undermine (and is now undermining) democracy itself.

A. Categories of Harm

The increasing use of AI algorithms in consumer markets and beyond gives rise to an ever-expanding list of possible harms. We offer a taxonomy of algorithmic harms, focusing on the decision that the algorithm is asked to make. In markets, the algorithm will generally be asked to maximize profits. The question is what decisions—decisions that affect profits—are placed in the algorithm's "hands." A major set of decisions that is increasingly allocated to algorithms involves *pricing*. Another important category of decisions relates to *targeting*, namely, deciding what type of product will be offered to a particular consumer or group of consumers. The decision can be a choice from existing items in the seller's product line or perhaps even a decision to invest in expanding the product line or shifting to a different product line.

We thus consider (1) algorithmic price discrimination and (2) algorithmic targeting. The essence of both categories is *differentiation*: the AI system sets different prices for different consumers or targets different products to different consumers. Such differentiation is fueled by individual-level data that is fed into the algorithm; for example, the AI may learn that an individual consumer is a tennis fan and thus would be willing to pay a high price for Wimbledon tickets, or that an individual consumer is worried and risk-averse and would be willing to pay a high price for certain insurance policies. We characterize the incidence of algorithmic harm for each category. To do so, we organize the analysis, for each category, into a 2×2 matrix. See Table I.1.

The two rows distinguish between two types of consumer markets—one that is populated by sophisticated consumers who are reasonably well-informed and make rational decisions (S markets) and another that is populated by unsophisticated consumers who suffer from significant information

Table I.1 General Framework for Analyzing Algorithmic Harm

	No Differentiation (Pre-AI World)	**Differentiation (AI World)**
Sophisticated Consumers	S Benchmark	Algorithmic Benefit
Unsophisticated Consumers	U Benchmark	Algorithmic Harm

and rationality deficits (U markets). Of course, these are theoretical archetypes, and we are dealing with a continuum, not a dichotomy. Real-world markets are populated by a mix of more sophisticated and less sophisticated consumers. Nevertheless, dividing the analysis in this way is useful as we explore the extent to which algorithmic harm depends on deviations from perfect information and perfect rationality.

As a practical matter, policymakers might well be able to distinguish between markets where the majority of consumers are more sophisticated and markets where the majority of consumers are less sophisticated. Note that the S versus U distinction is really about the likelihood of mistakes. This depends not only on consumer characteristics, that is, how sophisticated the consumers are in this market, but also on market or product characteristics. Some products are more complex, making it more likely that even relatively sophisticated consumers will make mistakes. (Compare the market for milk cartons to the mortgage market.) At the same time, relatively unsophisticated consumers might not make mistakes when choosing among simple products (e.g., whether to buy apples or oranges). Policymakers should focus on markets for complex products and services, where the likelihood of mistakes is greater.[3] When we speak of S consumers or U consumers, we should be understood to be using shorthand for the likelihood of mistakes.

For each type of consumer market (i.e., for each row in Table I.1), we start with the "No Differentiation" benchmark—a pre-AI world, where sellers offer the same product at the same price to everyone: medicines, clothing, laptops, food, hair loss treatments. We then compare this benchmark to a world where large data sets and AI algorithms allow for at least some degree of "Differentiation." In some cases, we even posit a science-fiction world of "Full Differentiation," where algorithms can perfectly identify each consumer's preferences and perceptions and offer a different product or set an individualized price for every consumer. The science-fiction world might of course be on the way. Our overarching conclusion will be that algorithmic differentiation is generally beneficial in S markets but often harmful in U markets.[4]

This conclusion relates to prior work on consumer harm that predates the rise of AI. First, differentiation was hardly discovered or invented yesterday, or the day before. On the contrary, some kinds of differentiation occurred long before AI algorithms were commonplace. Companies have long tried to market certain goods to certain populations—women rather than men, old rather than young, New Yorkers rather than Texans, Italians rather than Germans, Parisians rather than Londoners, Chinese rather than Russians, city dwellers rather than suburbanites. Our claim is that the increasing use of AI algorithms results in much higher degrees of differentiation, and we suggest that the large difference in quantity, that is, the much greater degree of differentiation, is sufficient to create a difference in quality. Our comparison between a "No Differentiation" benchmark and a world with some (or full) differentiation helps more clearly to identify the harms caused by AI-enhanced differentiation.

Second, the risk that less sophisticated—imperfectly informed and imperfectly rational—consumers might be exploited by unscrupulous sellers also predates the rise of AI. "There's a sucker born every minute," P. T. Barnum, the famous American showman of the eighteenth century, is said to have said. Here again we suggest that AI algorithms significantly amplify the risk, as, for example, by enabling the identification of specific information and rationality deficits that affect the demand of individual consumers.[5]

B. More Categories of Harm

Algorithmically Enhanced Misperceptions

We begin with the case in which AI exploits consumers' existing information or rationality deficits. We then consider the case where AI-based algorithms create or exacerbate those deficits. They might, for example, provide misleading or false information to certain people, and they might work to exploit or even to inculcate present bias or unrealistic optimism in other people. It is easily imaginable that AI would know which consumers are most likely to be susceptible to interventions of this kind. Worse still,

AI-powered large language models (LLMs), like ChatGPT, could be used to design communications that would effectively misinform consumers or trigger misperceptions. LLMs could easily attempt to persuade people to buy a weight-loss product that is worthless, perhaps by misinforming them, perhaps by inculcating unrealistic optimism. From a legal policy perspective, it is even easier to justify a strong regulatory response when AI creates misperceptions rather than "only" exploits existing misperceptions.

Algorithmic Coordination

There is another category of harm, one that is orthogonal to consumer sophistication and does not depend on consumer misperception. This harm arises when competing sellers use AI algorithms to set prices and feed these algorithms data on competitors' pricing strategies. Here the concern is about the risk of algorithmic coordination—the risk that the AI will learn to coordinate on super-competitive, oligopolistic prices. Some evidence suggests that this is already happening.

AI and Discrimination Based on Race and Sex

Our central proposition is that algorithmic harm is concentrated in U markets (except for the case of Algorithmic Coordination) and, more specifically, that policymakers should focus on differentiation, or discrimination, based on the consumer's information or rationality deficits. That proposition is quite different from what can be found in most prior work on algorithmic harm. That work has focused on the risk that AI algorithms will discriminate on the basis of race and sex, setting higher prices or offering inferior products to women and to members of minority groups.[6] We share that concern but suggest that a broader problem is far more interesting and far more complex. We will offer the full story in due course, but in brief, the rise of AI can be expected to have two sets of implications for discrimination based on race and sex.

On the one hand, compared to a human decision-maker, AI algorithms are less likely to exhibit what is called "taste-based discrimination." Human beings might prefer to hire men rather than women, or Whites rather than people of color. By contrast, the AI algorithm has only the "taste" that it is programmed to have—usually a "taste" for maximizing profits. Also, AI is less likely, compared to a human decision-maker, to engage in what is called "statistical discrimination," which means the use of (say) race or sex as a proxy for certain desirable characteristics. Human beings might think that people of some groups are likely to do or be better in some way than people of other groups, and in deciding with whom to deal they might choose members of groups believed likely to do or be better. But why should an AI algorithm rely on race or sex, which are rough and imprecise proxies for a consumer's profit-relevant characteristics, when the AI, fueled by big data, has access to much more accurate proxies? The conclusion is that AI algorithms might well be less likely to show discriminatory tastes or to engage in statistical discrimination than are human beings. (LLMs must be analyzed separately; they might turn out to be discriminators.)

On the other hand, in certain cases decisions made by AI algorithms might introduce new forms of race- and sex-based discrimination. Consider an online retailer who is unaware of the race or sex of its customers (because the retailer never interacts with these customers in person) and thus cannot discriminate on the basis of race or sex. If this retailer delegates pricing or targeting decisions to an AI algorithm, the algorithm will likely have access to reams of data, such as the customer's IP address and history of online purchases across multiple retailers, that might be correlated with race or sex. Thus the algorithm's pricing or targeting decisions that are calculated to maximize profits might create a disparate impact on people of color or women. For certain goods, women might be charged higher prices or be denied certain deals and opportunities. We will see other problems as well.

* * *

Beyond the specific categories of harm, we should note the cumulative and dynamic effects of the algorithmic harms that we identify. The use of AI-powered algorithms to price-discriminate, to engage in targeting, to coordinate prices, and so on allows sellers to make higher profits. (This effect exists in S markets, but it is even larger in U markets.) Over time, this might increase wealth disparity in the population and enhance the market power of those companies that were first to adopt AI-powered algorithms. The welfare implications, and the broader societal implications, of this dynamic should be considered alongside the more discrete harms that we identify and analyze.

Our focus is on AI algorithms deployed by sellers and service providers and the harm that they might impose on consumers. We emphasize, however, that there are also consumer-side algorithms that can help consumers make better choices and thus mitigate the algorithmic harms that we identify. Examples include "digital butlers" like Alexa, Siri, and Google Assistant that can help consumers make purchasing decisions, and more specialized apps that compare prices and help identify attractive options.[7] Innovations of this sort will inevitably become better over time, perhaps immeasurably better. Without discounting the importance of consumer-side algorithms, we believe that structural asymmetries between sellers and buyers will prevent such algorithms from eliminating the harms that we identify here. But we will have something to say about the positive side.

C. Policy Implications

We show that AI-driven differentiation can be harmful and thus merit legal intervention designed to reduce or eliminate the harms. We consider several different types of harms. First, we consider the consumer surplus, namely, the total gain, or loss, that consumers experience as a group. Here, algorithmic harm means that consumers, as a group, lose from the introduction of AI-driven differentiation. Second, we consider the distribution of gains and losses within the group of consumers, since AI-driven differentiation can benefit some consumers while harming others. Here, algorithmic harm might mean, for example, that poor consumers lose while rich consumers gain. Finally, we consider total surplus in the market, encompassing both the sellers' surplus and the consumers' surplus. (This total surplus measure is sometimes referred to as the "efficiency" measure.) Here, algorithmic harm means a reduction in the total surplus.

The three types of harms correspond to three different normative criteria, which can be balanced in an aggregate social welfare function. We do not endorse any particular balancing. Rather, we present the normative implications of AI-driven differentiation, given each of the three criteria. In some cases, all three criteria point in the same direction. In other cases, policymakers would need to trade off harm under one criterion against benefit under another. For example, we can imagine cases in which consumers lose as a group, but in which the total surplus in the market increases.[8]

While a major claim is that algorithmic harm is more likely in U markets, our analysis yields additional policy-relevant results. We show that, within U markets, algorithmic harm is more likely where most consumers overestimate rather than underestimate the benefits from the product or service. We also show that harm is more likely when AI-driven price discrimination is benefit-based, and less likely when it is cost-based (or risk-based). These insights should help policymakers to focus on the markets that are most vulnerable to algorithmic harm.

Once a target market has been identified, what are the regulatory tools available to policymakers? The increasing use of algorithms, and the harm that such use inflicts upon less sophisticated consumers, provide fresh support for existing efforts to reduce information and rationality deficits, especially through behaviorally informed disclosure mandates. An understanding of algorithmic harm also casts new light on protection of privacy, which influences the amount of data that is available to "fuel" the AI algorithms. That understanding also has implications for antitrust law, since market power is a necessary condition for algorithmic price discrimination. Of course, we should look to antitrust law to address concerns about algorithmic coordination.

But our main emphasis is on two main categories of AI-specific legal responses that might reduce algorithmic harm: (1) requirements of algorithmic transparency and (2) more direct intervention in the design and implementation of algorithms that are used in consumer markets, either through ex post policing or through ex ante regulation. The implementation of these regulatory responses is especially challenging, given the increasing prevalence of opaque machine-learning algorithms. Indeed, there is an ongoing debate in the computer science and economics literatures about whether meaningful transparency is even possible. We present this debate without taking sides and lay out some of the cutting-edge "transparency protocols" that have been developed in an attempt to open the algorithmic black box. If successful, these transparency protocols can be imposed by policymakers and then be used to trigger market responses or regulatory scrutiny and to overcome doctrinal (*mens rea*–type) hurdles to liability for algorithmic harm.

Even if meaningful transparency about the inner workings of AI algorithms is impossible, the algorithms can be policed by scrutinizing their outputs. This strategy has been used to identify and prevent disparate impact on the basis of race and sex. We argue that a similar approach can be used to police disparate impact on the basis of sophistication. For example, if the AI sets significantly higher prices for less sophisticated consumers than for similarly situated, highly sophisticated consumers, then the law should intervene. This disparate impact approach can be used ex post—in litigation or enforcement actions. It can also be used as the linchpin for ex ante regulation of AI-powered algorithms. In particular, regulators can require the incorporation of nondiscrimination constraints—including limiting any differences in outcomes experienced by less sophisticated consumers relative to highly sophisticated consumers—into the algorithm's code.

Our discussion of legal responses can inform policymakers in North America, in Europe, and around the world who are increasingly concerned about algorithmic harm in consumer markets and beyond (Smith 2020). Any account will quickly go out of date, but for a few glimpses, consider the following. In the United States, the Council of Economic Advisers issued an early report on the risks of differential pricing fueled by "big data" (Council of Economic Advisers 2015). The Federal Trade Commission (FTC) has held hearings and issued several reports and guidance letters about algorithmic decision-making (Smith 2020; FTC 2018). More recently, the FTC issued several investigative orders seeking information from companies that, the Commission believes, are using big data and AI-powered algorithms to set differentiated prices (FTC 2024). Financial regulators—the Federal Reserve Board, the Consumer Financial Protection Bureau, the Federal Deposit Insurance Corporation, the National Credit Union Administration, and the Office of the Comptroller of the Currency—have issued a request for information and comment on financial institutions' use of machine-learning AI algorithms.[9] The Office of Management and Budget has issued broad guidance about the regulation of algorithmic decision-making.[10] Congress is considering multiple bills on the regulation of AI-powered algorithms.[11] And President Biden has issued a sweeping Executive Order on the Safe, Secure, and Trustworthy Development and Use of Artificial Intelligence (White House 2023).[12]

Beyond the United States, the European Union has taken the lead in regulating algorithmic decision-making with its new Artificial Intelligence Act and related regulations.[13] In Canada, the Parliament has been considering the Artificial Intelligence and Data Act (AIDA), which would ban AI systems that cause "serious harm" to individuals and would impose additional transparency and regulatory requirements on a class of "high-risk" algorithmic activities.[14] We can expect increasing initiatives of this kind in many nations.[15]

D. Beyond Consumer Markets

While our focus is on consumer markets, AI is increasingly being deployed in other markets and causing similar types of harm. We extend our analysis to two such markets: labor markets and political markets.

Labor Markets

Employers are increasingly using AI to make, or assist in making, hiring and wage-setting decisions. The parallels between consumer markets and labor markets are obvious.[16] In both markets, the typical interaction is between a more sophisticated party, a seller or an employer, armed with AI algorithms and a less sophisticated party, a consumer or an employee. In addition, the employer's wage-setting decision is very similar to the seller's price-setting decision, and we can expect algorithmic wage discrimination, which will be particularly harmful when targeting employees' misperceptions in U markets. In such markets, employers might well be able to exploit employees' lack of information or biases, perhaps resulting in low wages, low benefits, or unsafe working conditions. In the same vein, the employer's hiring decision, or the decision of which job to offer to which applicant, is very similar to the seller's product-targeting decision. Other harms that we identified in consumer markets—algorithmically enhanced misperceptions, algorithmic coordination, and, obviously, algorithmic discrimination based on race and sex—also afflict labor markets.

Political Markets

Similar considerations arise in political markets. Here too we have sophisticated actors, politicians, party leaders, and their political advisors "selling" themselves or their policies to many less sophisticated actors: voters. Like sellers who target different products to different consumers, politicians seek to target their messaging to the preferences and misperceptions of different voters. They use AI algorithms to identify the messaging that would work best for each voter. In political markets, the use of AI to create or enhance misperceptions is of particular concern, especially with the increasingly powerful use of "fake news" and "alternative facts."[17] If voters are imperfectly informed or if they suffer from behavioral biases, they will be especially vulnerable. One result might be polarization; another might be extremism. Democratic processes, and political processes of multiple kinds, might be at risk in ways that even George Orwell could not possibly have envisaged.

PART I
ALGORITHMIC HARM IN CONSUMER MARKETS

We begin, in Part I, with consumer markets. The importance of these markets is obvious. They cover so many aspects of our lives: housing, motor vehicles, food products, clothes, laptops, smartphones, healthcare services, gym subscriptions, vacations, and much more. How will our experiences as consumers change when AI-powered algorithms increasingly dominate these markets? We start with algorithmic price discrimination in Chapters 1 and 2. We then consider algorithmic targeting in Chapter 3. In Chapter 4, we discuss algorithmically enhanced misperceptions. In Chapter 5, we review concerns about algorithmic coordination. The critically important topic of algorithmic discrimination based on race and sex is the subject of Chapter 6. Finally, in Chapter 7, we examine the promise, and limits, of consumer-side algorithms as a cure for the harm caused by the seller-side algorithms that are the focus of Part I.

Chapter 1
Algorithmic Price Discrimination

We begin with price discrimination.[18] Some of the discussion will be a bit technical, but the central claims should be clear. The simplest point is that if consumers are sophisticated, AI-powered price discrimination will significantly reduce the consumer surplus while increasing efficiency (understood as the overall surplus that includes both the consumer surplus and the seller's profits). If a company can charge different prices to different people, and if consumers have full information and are fully rational, people will pay what they are willing to pay.[19] Consumers with a higher willingness to pay (perhaps because they are richer) will be charged a higher price and pay more than they would without price discrimination, which is why the consumer surplus will be reduced. But more consumers will be served, and thus efficiency will be increased. Specifically, consumers with a lower willingness to pay who would have been priced out of the market in the absence of price discrimination will now face a lower price and be able to purchase the good or service. And since consumers with a lower willingness to pay are generally poorer, price discrimination will have some advantages on distributional grounds, even though the total consumer surplus is reduced.

The analysis is very different if consumers are unsophisticated. In that event, sellers can overcharge consumers—not merely reducing the consumer surplus but turning it negative. The willingness to pay of unsophisticated consumers includes a misperception component. Specifically, they might mistakenly overestimate the value of the product or service. For example, they might think that some healthcare product is more valuable than it is. Sellers will take advantage of this inflated willingness to pay and charge consumers more than the product or service is actually worth to them. Hence the negative surplus. Therefore, in U markets, the harm to consumers is significantly greater. Efficiency might also decrease. While AI-powered price discrimination brings into the market consumers who would otherwise be left out, in U markets price discrimination might bring in consumers who should not be in this market, namely, consumers for whom the

Algorithmic Harm. Oren Bar-Gill and Cass R. Sunstein, Oxford University Press. © Oren Bar-Gill and Cass R. Sunstein (2025). DOI: 10.1093/oso/9780197778197.003.0002

actual benefit (but not the overestimated benefit) from the product or service is lower than the cost to the seller of making the product or providing the service.

Empirical evidence suggests that sellers are increasingly using data and AI-powered algorithms to set personalized prices, that is, to price-discriminate.[20] In the domain of insurance, for example, different consumers are offered different prices on the basis of data indicating what they would be willing to pay for various policies (FCA 2019).[21] In the domain of travel, algorithms enable companies to offer higher or lower prices, depending on consumers' expected preferences for hotels, activities, and more (OECD 2018; Mundt 2020). Focusing on the airline industry, Aldo Ponticelli, head of distribution strategy and systems support at Alitalia, said, "The journey to personalization in the airline industry has begun, but this is a marathon, not a sprint, and we are just at the starting line" (Humphries 2019). We could easily imagine a situation in which many sellers offer people different prices for the same product (laptops, cell phones, vacations, meals, blankets, Labrador Retrievers), depending on what they know about those people.[22] These different prices track people's different willingness to pay (WTP), which might be driven by misperception. Policymakers are increasingly concerned about such algorithm-enabled price discrimination.[23]

To focus on price discrimination, we assume that the seller offers a uniform product (with uniform quality) to all consumers, such that differentiation, if it occurs, is limited to the price dimension. (We relax this assumption in Chapter 3.) Price discrimination requires some degree of market power.[24] For expositional simplicity, we focus on the extreme case of monopoly.[25]

A. S Markets

We first consider the effects of algorithmic pricing in markets with highly sophisticated consumers who are reasonably informed and make fully rational purchasing decisions. To do so, we start with the no-differentiation S Benchmark, and then compare this benchmark to the outcome with full differentiation, thus identifying the effects of AI in S markets. The S Benchmark is presented in Figure 1.1, using the most basic market setup with a linear, downward-sloping demand curve and a linear, horizontal supply

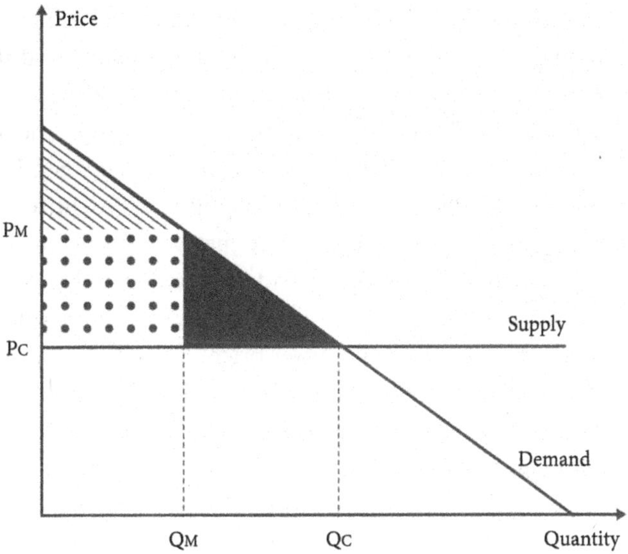

Figure 1.1 The "no differentiation," S Benchmark.

curve (reflecting a fixed-per-unit-cost assumption; let k denote the per-unit cost).[26] The intersection of the demand curve with the supply curve, at (Q_C, P_C), represents the perfect-competition equilibrium, where Q_C represents the equilibrium quantity and P_C represents the equilibrium price (which is equal to the per-unit cost, k). But, as explained above, we focus on the monopoly case. Compared to the perfect-competition case, a monopolist will set a higher price, $P_M > P_C$, and sell fewer units of the product, $Q_M < Q_C$.[27]

Consumer surplus is represented by the shaded triangle; it is equal to the difference between the consumer's WTP and the price, P_M, aggregated across all consumers. Some consumers have a high WTP. They are represented by the high points on the left side of the demand curve, and they enjoy more surplus. Other consumers have a lower WTP. They are represented by the lower points of the demand curve, close to Q_M, and they enjoy less surplus. The seller's surplus is represented by the dotted rectangle and is equal to the number of units sold multiplied by the difference between the monopoly price and the per-unit cost: $Q_M \cdot (P_M - k)$. Social welfare is, by definition, equal to the sum of the consumer surplus and the producer's (monopolist's) surplus. The black triangle represents the monopoly deadweight loss: because of the higher price that the monopolist charges, consumers who should buy the product refrain from purchasing it (specifically, the lost quantity is given by $Q_C - Q_M$); and the welfare that these lost purchases would have produced constitutes the monopoly deadweight loss.

Next, we consider the "full differentiation" outcome, where the monopolist charges each consumer a different, personalized price.[28] See Figure 1.2. Using big data and AI algorithms, the monopolist will identify each consumer's WTP and set a personalized price just below this WTP. Thus a consumer with a high WTP on the left side of the demand curve will pay a high price; a consumer with a lower WTP toward the middle or right side of the demand curve will pay a lower price. The seller's surplus is represented by the dotted triangle and is equal to the difference between the consumer's WTP and the per-unit cost, *k*, aggregated across all consumers. A price-discriminating monopolist keeps the entire surplus to itself; there is no consumer surplus. Observe that the quantity sold is Q_C, as in the competition case. Price discrimination allows the monopolist to increase the quantity sold—from Q_M to Q_C—thus eliminating the deadweight loss and increasing overall social welfare. However, this efficiency gain comes at a steep distributional price; the entire surplus goes to the monopolist, and consumers are left with nothing.[29] Still, the efficiency gain is worth

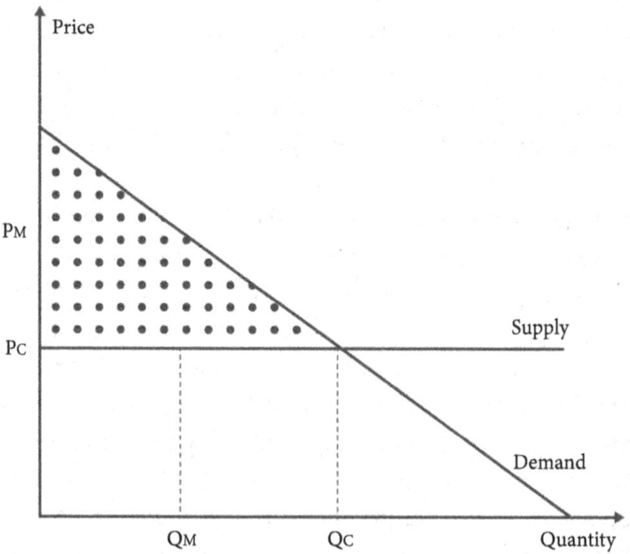

Figure 1.2 "Full differentiation" in S markets.

emphasizing. It is a powerful argument in favor of price discrimination in markets with highly sophisticated consumers.

Imperfect price discrimination. While perfect price discrimination may be coming in the not so distant future, it is useful to consider the current situation, where AI-powered algorithms are affecting a shift toward higher degrees of price discrimination but still falling short of perfect price discrimination. Such imperfect price discrimination implies a segmentation of the market into increasingly small groups of consumers, where each group pays a different price. Importantly, because pricing is group-based rather than individualized, within each group there are consumers who pay a price below their WTP and enjoy a positive surplus. Therefore, in S markets, increased yet imperfect price discrimination can be even more attractive than perfect price discrimination. On the one hand, imperfect price discrimination reduces but does not eliminate the monopoly deadweight loss (which is entirely eliminated with perfect price discrimination). On the other hand, consumers enjoy a positive surplus (where they are left with zero surplus under perfect price discrimination).

Moreover, imperfect price discrimination results in progressive redistribution among consumers: richer consumers face a higher price (because they have a higher WTP), and poorer consumers face a lower price (because they have a lower WTP). If the rich pay more than the poor for (say) electricity, food, and automobiles, there are gains in terms of both efficiency and fair distribution. The poor who were excluded from the market in the "no differentiation" benchmark now enter the market, and, unlike in the "full differentiation" case, they enjoy a positive surplus.[30]

B. U Markets

We now consider the effect of algorithmic pricing in markets where consumers are less sophisticated and suffer from information or rationality deficits (or both). To do so, we first derive the no-differentiation U Benchmark, and then compare this benchmark to the outcome with full differentiation, thus identifying the algorithmic harm in U markets.

Before proceeding, we must consider how imperfect information and imperfect rationality manifest in our analytical-graphical framework. These imperfections affect consumers' WTP. A consumer who overestimates the benefit from the product will have a higher WTP, and a consumer who underestimates the benefit from the product will have a lower WTP. We begin with overestimation, which is probably the more prevalent problem (as sellers have an incentive to promote overestimation and fight underestimation); the underestimation case is discussed in the next chapter. We initially assume that the degree of overestimation is not correlated with consumers' no-misperception, preference-based WTP, namely, that the average bias level is the same for consumers with a higher preference-based WTP at the left-hand side of the demand curve and for consumers with a lower preference-based WTP toward the middle and right-hand side of the demand curve. (This assumption is relaxed in the next chapter.) Now, in addition to the actual demand curve, we have a perceived demand curve. In Figures 1.3 and 1.4, the actual demand curve is represented by the solid downward-sloping line, and the perceived demand curve is represented by the dashed downward-sloping line.

The U Benchmark is presented in Figure 1.3. In the S Benchmark, the monopoly price was determined by the demand curve. In the U Benchmark, the price is determined by the perceived demand curve. Therefore, the monopoly price with misperception, $P_M{}'$, is higher than the

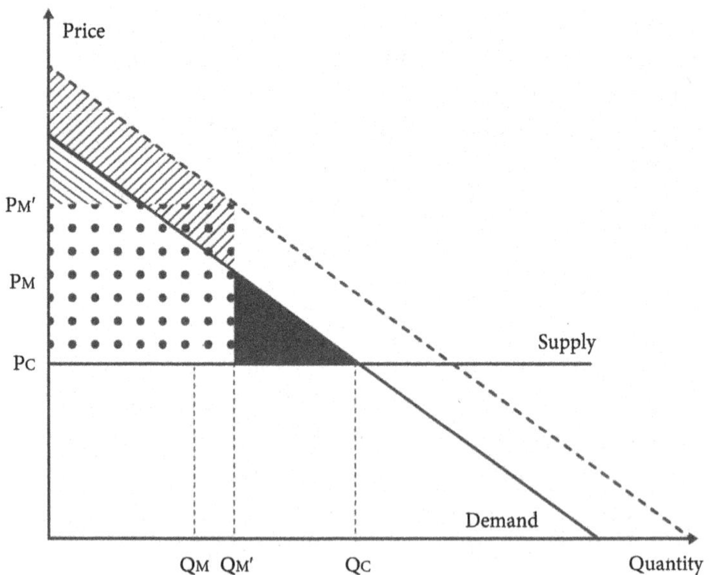

Figure 1.3 The "no differentiation," U Benchmark.

monopoly price without misperception, P_M. The quantity sold with misperception, Q_M', is also higher than the quantity sold without misperception, Q_M.[31] Turning to welfare: the higher price reduces the actual consumer surplus, which is represented by the shaded triangle. (More precisely, the shaded triangle represents transactions that create positive consumer surplus; to see the full consumer surplus, we need to subtract transactions that create negative consumer surplus, as described below.) The *perceived* surplus is larger—the perceived extra surplus is represented by the shaded trapezoid. Overestimation causes some consumers to purchase the product even though its actual value to them is lower than the price, P_M'.

The loss incurred by these consumers is represented by the dotted and shaded triangle. This loss reduces the (actual) consumer surplus. Indeed, the consumer surplus might be negative—the dotted and shaded triangle might be larger than the shaded triangle. But whatever consumers lose, the monopolist gains. The dotted and shaded triangle is part of the dotted rectangle, which represents the monopolist's surplus. Therefore, we have a distributional effect but no reduction in efficiency. Indeed, misperception increases efficiency. By inflating demand, the overestimation bias increases the quantity sold—from Q_M to Q_M'—and thus reduces the monopoly deadweight loss, which is represented by the black triangle. Notice that the black triangle in Figure 1.3 is smaller than the black triangle in Figure 1.1.[32]

Next, we consider the "full differentiation" outcome, where the monopolist charges each consumer a different, personalized price, equal to the consumer's WTP. See Figure 1.4. Whereas WTP derived only from preferences in the S case, now WTP is a product of both preferences and misperceptions. Price discrimination allows the monopolist to "march down" the demand curve, setting different prices for different consumers. In the S case, the monopolist marched down the *actual* demand curve. In the U case, the monopolist is marching down the *perceived* demand curve. Turning to welfare: in the S case the monopolist extracted the entire surplus. Consumers gained nothing, but also lost nothing. In the U case, the monopolist is also extracting perceived surplus, which is represented by the dotted and shaded trapezoid. This extra gain to the monopolist is a loss to consumers; the dotted and shaded trapezoid represents a transfer from consumers to the monopolist—a distributional effect with no efficiency implications.[33] But there are also efficiency implications. Consumers in the

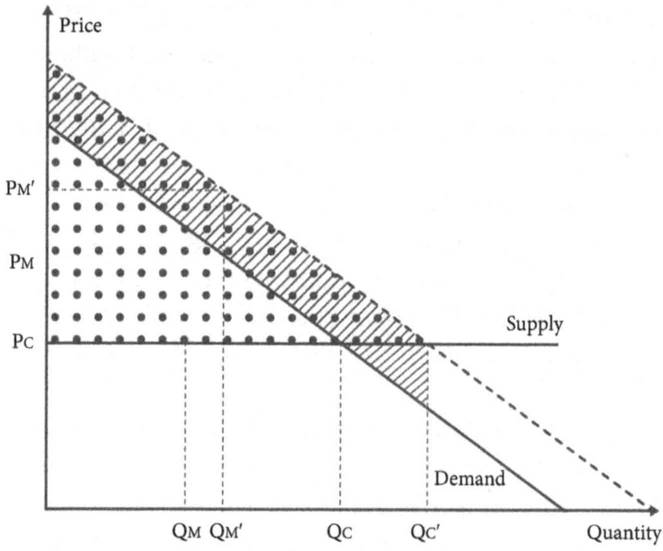

Figure 1.4 "Full differentiation" in U markets.

$[Q_C, Q_C']$ range should not purchase the product. They buy only because of their misperception, because they overestimate the product's value. These purchases create an efficiency loss, which is borne entirely by consumers. This loss is represented by the upward-sloping shaded triangle below the supply curve.

In the S case, where WTP is derived from preferences alone (see supra Section A), price discrimination hurts consumers but increases efficiency. Specifically, consumers enjoy no surplus at all, but deadweight loss is eliminated. In the U case, price discrimination hurts consumers even more and may either increase or decrease efficiency. Consumers are hurt more because now they give up surplus that they do not have—perceived surplus—and thus end up with a loss. In terms of efficiency, the insufficient quantity problem is avoided, but an excessive quantity problem is created. Whether price discrimination increases or decreases efficiency depends on the relative magnitudes of the black triangle in Figure 1.3 and the upward-sloping shaded triangle in Figure 1.4.[34]

Imperfect price discrimination. The analysis remains largely unchanged when we consider imperfect price discrimination. In U markets, there is a risk that the poor, and the rich, will end up paying more than their preference-based WTP. Therefore, our basic result—that a higher degree of price discrimination is more harmful to consumers in U markets and may or may not increase efficiency in such markets (as compared to S markets, where it generally increases efficiency)—extends to the imperfect price discrimination case, with linear demand curves.[35]

C. The Central Story

In the S case, AI-powered algorithms increase efficiency by eliminating the monopoly deadweight loss, or reducing it in the imperfect price discrimination case. At the same time, they harm consumers by erasing the consumer surplus. In the imperfect price discrimination case, the overall consumer surplus likely decreases, but poorer consumers benefit. In the U case, algorithms harm consumers even more—not only do they erase the consumer surplus, but they also create a negative consumer surplus by setting prices above the consumer's actual benefit. In addition, the AI-enabled price discrimination might reduce rather than increase efficiency in the U case.

It is important to note that the AI algorithm does not set out to harm consumers; it is programmed to maximize profit. To maximize profit, the algorithm seeks out consumers' WTP for different products and services. The extent and nature of the resulting algorithmic harm depend on different factors that determine the WTP. In particular, a consumer's WTP depends on (1) preferences—a consumer will pay more for a product that generates a greater benefit in terms of preference satisfaction, broadly understood; (2) wealth (or budget constraints)—a rich consumer will be able (and willing) to pay more than a poor consumer; and (3) misperceptions—a consumer who overestimates the benefit from a product, because of some information or rationality deficit, will pay more for that product.[36]

An AI algorithm designed to maximize profit cares only about the bottom-line WTP, not about the factors that influence the WTP.[37] But the harm that this algorithm causes very much depends on these underlying factors. As we have seen, when WTP is largely determined by preferences and wealth (the S case), the algorithm causes limited harm and may even generate socially desirable outcomes. It is when WTP is significantly influenced by misperceptions (the U case) that algorithms raise particular concern.

Chapter 2
Algorithmic Price Discrimination: Extensions

The main lesson of the analysis in Chapter 1 is that algorithmic price discrimination is more likely to be harmful in U markets and more likely to be beneficial in S markets. We now study several extensions of the baseline Chapter 1 model to explore the robustness of this main result and its limitations. In addition, the analysis of extensions in this chapter allows us to formulate more precise guidelines for policymakers.

We show that the main result—that algorithmic price discrimination is more likely to be harmful in U markets—holds, when misperceptions are correlated with the preference-based WTP (Section A) and when the price discrimination is based on consumers' past behavior, that is, in the case of behavior-based pricing (Section C). We also show (in Section E) that our main result extends, with appropriate adjustments, to (1) markets where the misperception is about the product's price (rather than the benefit that the consumer would gain from the product), (2) markets where only a subgroup of consumers suffers from information and rationality deficits, (3) markets that exhibit some competition among sellers, and (4) markets where the price discrimination is based on consumers' misperceived outside options. In contrast, we show that there is less cause for concern about algorithmic price discrimination when the misperception takes the form of underestimation rather than overestimation (Section B) and when the price discrimination is based on the cost, to the seller, of serving different consumers rather than on the WTP of different consumers (Section D).

The intuition for these last two observations is worth highlighting up front, since they should prove crucial for policymakers. First, it should be emphasized that our baseline analysis, in Chapter 1, assumed that AI-powered algorithms set prices just below the consumer's WTP. Therefore, if misperceptions inflate consumers' WTP, that is, if consumers overestimate the benefit from the product or service, then such algorithmic pricing harms

Algorithmic Harm. Oren Bar-Gill and Cass R. Sunstein, Oxford University Press. © Oren Bar-Gill and Cass R. Sunstein (2025). DOI: 10.1093/oso/9780197778197.003.0003

consumers. While in many markets pricing tracks the consumer's benefit, in other markets pricing tracks the seller's cost. For instance, lenders routinely employ AI-powered algorithms to estimate the risk that a potential borrower will fail to repay the loan, and then fold this estimate into a risk-adjusted cost of lending to this borrower. The algorithm then sets a price, or interest rate, that reflects the lender's risk-adjusted cost. This type of algorithmic pricing is much less troubling, in large part because the focus on seller costs rather than consumer benefits implies that consumer sophistication, or lack thereof, does not affect the price that the algorithm sets.

Second, in markets where algorithmic pricing tracks the consumer's benefit and thus reflects the consumer's information and rationality deficits, it is important to distinguish between a lack of sophistication that results in overestimation and a lack that results in underestimation of benefits. Our baseline analysis, in Chapter 1, focused on the overestimation case, which is likely the most common simply because sellers have strong incentives to encourage overestimation of the benefit from their products and to counter underestimation of such benefit. Still, there are important markets where underestimation is probably the dominant misperception. Think about the market for health insurance, where optimistic consumers underestimate the likelihood that they will get sick or the cost of care when they do, and thus underestimate the benefit from health insurance. In such markets, algorithmic pricing would help, not harm, consumers, because the algorithm that identifies the underestimation will set a lower price.

Combining these two observations provides important guidance to regulators who, faced with limited enforcement budgets, must triage and focus on the markets where algorithmic harm is most likely. We can now tell these regulators to focus on markets where algorithmic pricing is benefit-based, not cost-based, and on markets where the benefit is overestimated, not underestimated.

A. Misperceptions That Are Correlated with the Preference-Based WTP

Our baseline analysis above assumed that the degree of misperception is not correlated with the consumer's preference-based WTP. Graphically, this assumption was represented by a perceived demand curve that was parallel to the actual demand curve. Put differently, the perceived demand curve was represented by an upward shift from the actual demand curve. If there is a positive correlation between the degree of misperception and preference-based WTP, then the distance between the perceived and actual demand curves is larger at the left-hand side of the graph and smaller at the right-hand side of the graph. See Figure 2.1a. Conversely, if there is a negative correlation between the degree of misperception and preference-based WTP, then the distance between the perceived and actual demand curves is smaller at the left-hand side of the graph and larger at the right-hand side of the graph. See Figure 2.1b.[38]

Our main result—that algorithmic price discrimination is likely harmful in U markets—extends to the case where misperceptions are correlated with the preference-based WTP. Still, correlation between the degree of misperception and the preference-based WTP adds nuance to the normative assessment of algorithmic price discrimination. The extra harm that consumers incur is larger in the positive correlation case and smaller in the negative correlation case. The positive per-unit production cost, that is, the supply curve, truncates the perceived demand curve and the overestimation bias, and thus the consumer harm from overpayment. This truncation effect is smaller in the positive correlation case and larger in the negative correlation case. Shifting to distributional effects among consumers: if higher preference-based WTP (at the left-hand side of the demand curve) represent richer consumers, and lower preference-based WTP (at the right-hand side of the demand curve) represent poorer consumers, then richer consumers incur relatively larger harm in the positive correlation case and poorer consumers incur relatively larger harm in the negative correlation case.

In terms of efficiency, the cost of price discrimination is measured by the welfare-reducing transactions that are entered into by overestimating consumers (represented by the upward-sloping shaded triangles in Figure 2.1)—a cost that needs to be compared to the monopoly deadweight loss in the absence of price discrimination. Price discrimination is more likely to reduce efficiency when the cost from the welfare-reducing transactions is higher (i.e., when the upward-sloping shaded triangle is larger). In the positive correlation case, the welfare loss from inefficient transactions is higher when the per-unit production cost is high; in the negative correlation case, the loss is higher when the per-unit production cost is low.

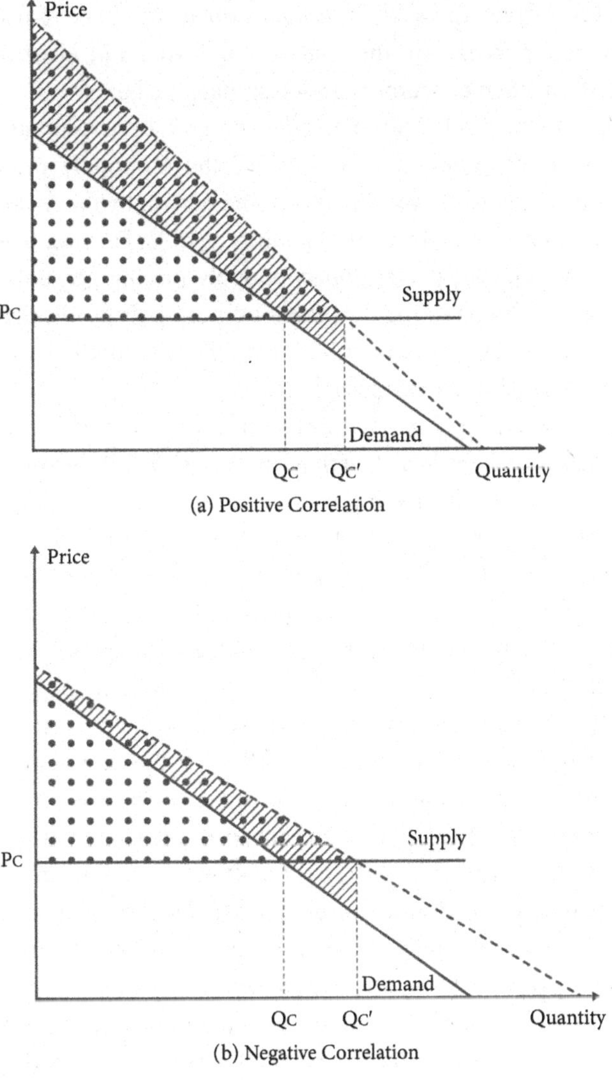

(a) Positive Correlation

(b) Negative Correlation

Figure 2.1 Correlated misperceptions.

B. Underestimation

Our baseline analysis assumed that consumers overestimate the benefit from a product or service. But in some markets, we can expect underestimation. For example, consumers likely underestimate the benefit from health insurance (e.g., because they underestimate future healthcare costs). And present-biased consumers likely underestimate the benefit from a more fuel-efficient car. What are the welfare implications of algorithmic price discrimination when consumers underestimate the benefit?

Starting with the no-discrimination benchmark: underestimation reduces the price that the monopolist sets (since the monopoly price is determined by the demand curve, which is pushed down by the misperception). Underestimation also reduces the quantity sold.[39] Turning to welfare: in the S case, without misperception, monopoly pricing prevents some efficient purchases, thus creating the infamous monopoly deadweight loss. The underestimation bias prevents additional efficient purchases from taking place, thus increasing the deadweight loss.[40]

Now add (perfect) price discrimination: the monopolist sets a different price for each consumer, based on that consumer's WTP. Turning to welfare: price discrimination clearly increases efficiency, as it reduces the deadweight loss; that is, more consumers purchase the product. The effect on the consumer surplus, however, is ambiguous. In the S case the monopolist extracted the entire surplus. Consumers gained nothing. Here the monopolist can extract only the underestimated perceived surplus. The consumers are left with the difference between the actual surplus and the perceived surplus. So consumers enjoy a positive surplus, but it is not clear whether this surplus is larger or smaller than the surplus that they enjoy in the absence of price discrimination. On the one hand, more consumers buy the product and enjoy this difference between the actual and perceived surplus. On the other hand, the consumers who would have purchased the product also in the absence of price discrimination enjoy a smaller surplus (because they are charged a higher, personalized price). Within the group of consumers, the benefit from price discrimination is concentrated among poor consumers (who are excluded from the market in the absence of price discrimination), which suggests that price discrimination is beneficial on distributional grounds.

To conclude: in the S case, price discrimination hurts consumers but increases efficiency. Specifically, consumers enjoy no surplus at all, but there is no deadweight loss. With overestimation, price discrimination hurts consumers even more and may either increase or decrease efficiency. Here, with underestimation, price discrimination clearly increases efficiency and may or may not hurt consumers (and is likely to benefit poorer consumers). Therefore, algorithmic price discrimination is less worrisome, and thus legal intervention is less needed, in markets with underestimation.

We note that, while some markets can be characterized by either over- or underestimation, in other markets both types of misperception occur simultaneously; that is, some consumers will overestimate the benefits from the product, whereas others will underestimate these benefits. In such markets, the algorithm will distinguish between these two types of consumers, setting higher prices for the overestimators and lower prices for the underestimators. The former will be harmed by the algorithmic price discrimination, while the latter will benefit. The overall welfare assessment will depend on the relative number of over- versus underestimators, as well as on the magnitude of the bias in each group.

C. Behavior-Based Pricing

We now consider behavior-based pricing (BBP), where the algorithm discriminates based on the consumer's past behavior.[41] To clarify, our baseline analysis of algorithmic price discrimination did not specify the source of the WTP information that the algorithm used to price-discriminate; and the baseline analysis applies to situations where the WTP information is based on the consumer's past behavior. But when sellers' information about consumers' WTP is based on the consumers' past purchasing decisions, there are additional welfare effects to consider. First, the welfare analysis now includes a dynamic component: over time, as sellers and their AI-powered algorithms accumulate more information about consumers' past behavior, the degree of price discrimination increases. Second, in S markets consumers will strategically adjust their purchasing behavior in earlier periods in order to obtain lower prices in later periods. Such strategic response mitigates, and may even eliminate, algorithmic harm from BBP in S markets.[42] As before, the harm to consumers is concentrated in U markets, where many consumers are unaware of the algorithm's BBP and do not respond strategically. (Indeed, in the BBP extension, we define S markets as those where most consumers are aware of the seller's BBP and respond strategically, and we define U markets as those where most consumers are unaware of the seller's BBP and thus do not respond strategically. Of course, other manifestations of information and rationality deficits will continue to cause algorithmic harms—the harms that we identified in Chapter 1—also with behavior-based pricing.)

BBP is already practiced in certain consumer markets, and its prevalence is likely to increase. Amazon experimented with BBP in 2000, setting higher prices for consumers who purchased certain DVDs.[43] More recently, Uber has been accused of engaging in BBP (Mahdawi 2018), but there is no clear proof of this. And the Airline Tariff Publishing Company, which is co-owned by several large airlines, announced in October 2019 that it is developing a dynamic pricing tool which can adjust pricing based on consumers' prior transactions (Peterson 2019). Finally, it is quite clear that large tech companies like Amazon and Apple collect data on consumers' purchasing behavior and that data aggregators collect and sell similar data to smaller companies.[44] It would be surprising if these data are not fed into sellers' pricing algorithms.

To illustrate the equilibrium outcomes and welfare implications of algorithmic BBP, we consider a simple two-period model. In the earlier period, the (monopolist) seller has limited information and thus sets a single price for all potential customers. In the later period, the seller sets two prices—a higher price for consumers who purchased in the earlier period and a lower price for those who did not. Suppose, for example, that in the earlier period Uber sets a single price for all potential riders. Uber then observes that a certain consumer declined a ride at this price. The Uber algorithm will identify this consumer as a low-WTP consumer and offer her a lower price in the later period. In contrast, another consumer who took the ride in the earlier period will be identified as a high-WTP consumer and offered a higher price in the later period.

To ascertain the welfare effects of algorithmic BBP, we begin with the pre-AI benchmark. In this pre-AI world, a monopolistic seller will set the same single (monopoly) price in both the early and late periods. This means that the same, higher-WTP consumers purchase the product in both periods; and the same, lower-WTP consumers are excluded from the market in both periods. With algorithmic BBP, in the earlier period fewer consumers will purchase the product. In U markets this is because the seller will increase the early-period price (relative to the pre-AI benchmark) in order to more effectively discriminate between low- and high-WTP consumers in the later period. In S markets this is because a group of strategic consumers will not purchase the product even though they value it more than the charged price. Specifically, these consumers will strategically decline the Uber ride offer, even if the benefit from the ride exceeds the offered price, in order to secure lower price offers in the future.

In the later period more consumers purchase the product under BBP. Specifically, low-WTP consumers who were excluded from the market in the earlier period will face a lower price in the later period and thus enter the market. In terms of total surplus, in both S markets and U markets BBP increases the total number of transactions across the two periods; that is, the increase in the number of later-period transactions outweighs the decrease in earlier-period transactions, and thus the total surplus increases.

In terms of consumer surplus, in both S markets and U markets consumers with lower WTP, who are likely poorer, benefit from BBP because they face a lower price and thus can enter the market even if only in the later period, whereas they are excluded from the market in both periods without BBP. The main difference between S markets and U markets is with respect to consumers with higher WTP who are likely richer. In U markets, these consumers are harmed by BBP because they now face a higher price in the later period. In S markets, these consumers also pay a higher price in the later period. But they pay a lower price in the earlier period because sellers reduce the earlier-period price to limit the number of consumers who strategically refrain from purchasing. Across both periods, consumers with higher WTP benefit from BBP in S markets. Therefore, algorithmic BBP increases the overall consumer surplus in S markets.[45] In contrast, algorithmic BBP reduces the overall consumer surplus in U markets, as the harm to the higher-WTP consumers exceeds the benefit to the lower-WTP consumers. Still, if our social welfare function places greater weight on lower-WTP consumers who are likely poorer, then BBP can be desirable, or at least less undesirable, even in U markets. In any event, we see, once again, that concern about algorithmic harm should be smaller in S markets and greater in U markets.

D. Cost-Based Price Discrimination

We have thus far focused on situations where the cost to the seller of providing the good or the service does not depend on the consumer's characteristics and where the algorithmic pricing tracks the consumer's WTP. But there are also important situations where the seller's cost depends on the consumer's characteristics, and the algorithm tracks these cost-affecting characteristics, setting higher prices for higher-cost consumers and lower prices for lower-cost consumers. Consumer credit markets are perhaps the leading example. When a lender offers a loan to a borrower, the cost to the lender of this loan depends on the likelihood that the borrower will repay the loan. When the probability of repayment is higher, the cost to the lender is lower, and thus the lender can offer a lower price, that is, a lower interest rate. And when the probability of repayment is lower, the cost to the lender is higher, and thus the lender will set a higher interest rate. The pricing algorithms thus track borrower characteristics that predict the probability of repayment, such as income, debt overhang, and the consumer's history of debt repayment across multiple lenders. This is what credit scoring models do, and these models are increasingly AI-based.[46]

When algorithmic pricing tracks cost rather than WTP, the concern about algorithmic harm is diminished. It is less objectionable for sellers or lenders to charge higher prices when they face higher costs. As before, in assessing the welfare implications of algorithmic pricing a comparison to the pre-AI world is instructive. If lenders cannot distinguish between low-risk and high-risk borrowers, then they would set a single interest rate that reflects average risk. Low-risk borrowers would then cross-subsidize high-risk borrowers, creating both winners (high-risk borrowers) and losers (low-risk borrowers). If high-risk borrowers are generally poorer, then this pre-AI outcome can be distributionally attractive, and pricing algorithms that eliminate the cross-subsidization would then be socially harmful. But it is also possible that, in the pre-AI world, low-risk borrowers would reject the single interest rate and exit the market. Realizing that only high-risk borrowers remain, lenders would then increase the interest rate. There would be no cross-subsidization, only a smaller market serving only high-risk borrowers. If this is the pre-AI benchmark, then algorithmic pricing would increase welfare by expanding the market to low-risk borrowers.[47]

Another possibility is that AI-powered algorithms, using big data, can identify low-risk borrowers that were falsely categorized as high-risk in a pre-AI world. This outcome is especially attractive if the falsely categorized borrowers disproportionately come from traditionally disadvantaged groups. On the flip side, there is a concern that biased algorithms would mistakenly attribute high risk to members of traditionally disadvantaged groups. (See Chapter 6 for further discussion.)[48]

It is important to emphasize that our leading distinction between S markets and U markets is less important when price discrimination tracks cost, or risk, rather than WTP. WTP is a consumer-side feature that is commonly influenced by consumer sophistication. Imperfectly informed and imperfectly rational consumers often overestimate the benefits of a product, resulting in an inflated WTP. In contrast, cost is a seller-side feature, even though it is influenced by certain consumer characteristics. When AI-powered algorithms allow sellers to adjust the price so that it matches the cost of serving the particular consumer, the consumer's sophistication does not enter the equation (at least not directly). Therefore, the welfare analysis of algorithmic cost-based pricing is similar in both S markets and U markets. And in both types of markets, we should be less concerned about algorithmic harm.

E. Additional Extensions

Misperception about the Price

In important consumer markets—think mortgages, credit cards, cellular services, broadband, insurance—pricing is complex and multidimensional. In these markets, the main concern is about price misperception, namely, that consumers might not fully understand the pricing structure and thus underestimate the overall price that they will end up paying for the product or service. Consumers might not pay attention to certain components of the pricing structure; some of those components might be in some sense shrouded or not highly visible. Or consumers might underestimate the probability of triggering a certain price dimension, such as a late fee on a credit card or mortgage. When AI-powered algorithms can be used to identify and exploit such price misperceptions, consumers will incur harm that is similar to the harm analyzed above. Indeed, the effects of price underestimation are analytically identical to the effects of value overestimation that we analyzed above.

Discriminating between Sophisticated and Unsophisticated Consumers

For analytical purposes, we distinguished between S markets and U markets. But we have also noted that in practice, most markets include both more and less sophisticated consumers. In these markets, sellers will use AI to discriminate between these groups of consumers—offering good deals to the more sophisticated consumers and bad deals to the less sophisticated consumers.[49] For example, sellers can offer generally high-priced products with a few good deals hidden among their offerings. More sophisticated consumers will find those good deals, whereas less sophisticated consumers will not.[50] The welfare implications of such discrimination depend on what sellers will do if they cannot discriminate—will they offer the better deal to everyone or the worse deal to everyone?

Competition

As explained above, some degree of market power is a precondition for price discrimination, and for simplicity, we analyzed a monopolistic market. How would the analysis change if sellers, while enjoying some market power, are still subject to the forces of competition? On the one hand, competition might force algorithmic harm, as sellers who fail to utilize AI-powered algorithms will lose out to competitors who do (compare Bar-Gill 2012, 16). On the other hand, competition can reduce algorithmic harm by constraining sellers' ability to engage in price discrimination. In addition, one seller might reveal algorithmic abuses by her competitor in an attempt to win over consumers. Overall, as long as the competition does not preclude price discrimination, our main result—that algorithmic price discrimination is more harmful in U markets—holds.[51]

Outside Options

The preceding analysis assumed a monopoly seller, such that the only outside option was "no purchase." If we relax the monopoly assumption, WTP can be influenced by the consumer's actual and perceived outside options. For example, if a consumer can purchase the product from Seller #1 at a price of $100, that is, if the consumer has an "outside option" of getting the product for $100, then her WTP, when facing Seller #2, will never exceed $100. Some consumers have access to multiple, competing sellers. These consumers will have a lower WTP. Other consumers do not have access to competing sellers (e.g., because they don't have a car or don't have internet access or don't have a bank account). These consumers will have a higher WTP.

AI-powered algorithms will be able to identify consumers with fewer, or less attractive, outside options and offer them higher prices.[52] And, like other factors that influence the WTP, the existence and features of outside options might be subject to misperception. Specifically, an unsophisticated consumer might underestimate her outside options (e.g., she might underestimate her ability to get a lower price from a competing seller). As a result, the consumer will have a higher WTP. An algorithm trained to track WTP would set a higher price for this consumer, even if the consumer could in fact get a lower price from a competing seller.

The normative evaluation of algorithmic price discrimination may change when WTP is influenced by consumers' outside options. For example, when WTP is determined by preferences and by budget constraints, it is likely that rich consumers will have a higher WTP and poor consumers will have a lower WTP. Accordingly, the algorithm will set higher prices for the rich and lower prices for the poor, which is distributionally attractive. In contrast, when WTP is determined by outside options, it is likely that rich consumers will have a lower WTP and poor consumers will have a higher WTP. The algorithm will then set higher prices for the poor and lower prices for the rich, which is distributionally unattractive. Note that these distributional concerns apply in both S markets and U markets. Still, overall algorithmic harm will be greater in U markets to the extent that underestimation of outside options will further increase WTP both for richer consumers and for poorer consumers.

F. Summary

The extensions studied in this chapter hold several key lessons for policymakers: First, the basic insight—that AI-powered price discrimination is more troubling in U markets—is robust to several real-world variations on the assumptions that underlie the baseline Chapter 1 analysis. Policymakers should thus focus their attention, and their limited enforcement budget, on U markets. Second, not all U markets are created equal. In some U markets, most unsophisticated consumers overestimate the benefit from the product or service, whereas in other U markets most unsophisticated consumers *under*estimate the benefit from the product or service. The welfare costs of AI-powered price discrimination are significantly larger in the former, where the problem is overestimation. Therefore, policymakers should focus on the subset of U markets where overestimation is the more common problem. Finally, AI-powered price discrimination can be either benefit-based or cost-based. Algorithmic harm is larger when price discrimination is benefit-based and smaller when price discrimination is cost-based. To conclude: policymakers should focus on markets where AI algorithms set prices based on the consumers' perceived benefit levels, and these perceived benefits are overestimated.

Appendix

In this Appendix, we offer a formal analysis of the BBP extension (Section C). For reasons that were explained in Section C, we start with U markets and then proceed to analyze S markets.

A. U Markets

With BBP, it is easier to start with U markets, where unsophisticated consumers are not aware of the seller's BBP. These consumers will not adjust their early-period purchasing decisions to secure lower later-period prices. To ascertain the effect of algorithmic BBP, we begin with the pre-algorithmic benchmark. In this pre-algorithmic world, a monopolistic seller will set the same (monopoly) uniform price in both the early and late periods. With algorithmic BBP, the seller will set a uniform, higher early-period price and two late-period prices: a higher price for consumers who purchased in the early period and a lower price for those who did not. The lower late-period price allows poorer, lower-WTP consumers who did not purchase in the early period to enter the market. The higher late-period price extracts more surplus from the richer, higher-WTP consumers who made an early-period purchase.

The overall welfare effects of BBP are nuanced. From an efficiency perspective, with BBP sellers serve more consumers in the later period (thanks to the differentiated pricing) but fewer consumers in the early period (because of the higher early-period price). From a distributional perspective, higher-WTP consumers who are likely richer are harmed by the higher prices in both the early and late periods. At the same time, some lower-WTP consumers, who are likely poorer and were excluded from the market without BBP, are able to participate in the market and gain surplus with BBP. It will often be the case that consumers as a group are harmed by BBP, whereas a subgroup of poorer consumers benefits. The overall welfare assessment of algorithmic BBP is complicated by these trade-offs. To illustrate the effects of BBP and gain further insight into the trade-offs that determine the normative evaluation of this practice, we next study a detailed example of BBP.

Setup. Consider a product that gives each consumer a value, $v \in [0, V]$, and let the probability density function, $f(v)$, and the corresponding cumulative distribution function, $F(v)$, represent the distribution of values across a unit mass of consumers. For simplicity, we assume a uniform distribution, such that $f(v) = \frac{1}{V}$ and $F(v) = \frac{v}{V}$.[53] The distribution of values determines the demand for this product: for any price p, the quantity sold is given by $q(p) = 1 - F(p)$; that is, consumers with a value that exceeds the price will purchase the product. At this price p, the monopolistic seller makes a profit of $\pi(p) = p \cdot q(p)$ if we normalize the per-unit cost of production to zero; the consumer surplus is $\int_p^V (v - p) f(v)\, dv$, aggregating the net benefit, $v - p$, across consumers with values $v \in [p, V]$ who purchase the product at the price p. There are two time periods, period 1 and period 2. We assume that, in each period, each consumer purchases one unit of the product, at most. For simplicity, we assume no time discounting.

Pre-algorithmic world. In the pre-algorithmic world, the monopolist cannot engage in BBP. Therefore, it will set the same price in both periods, and this price will be offered to all consumers. Specifically, the offered price will be the standard monopoly price, which is $p^S = \frac{V}{2}$ in our setup.[54] Accordingly, consumers with above-median values purchase the good, whereas consumers with below-median values are excluded from the market. The monopolist's profit is $\pi(p^S) = p^S \cdot q(p^S) = \frac{1}{4}V$ in each period, for a total profit of $\frac{1}{2}V$. And the consumer surplus is $CS(p^S) = \int_{p^S}^V (v - p^S) f(v)\, dv = \frac{1}{8}V$ in each period, for a total consumer surplus of $\frac{1}{4}V$.

Post-algorithmic world. In the post-algorithmic world, the monopolist engages in BBP. It will set a period 1 price p_1, such that high-value consumers, with $v \in [p_1, V]$, buy the product in period 1; low-value consumers, with $v \in [0, p_1]$, do not buy the product in period 1. The monopolist will then set two different period 2 prices—one price p_2^H for the high-value consumers who bought the product in period 1, and another, lower price p_2^L for the low-value consumers who did not buy the product in period 1. In period 1, the seller is facing the entire market, and demand is given by $q_1(p_1) = 1 - F(p_1)$. The seller's profit is $\pi_1(p_1) = p_1 \cdot q_1(p_1)$; the consumer surplus is $CS_1(p_1) = \int_{p_1}^V (v - p_1) f(v)\, dv$.

In period 2, for the high-value segment, covering all consumers with $v \in [p_1, V]$, demand is given by $q_2^H(p_2^H) = 1 - F(p_2^H)$.[55] The seller's profit is $\pi_2^H(p_2^H) = p_2^H \cdot q_2^H(p_2^H)$; the consumer surplus is $CS_2^H(p_2^H) = \int_{p_2^H}^{V}(v - p_2^H)f(v)\,dv$. In our setup, the profit-maximizing price is $p_2^H = p_1$.[56] All of the high-value consumers, with $v \in [p_1, V]$, who purchase the product in period 1 will also purchase the product in period 2. Therefore, we can rewrite the monopolist's profit as $\pi_2^H(p_1) = p_1 \cdot q_2^H(p_1)$ and the consumer surplus as $CS_2^H(p_1) = \int_{p_1}^{V}(v - p_1)f(v)\,dv$. In the low-value segment, covering all consumers with $v \in [0, p_1]$, demand is given by $q_2^L(p_2^L) = F(p_1) - F(p_2^L)$. The seller's profit is $\pi_2^L(p_2^L) = p_2^L \cdot q_2^L(p_2^L)$; the consumer surplus is $CS_2^L(p_2^L) = \int_{p_2^L}^{p_1}(v - p_2^L)f(v)\,dv$. In our setup, the profit-maximizing price is $p_2^L = \frac{p_1}{2}$.[57] Of the low-value consumers who did not buy in period 1, the upper half, that is, consumers with $v \in \left[\frac{p_1}{2}, p_1\right]$, buy the product in period 2. Therefore, we can rewrite the monopolist's profit as $\pi_2^L\left(\frac{p_1}{2}\right) = \frac{p_1}{2} \cdot q_2^L\left(\frac{p_1}{2}\right)$ and the consumer surplus as $CS_2^L(p_1) = \int_{p_1/2}^{p_1}\left(v - \frac{p_1}{2}\right)f(v)\,dv$.

We can now derive the period 1 price. The seller sets this price to maximize the sum of its period 1 profit, $\pi_1(p_1)$, together with the two period 2 profits—$\pi_2^H(p_1)$ for the high-value segment and $\pi_2^L\left(\frac{p_1}{2}\right)$ for the low-value segment.[58] In our setup, the profit-maximizing price is $p_1 = \frac{4V}{7}$, such that the upper $\frac{3}{7}$ of consumers, with values $v \in \left[\frac{4V}{7}, V\right]$, buy the good in period 1. Then, in period 2, the seller will set $p_2^H = p_1 = \frac{4V}{7}$ for the consumers who bought the product in period 1, such that the same consumers, with values $v \in \left[\frac{4V}{7}, V\right]$ buy also in period 2; the seller will set $p_2^L = \frac{p_1}{2} = \frac{2V}{7}$ for the consumers who did not buy the product in period 1, such that consumers with values $v \in \left[\frac{2V}{7}, \frac{4V}{7}\right]$ buy in period 2.

Comparison. BBP clearly increases the seller's profit; otherwise, the seller would avoid BBP and set prices as in the pre-algorithmic world. Specifically, whereas the seller's profit was $\frac{1}{2}V$ without BBP, it is $\pi_1(p_1) + \pi_2^H(p_1) + \pi_2^L\left(\frac{p_1}{2}\right) = \frac{28}{49}V$ with BBP. But while the seller benefits from BBP, consumers are harmed. Without BBP, consumer surplus was $\frac{1}{4}V$. With BBP, consumer surplus is $CS_1(p_1) + CS_2^H(p_1) + CS_2^L\left(\frac{p_1}{2}\right) = \frac{11}{49}V$. In our setup, the harm to consumers from BBP, that is, the reduction in consumer surplus $\left(\frac{1}{4}V - \frac{11}{49}V\right)$, is smaller than the benefit to the seller, that is, the increase in the seller's profit $\left(\frac{28}{49}V - \frac{1}{2}V\right)$, such that BBP increases overall efficiency.[59] Yet, given the adverse distributional effect, BBP may still be socially undesirable.

Table 2.1 Disaggregated Effects of BBP in U Markets

Consumers with	Consumer Surplus		Seller's Profit		Total	
	No BBP	BBP	No BBP	BBP	No BBP	BBP
$v \in \left[\frac{4V}{7}, V\right]$	$\frac{96}{392}V$	$\frac{72}{392}V$	$\frac{168}{392}V$	$\frac{192}{392}V$	$\frac{264}{392}V$	$\frac{264}{392}V$
$v \in \left[\frac{V}{2}, \frac{4V}{7}\right]$	$\frac{2}{392}V$	$\frac{7}{392}V$	$\frac{28}{392}V$	$\frac{8}{392}V$	$\frac{30}{392}V$	$\frac{15}{392}V$
$v \in \left[\frac{2V}{7}, \frac{V}{2}\right]$	0	$\frac{9}{392}V$	0	$\frac{24}{392}V$	0	$\frac{33}{392}V$
$v \in \left[0, \frac{2V}{7}\right]$	0	0	0	0	0	0

Drilling down further, we can distinguish between four groups of consumers, as shown in Table 2.1. The table also presents, for each group, the consumer surplus, the seller's profit, and the total surplus (which combines the consumer surplus and the seller's profit), with and without BBP.

We can now summarize the effect of BBP on each group. (1) Consumers with $v \in \left[0, \frac{2V}{7}\right]$ would be excluded from the market with and without BBP. (2) Consumers with $v \in \left[\frac{2V}{7}, \frac{V}{2}\right]$ would be excluded without BBP and served, albeit only in the second period, with BBP. (3) Consumers with $v \in \left[\frac{V}{2}, \frac{4V}{7}\right]$ would be served in both periods without BBP and only in the second period with BBP. Still, because of the lower price charged with BBP in the second period, they enjoy a higher consumer surplus, and the seller's profit from serving these consumers is lower. (4) Consumers with $v \in \left[\frac{4V}{7}, V\right]$ would be served, in both periods, with and without BBP. BBP allows the seller to charge a higher price, thus shifting surplus from consumers to the seller. (The total surplus is not changed by the introduction of BBP.) While BBP harms consumers as a group, the distributional effects are more subtle: consumers with $v \in \left[\frac{4V}{7}, V\right]$ who are likely richer are harmed by BBP, whereas consumers with $v \in \left[\frac{V}{2}, \frac{4V}{7}\right]$ and with $v \in \left[\frac{2V}{7}, \frac{V}{2}\right]$ who are likely poorer benefit from BBP.[60] (Consumers as a group are harmed because the group with $v \in \left[\frac{4V}{7}, V\right]$ is larger.)

B. S Markets

We next turn to S markets, where consumers are aware of the seller's BBP. As noted above, some high-WTP consumers will strategically refrain from making an early-period purchase in order to secure a lower price in the later period. This reduces efficiency and consumer surplus in the early period. In the later period, the algorithm segments the market, with a higher price for consumers who purchased in the early period and a lower price for those who did not. (From a distributional perspective, the outcome in S markets is somewhat less attractive, as the lower, later-period price is enjoyed by some relatively wealthy consumers who strategically refrained from purchasing in the early period.) When consumers are aware of the seller's use of BBP and respond strategically, BBP helps consumers and harms sellers. Therefore, in the early period, sellers would prefer to commit to refraining from using BBP, if they could. But such a commitment may well prove impossible: in the later period, armed with reams of data and the algorithms to analyze it, sellers will have a strong incentive to engage in BBP, and sophisticated consumers will anticipate this in the early period and respond accordingly. From a social welfare perspective, algorithmic BBP can be desirable in S markets.

Post-algorithmic world. Whereas in U markets in period 1 consumers bought the product whenever the value that they gained from the product exceeded its price, in S markets consumers might refrain from making a period 1 purchase even if value exceeds price. Therefore, we need to derive a value threshold, $\tilde{v}_1$, such that only consumers with $v \in [\tilde{v}_1, V]$ will buy the product in period 1. (Note that $\tilde{v}_1$ will exceed the period 1 price, p_1.) At this threshold, the loss from forgoing a beneficial period 1 purchase exactly equals the gain from a lower period 2 price: $\tilde{v}_1 - p_1 = p_2^H - p_2^L$; we call this the "threshold equation." The period 2 prices also need to be adjusted, relative to the U markets case, such that the threshold $\tilde{v}_1$ replaces p_1. Specifically, we have $p_2^H = \tilde{v}_1$ and $p_2^L = \frac{\tilde{v}_1}{2}$. Plugging these period 2 prices into the threshold equation, we get $\tilde{v}_1(p_1) = 2p_1$. We can also rewrite the period 2 prices as a function of p_1: $p_2^H(p_1) = 2p_1$ and $p_2^L(p_1) = p_1$.

The seller sets p_1 to maximize the sum of its period 1 profit, $\pi_1(p_1)$, together with the two period 2 profits—$\pi_2^H(2p_1)$ for the high-value segment and $\pi_2^L(p_1)$ for the low-value segment.[61] In our setup, the profit-maximizing price is $p_1 = \frac{3V}{10}$ and the threshold is $\tilde{v}_1(p_1) = \frac{6V}{10}$, such that the upper 40% of consumers, with values $v \in \left[\frac{6V}{10}, V\right]$, buy the good in period 1. Then, in period 2, the seller sets $p_2^H(p_1) = \frac{6V}{10}$ for the consumers who bought the product in period 1, such that the same consumers, with values $v \in \left[\frac{6V}{10}, V\right]$, buy also in period 2, and $p_2^L(p_1) = \frac{3V}{10}$ for the consumers who did not buy the product in period 1, such that consumers with values $v \in \left[\frac{3V}{10}, \frac{6V}{10}\right]$, buy in period 2. As compared to the U markets case, we have fewer period 1 purchases and fewer period 2 purchases.

Comparison. What are the effects of BBP in S markets? Whereas the seller's profit was $\frac{1}{2}V$ without BBP, it is $\pi_1(p_1) + \pi_2^H(2p_1) + \pi_2^L(p_1) = 0.45V$ with BBP. In terms of consumer surplus, as compared to a surplus of 0.25V without BBP, we have $CS_1(p_1) + CS_2^H(2p_1) + CS_2^L(p_1) = 0.325V$ with BBP. When consumers are aware of the seller's use of BBP and respond strategically, BBP helps consumers and harms sellers. (This is why sellers would prefer to commit to refraining from using BBP, if they could.)

Drilling down further, we can distinguish between four groups of consumers, as shown in Table 2.2. The table also presents, for each group, the consumer surplus, the seller's profit, and the total surplus (which combines the consumer surplus and the seller's profit), with and without BBP.

We can now summarize the effect of BBP on each group. (1) Consumers with $v \in \left[0, \frac{3V}{10}\right]$ would be excluded from the market with and without BBP. (2) Consumers with $v \in \left[\frac{3V}{10}, \frac{V}{2}\right]$ would be excluded without BBP and served, albeit only in the second period, with BBP. (3) Consumers with $v \in \left[\frac{V}{2}, \frac{6V}{10}\right]$ would be served in both periods without BBP and only in the second period with BBP. Still, because of the lower price charged with BBP in the second period, they enjoy a higher consumer surplus; the seller's profit from serving these consumers is lower. (4) Consumers with $v \in \left[\frac{6V}{10}, V\right]$ would be served, in both periods, with and without BBP. BBP allows the seller to charge a higher price in the second period but pushes the price down in the first period. Overall, in group (4), BBP shifts surplus from the seller

Table 2.2 Disaggregated Effects of BBP in S Markets

Consumers with	Consumer Surplus		Seller's Profit		Total	
	No BBP	BBP	No BBP	BBP	No BBP	BBP
$v \in \left[\frac{6V}{10}, V\right]$	0.24V	0.28V	0.4V	0.36V	0.64V	0.64V
$v \in \left[\frac{V}{2}, \frac{6V}{10}\right]$	0.01V	0.025V	0.1V	0.03V	0.11V	0.055V
$v \in \left[\frac{3V}{10}, \frac{V}{2}\right]$	0	0.02V	0	0.06V	0	0.08V
$v \in \left[0, \frac{3V}{10}\right]$	0	0	0	0	0	0

to consumers. (The total surplus is not changed by the introduction of BBP.) Looking across the four groups, BBP harms the seller and helps consumers, and, unlike in U markets, all groups of consumers benefit.

C. Summary

In S markets, algorithmic behavior-based price discrimination is welfare enhancing, increasing both the consumer surplus and overall welfare. In U markets, the welfare effects are more subtle. BBP reduces overall consumer surplus, but the harm is concentrated in the group of high-WTP consumers who are likely richer, whereas low-WTP consumers who are likely poorer benefit from BBP.

Chapter 3
Algorithmic Targeting

In this chapter, we shift our focus from price discrimination to product targeting. (Although, as we will see, prices may also vary.) The AI-powered algorithm matches different consumers with different products or different product designs. Our analysis covers targeted advertising, which is one of the major examples of algorithmic decision-making in consumer markets.[62]

As with algorithmic price discrimination, the most fundamental conclusion is that algorithmic targeting is largely beneficial in S markets, where most consumers are sophisticated, but potentially harmful in U markets, where many consumers are unsophisticated (although there are also sophisticated consumers). Moreover, as with algorithmic price discrimination, we will show that algorithmic targeting might be harmful in U markets where the unsophisticated consumers overestimate the product's benefit; targeting may actually help consumers when information and rationality deficits lead to underestimation of the product's benefits.

Intuitively, in S markets, algorithmic targeting is welfare enhancing, as it allows for a better matching between products and consumers. If some consumers like tablets and other consumers like laptops, algorithmic targeting can help both to get what they want. In U markets with overestimated benefits, algorithmic targeting might harm biased consumers by offering them an inferior product whose benefits they overestimate. Consumers might be offered an outmoded laptop at an inflated price, and they might like what they see. These biased consumers are harmed, relative to a pre-algorithmic, no-differentiation world, where the superior product would have been offered to all consumers. But even in U markets with overestimated benefits, algorithmic targeting is not always harmful. Specifically, targeting can help consumers, if in the pre-algorithmic, no-differentiation world the seller would offer only the inferior product to the biased consumers at an inflated price. (In this case, algorithmic targeting helps the unbiased consumers and does not harm the biased consumers.) In U markets where some consumers *under*estimate the benefit from a superior product, algorithmic targeting helps consumers because, in a pre-algorithmic,

Algorithmic Harm. Oren Bar-Gill and Cass R. Sunstein, Oxford University Press. © Oren Bar-Gill and Cass R. Sunstein (2025). DOI: 10.1093/oso/9780197778197.003.0004

no-differentiation world either (i) the inferior product would have been offered to all consumers or (ii) the superior product would have been offered at a price that completely excludes biased consumers from the market (whereas targeting allows biased consumers to at least get the inferior product).

AI-powered algorithms are increasingly being used in U markets to target vulnerable consumers and exploit their overestimation bias.[63] The company EyeQ, which counts VinMart and Unilever among its "partners," developed an "Emotional Recognition" algorithm that scans the faces of in-store shoppers "to measure six basic emotions, detect genders and ages," and then "optimize[s] the advertisement targeting effect."[64] A leaked internal Facebook strategy document boasted, "By monitoring posts, pictures, interactions and internet activity in real-time, Facebook can work out when young people feel 'stressed,' 'defeated,' 'overwhelmed,' 'anxious,' 'nervous,' 'stupid,' 'silly,' 'useless,' and a 'failure.'" According to the leaked document, this can be used to micro-target ads at "moments when young people need a confidence boost."[65] Another example involves Target Corporation, which allegedly used big data and algorithms to identify pregnant consumers and new parents and then sent them special coupons (Duhigg 2013). This could be good for S consumers but bad for U consumers or for consumers who temporarily become U consumers as sleep-deprived new parents.

A. S Markets

In S markets, where most consumers are sophisticated, algorithmic targeting can be welfare enhancing. Consider the market for laptops and assume, for simplicity, that there are two types of laptops. The first has a large, super-high-definition screen and a powerful graphics card. The second has a lower-end screen and graphics card, but a super-fast central processing unit and extra random-access memory. It would be welfare enhancing if the algorithm were to offer the first laptop to a graphic designer and the second to a computer scientist who needs to analyze large data sets. Or consider a market for cars and assume, for simplicity, that there are two types of cars: a larger car with more legroom and a bigger trunk, and a smaller car that comes with a higher-end entertainment system. It would be welfare enhancing if the algorithm were to offer the larger car to a suburban family and the smaller car to an unmarried city dweller who enjoys listening to opera (and struggles with parking in the city). In more extreme cases, every consumer could be offered the specific laptop or the specific car that is most likely to fit their particular needs.[66]

The examples could easily be proliferated. The central point is that in light of the immense diversity of both preferences and products, a great deal might be gained in terms of welfare if an algorithm could help to "match" particular desires and needs with particular offerings. So long as we are dealing with S markets, there are welfare gains if the matches are accurate. To be sure, we would have little need for the assistance of an algorithm if search costs were zero; in that case, people could find the right product. A key advantage of the algorithm, under the circumstances we are assuming, is that it reduces search costs.

B. U Markets

With respect to algorithmic targeting, the interesting U markets are those where unsophisticated consumers appear alongside a significant number of sophisticated consumers. In these markets, algorithmic targeting might be welfare reducing. Suppose that unsophisticated consumers overestimate the benefit from a lower-quality product, mistakenly preferring this product over an objectively superior product. If so, the algorithm would offer the superior product to the sophisticated consumers while offering the lower-quality product to the unsophisticated consumers. This algorithmic outcome is harmful if, in a pre-algorithmic world with no product targeting, sellers would offer the superior product to *all* consumers.

In these scenarios, one group of consumers is offered lower-quality products rather than just different-quality products (as in the laptops and cars examples from Section A above). But algorithmic targeting can also help consumers in U markets. For instance, if a sufficiently large number of unsophisticated consumers *under*estimate the benefit from a higher-quality product, mistakenly preferring a lower-quality product, then in a pre-algorithmic world all consumers would be offered the lower-quality product. The advantage of algorithmic targeting is that it allows the seller to offer the higher-quality product at least to the sophisticated consumers.

Consider a market with two products, P1 and P2, where the benefit (to consumers) from P1 is larger than the benefit from P2. To focus on the effect of benefit and perceived benefit, we assume that the cost, to Seller, of manufacturing the two products is identical, and for expositional purposes we let this cost be zero. We assume that some of the consumers are sophisticated, and thus accurately identify the benefits that they would derive from each product, while others are unsophisticated, and thus misperceive the benefit from one of the products. We distinguish between the case where the lower, P2 benefit is overestimated and the case where the higher, P1 benefit is underestimated. Market power is such that Seller gets half of the perceived surplus and the consumer gets half of the perceived surplus. (Note that, since the cost is zero, half of the perceived surplus is equal to half of the perceived benefit.) This equal division of the perceived surplus is achieved by setting the price equal to half of the perceived benefit.[67]

1. Overestimation

Consider the following examples:

Example 3.1a

There are two types of cars: (i) a larger car with more legroom and a bigger trunk (P1), which provides a benefit of 200, and (ii) a smaller car that comes with a higher-end entertainment system (P2), which provides a benefit of 100. One half (1/2) of consumers are sophisticated, and thus accurately identify the benefits that they would derive from each car. The other half (1/2) of consumers overestimate the number of hours that they will spend listening to opera in the car and thus overestimate the benefit from P2, mistakenly thinking that it is 300 (rather than 100).[68]

Example 3.1b

Same as Example 3.1a, except that one quarter (1/4) of consumers are sophisticated, and the other three quarters (3/4) overestimate the benefit from P2, mistakenly thinking that it is 300 (rather than 100).

In a world with big data and AI-powered algorithms, Seller can distinguish between the biased and unbiased consumers. Therefore, Seller will offer the larger vehicle to the unbiased consumers, at a price of 100 (which is half of the actual benefit, 200). And Seller will offer the smaller car with the high-end entertainment system to the biased consumers who overestimate the benefit from the entertainment system, at a price of 150 (which is half of the perceived benefit, 300). In an algorithmic world, in Example 3.1a, Seller's overall profit is $\frac{1}{2} \times 100 + \frac{1}{2} \times 150 = 125$, and the overall consumer surplus is $\frac{1}{2} \times (200 - 100) + \frac{1}{2} \times (100 - 150) = 25$. And, in Example 3.1b, Seller's overall profit is $\frac{1}{4} \times 100 + \frac{3}{4} \times 150 = 137.5$, and the overall consumer surplus is $\frac{1}{4} \times (200 - 100) + \frac{3}{4} \times (100 - 150) = -12.5$.

To appreciate the potential algorithmic harm (or benefit) in such cases, we must compare the targeting outcome to the no-differentiation benchmark. What would car sellers do in a pre-algorithmic world, where they cannot distinguish the biased consumers from the unbiased consumers? Unable to discriminate, the sellers would offer the same car to all consumers.[69] But which car will they offer? Would they offer the larger car or the smaller? And what price will they set? If Seller offers P1, then misperception doesn't play a role (since only the benefit from P2 is misperceived). Seller sets a price of 100 and earns a profit of 100. Note that all consumers buy P1. If Seller offers P2, then Seller would forgo the business generated by the unbiased consumers and set a price of 150, at which only overestimators would make the purchase. Seller's profit would then be $\frac{1}{2} \times 150 = 75$ in Example 3.1a and $\frac{3}{4} \times 150 = 112.5$ in Example 3.1b, reflecting a higher per-unit profit but a smaller number of units sold.[70] Since $75 < 100$, in Example 3.1a Seller will offer the larger car to all consumers, and the consumer surplus will be $200 - 100 = 100$. And, since $112.5 > 100$, in Example 3.1b Seller will offer the smaller car at a price that will attract only the biased consumers, and the consumer surplus will be $\frac{3}{4} \times (100 - 150) = -37.5$.

To assess the welfare effects of algorithmic targeting, we compare the pre- and post-algorithmic worlds. In Example 3.1a, targeting harms consumers who enjoy a surplus of 100 in the pre-algorithmic world and only 25 in the post-algorithmic world. In a pre-algorithmic world, all consumers get the superior product (the larger car), P1, whereas in the post-algorithmic world, the biased consumers get the inferior product (the smaller car), P2, and overpay for it. In contrast, in Example 3.1b, targeting helps consumers, who lose 37.5 in the pre-algorithmic world and lose only 12.5 in the post-algorithmic world. In a pre-algorithmic world, unbiased consumers are left out of the market, whereas in the post-algorithmic world they get the larger car, P1, and their purchases increase the overall consumer surplus. (In both worlds, biased consumers get the smaller car, P2, and overpay for it.)

2. Underestimation

Consider the following examples:

Example 3.2a

There are two types of cars: (i) a highly fuel-efficient hybrid vehicle (P1), which provides a benefit of 300, and (ii) a gas guzzler, but one that comes with fancier seats and a higher-end entertainment system (P2) and provides a benefit of 200. One-half (1/2) of consumers are sophisticated and thus accurately identify the benefits that they would derive from each car. The other half (1/2) of consumers are present-biased and thus underestimate the fuel-efficiency advantage of P1; these consumers mistakenly think that the benefit from P1 is 100 (rather than 300).[71]

Example 3.2b

Same as Example 3.2a, except that three-quarters (3/4) of consumers are sophisticated, and the other one-quarter (1/4) underestimate the benefit from P2, mistakenly thinking that it is 100 (rather than 300).

In a world with big data and AI-powered algorithms, Seller can distinguish between the biased and unbiased consumers. Therefore, Seller will offer the hybrid vehicle to the unbiased consumers, at a price of 150 (which is half of the actual benefit, 300). And Seller will offer the gas guzzler with the fancy seats and the high-end entertainment system to the biased consumers who underestimate the fuel-efficiency advantage of the hybrid car, at a price of 100 (which is half of the actual benefit, 200). In an algorithmic world, in Example 3.2a, Seller's overall profit is $\frac{1}{2} \times 150 + \frac{1}{2} \times 100 = 125$, and the overall consumer surplus is $\frac{1}{2} \times (300 - 150) + \frac{1}{2} \times (200 - 100) = 125$. And in Example 3.2b, Seller's overall profit is $\frac{3}{4} \times 150 + \frac{1}{4} \times 100 = 137.5$, and the overall consumer surplus is $\frac{3}{4} \times (300 - 150) + \frac{1}{4} \times (200 - 100) = 137.5$.

To appreciate the potential algorithmic harm (or benefit) in such cases, we must compare the targeting outcome to the no-differentiation benchmark—to a pre-algorithmic world where, unable to distinguish between the biased and unbiased consumers, sellers must offer the same car to all consumers. If Seller offers the gas guzzler (P2), then misperception doesn't play a role (since only the benefit from P1 is misperceived). Seller sets a price 100 and earns a profit of 100. Note that all consumers buy P2. If Seller offers the hybrid vehicle (P1), then Seller would forgo the business generated by the biased consumers and set a price of 150, at which only unbiased consumers would make the purchase. Seller's profit would then be $\frac{1}{2} \times 150 = 75$ in Example 3.2a and $\frac{3}{4} \times 150 = 112.5$ in Example 3.2b, reflecting a higher per-unit profit but a smaller number of units sold.[72] Since $75 < 100$, in Example 3.2a Seller will offer the gas guzzler to all consumers, and the consumer surplus will be $200 - 100 = 100$. And since $112.5 > 100$, in Example 3.2b Seller will offer the hybrid car at a price that will attract only the unbiased consumers, and the consumer surplus will be $\frac{3}{4} \times (300 - 150) = 112.5$.

To assess the welfare effects of algorithmic targeting, we compare the pre- and post-algorithmic worlds. In Example 3.2a, targeting helps consumers, who enjoy a surplus of 100 in the pre-algorithmic world and a higher surplus of 125 in the post-algorithmic world. In a pre-algorithmic world, all consumers get the inferior product (the gas guzzler), P2, whereas in the post-algorithmic world, the unbiased consumers get the better product (the hybrid), P1. Also, in Example 3.2b, targeting helps consumers, who enjoy a surplus of 112.5 in the pre-algorithmic world and a higher surplus of 137.5 in the post-algorithmic world. In a pre-algorithmic world, biased consumers are left out of the market, whereas in the post-algorithmic world they at least get the gas guzzler, P2 (which still provides a positive benefit).

C. In Brief

In S markets, algorithmic targeting is welfare enhancing, as it allows for a better matching between products and consumers. In U markets, the picture is more complicated. When some consumers overestimate the benefit from an inferior product, algorithmic targeting harms consumers if the superior product would have been offered to all consumers in a pre-algorithmic, no-differentiation world. If the inferior product would have been offered at an inflated price only to the biased consumers, then algorithmic targeting helps the unbiased consumers (and does not harm the biased consumers). When some consumers underestimate the benefit from a superior product, algorithmic targeting helps consumers because, in a pre-algorithmic, no-differentiation world either (i) the inferior product would have been offered to all consumers or (ii) the superior product would have been offered at a price that completely excludes biased consumers from the market (whereas targeting allows biased consumers to at least get the inferior product).

Cases where benefits are overestimated and there is a significant risk of algorithmic harm are quite common. For example, a seller may offer to such biased consumers excessively expensive or unneeded life insurance, extended warranties, home protection plans, or 1,001 dance lessons. In all of these cases, biased consumers might overestimate the benefits of the relevant offerings.[73]

There is another set of cases where algorithmic targeting can help unsophisticated consumers. An algorithm that identifies a bias may respond in a way that both maximizes the seller's profits and helps the biased consumer. For example, an algorithm may identify a present-biased consumer who would not purchase a gym subscription because he underestimates the long-term benefits of gym membership. If the algorithm offers this consumer a low introductory rate (and a high long-term rate), which is especially attractive to the present-biased consumer, then the consumer may purchase the gym membership—to the benefit of both seller and buyer. Or assume that a bank's algorithm identifies less sophisticated consumers who are likely to spend excessively and offers them a product that helps them manage their finances more responsibly (and thus also avoid defaulting on their bank loans). This could be beneficial to both the bank and the consumer.

D. Shifting Preferences

There is an independent problem which raises fundamental questions. Focusing on markets with sophisticated consumers, where we touted the welfare benefits of algorithmic targeting, our central assumption was that an algorithm should be in a good position to know, at a given time, what people will like, and how much they will like it. It will therefore be able to offer them goods and services that are well-matched to previously registered preferences, for example, preferences expressed through prior purchases. If a consumer likes specific books—say, about World War II or about the wonderfulness or terribleness of a particular politician—the algorithm will be able to display, to that consumer, books that fit those preferences, and at the right prices. From one perspective, that is highly desirable. From another perspective, this could be harmful, for instance, if the consumer would also enjoy books about economics or psychology, even though she never purchased such books before. By offering only books that match previously registered preferences, the algorithm might prevent the consumer from learning that she would also enjoy other books. Things become even more complicated if we shift from a learning story to a preference-changing story.[74]

In ordinary markets, people are continuously learning about their preferences, and also their preferences change over time. One reason is that consumers often expand their own horizons. They may do so after seeing a range of diverse offerings that might not be included in an algorithm's choices or after serendipitous encounters that pique interest and curiosity. An algorithm might limit itself to products that match previously registered preferences, which might not be in consumers' interest and which might not increase their welfare.

It is challenging to undertake welfare analysis that is unmoored from previously registered preferences (Oishi & Westgate 2022; Dolan 2015). But we could easily imagine situations in which new and expanded horizons improve welfare; an algorithm might not help on that score and could even hurt. To be sure, an especially sophisticated algorithm might anticipate this problem, and might solve it. It might know not only what consumers have liked in the past, but also what they might end up liking in the future, even if the latter diverges from the former. It is a nice question whether and when algorithms will achieve that level of sophistication.[75]

Appendix

The Appendix provides a formal analysis of algorithmic targeting in U markets to complement the informal discussion from Section B. Consider a market with two products, P1 and P2. The cost, to Seller, of manufacturing P1 is c_1 and the cost of manufacturing P2 is c_2. To focus on the effect of benefit and perceived benefit, we assume that $c_1 = c_2 \equiv c$. Consumers enjoy a benefit b_1 from P1 and b_2 from P2; assume that $b_1 > b_2$.[76] We analyze two types of misperception:

(a) Overestimation: Biased consumers (mistakenly) think that the benefit from P2 is δb_2, where $\delta > 1$. For example, consider the market for new cars and assume, for simplicity, that there are two types of cars—one is larger with more legroom and a bigger trunk (P1), whereas the other is smaller but comes with a higher-end entertainment system (P2). Consumers who overestimate the number of hours that they will spend listening to opera in the car will overestimate the benefit from P2. To focus on situations where the overestimation bias is potentially most troubling, we assume that $b_2 < b_1 < \delta b_2$, that is, that the bias flips the relative desirability of the two products.

(b) Underestimation: Biased consumers (mistakenly) think that the benefit from P1 is δb_1, where $\delta < 1$. Consider, again, the market for new cars and assume, for simplicity, that there are two types of cars—one is a highly fuel-efficient hybrid vehicle (P1), whereas the other is much less fuel-efficient but comes with fancier seats and a higher-end entertainment system (P2). Since the benefit from P1 accrues over time, present-biased consumers will underestimate this benefit. To focus on situations where the underestimation bias is potentially most troubling, we assume that $\delta b_1 < b_2 < b_1$, that is, that the bias flips the relative desirability of the two products.

In both cases, we assume that a share α_U of consumers are unbiased and recognize the true benefit (b_1 or b_2), whereas the remaining share α_B ($= 1 - \alpha_U$) of consumers are biased and misperceive the benefit, as δb_2 in the overestimation case or as δb_1 in the underestimation case. Market power is such that Seller can set a price equal to a percentage $\gamma < 1$ of the consumers' benefit (or WTP).[77]

1. Overestimation

In a world with big data and sophisticated algorithms, Seller can distinguish between the biased and unbiased consumers, offering P1 to the unbiased consumers and P2 to the biased consumers.[78] In our example, the algorithm offers the larger vehicle to the unbiased consumers, at a price of $p_1 = \gamma b_1$. At the same time, the algorithm offers the smaller car with the high-end entertainment system to consumers who are identified as those who are likely to overestimate the benefit from the entertainment system. Moreover, the algorithm will set a high price for the smaller car with the high-end entertainment system, reflecting the biased consumers' inflated WTP: $p_2^B = \gamma\delta b_2$. Seller's overall profit, in an algorithmic world, is $\pi^A = \alpha_U(p_1 - c) + \alpha_B(p_2^B - c) = \alpha_U(\gamma b_1 - c) + \alpha_B(\gamma\delta b_2 - c)$, and the overall consumer surplus is $CS^A = \alpha_U(b_1 - p_1) + \alpha_B(b_2 - p_2^B) = \alpha_U(1-\gamma)b_1 + \alpha_B(1-\delta\gamma)b_2$.

To appreciate the potential algorithmic harm in such cases, we must compare the algorithmic targeting outcome to the no-differentiation benchmark. What would car sellers do in a pre-algorithmic world, where they cannot distinguish the biased consumers from the unbiased consumers? Unable to discriminate, the sellers would offer the same car to all consumers.[79] But which car will they offer? Will they offer the larger car (P1) or the smaller (P2)? And what price will they set? The answer depends on market conditions—on the aggregate demand for each car model, which depends on the number of biased versus unbiased consumers.[80]

Which product will Seller offer—P1 or P2? If Seller offers P1, then misperception doesn't play a role (since only the benefit from P2 is overestimated). Seller sets a price of $p_1 = \gamma b_1$ and earns a profit of $\pi_1^{PA} = \gamma b_1 - c$ (where the superscript "PA" refers to the pre-algorithmic world). Note that all consumers buy P1. If Seller offers P2, then she must choose which consumers she wants to serve. If Seller wants to serve all consumers, she will set a price of $p_2 = \gamma b_2$ and earn a profit of $\pi_2^{PA} = \gamma b_2 - c$. Alternatively, Seller could forgo the business generated by the unbiased consumers and set a higher price, $p_{2B} = \gamma\delta b_2$ (the subscript "2B" stands for a P2 price targeting biased consumers), at which only overestimators would make the purchase. Seller's profit will then be $\pi_{2B}^{PA} = \alpha_B(\gamma\delta b_2 - c)$, reflecting a higher per-unit profit but a smaller number of units sold.

Note that, since $\pi_1^{PA} > \pi_2^{PA}$, Seller will never offer P2 at a price that will attract all consumers. Intuitively, in order to sell the smaller car to all consumers, Seller would have to reduce the price to a level that even unbiased consumers would be willing to pay. But if such a low price is needed to capture the entire market with the smaller car, it is more profitable for Seller to capture the entire market with the larger car that can fetch a higher price. Therefore, in a pre-algorithmic world:

(i) Seller will offer P1, the larger car, to all consumers, if the profit that Seller can make from offering the larger car to all consumers exceeds the profit that she can make from offering the smaller car only to overestimators, that is, if $\pi_1^{PA} > \pi_{2B}^{PA}$. In this case, consumer surplus will be $CS_1^{PA} = (1 - \gamma)\, b_1$.

(ii) Seller will offer P2, the smaller car, at a price that will attract only biased consumers, if the profit that she can make from offering the smaller car only to overestimators exceeds the profit that she can make from offering the larger car to all consumers, that is, if $\pi_{2B}^{PA} > \pi_1^{PA}$. In this case, consumer surplus will be $CS_{2B}^{PA} = \alpha_B (1 - \delta\gamma)\, b_2$.

And since $\pi_1^{PA} > \pi_{2B}^{PA}$ is equivalent to $\gamma b_1 - c > \alpha_B (\gamma\delta b_2 - c)$, there exists a threshold $\hat{\alpha}_B = \frac{\gamma b_1 - c}{\gamma\delta b_2 - c}$, such that P1 will be offered to all consumers when $\alpha_B < \hat{\alpha}_B$, and P2 will be offered only to biased consumers when $\alpha_B > \hat{\alpha}_B$. We can thus write:

$$CS^{PA} = \begin{cases} CS_1^{PA} = (1 - \gamma)\, b_1 & , \quad \alpha_B < \hat{\alpha}_B \\ CS_{2B}^{PA} = \alpha_B (1 - \delta\gamma)\, b_2 & , \quad \alpha_B > \hat{\alpha}_B \end{cases}$$

To assess the welfare effects of algorithmic targeting, we compare the pre- and post-algorithmic worlds. In case (i), when $\alpha_B < \hat{\alpha}_B$, algorithmic targeting harms consumers, since $CS^A < CS_1^{PA}$. In a pre-algorithmic world, all consumers get the superior product (the larger car), P1, whereas in the post-algorithmic world, the biased consumers get the inferior product (the smaller car), P2, and overpay for it. In contrast, in case (ii), when $\alpha_B > \hat{\alpha}_B$, algorithmic targeting helps consumers, since $CS^A > CS_{2B}^{PA}$. In a pre-algorithmic world, unbiased consumers are left out of the market, whereas in the post-algorithmic world, they get P1. (In both worlds, biased consumers get P2 and overpay for it.)

To conclude, algorithmic targeting harms consumers when $\alpha_B < \hat{\alpha}_B$ and helps consumers when $\alpha_B > \hat{\alpha}_B$. In other words, algorithmic targeting is more likely to harm consumers when the share of biased consumers is small, that is, when α_B is small. Note that the threshold, $\hat{\alpha}_B$, is decreasing in the magnitude of the misperception (δ); that is, the range of scenarios where algorithmic targeting is harmful is smaller when the misperception is greater. Combining these results: algorithmic targeting is more likely

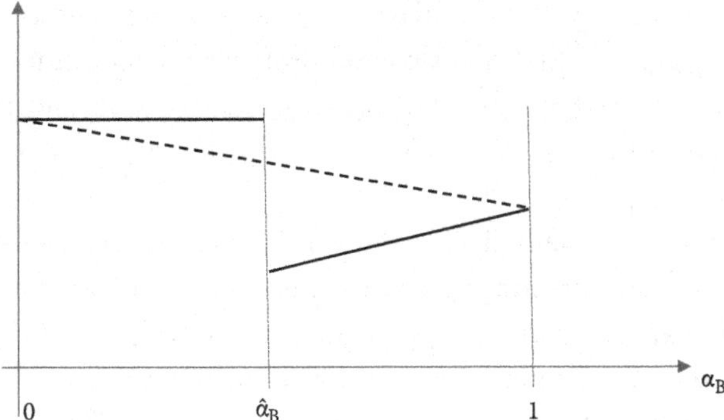

Figure 3.1 CS^{PA} (solid line) and CS^{A} (dashed line) as a function of α_B.

to harm consumers when the share of biased consumers is small and the magnitude of the bias is small.

With respect to the no-differentiation consumer surplus (CS^{PA}), we note that (i) $CS_{2B}^{PA}(\hat{\alpha}_B) = \frac{\gamma b_1 - c}{\gamma \delta b_2 - c}(1-\delta\gamma)\, b_2 < (1-\gamma)\, b_1 = CS_1^{PA}$,[81] (ii) $CS_{2B}^{PA}(\alpha_B)$ is linearly increasing in α_B when $\delta\gamma < 1$ and linearly decreasing in α_B when $\delta\gamma > 1$, and (iii) $CS_{2B}^{PA}(\alpha_B = 1) < (1-\gamma)\, b_1 = CS_1^{PA}$.[82] Comparing to the consumer surplus with algorithmic targeting, we note that (i) $CS^{PA}(\alpha_B = 0) = CS^{A}(\alpha_B = 0)$, (ii) $CS^{A}(\alpha_B)$ is linearly decreasing in α_B, and (iii) $CS^{PA}(\alpha_B = 1) = CS^{A}(\alpha_B = 1)$.[83] We can now graph the no-differentiation consumer surplus (CS^{PA}) as a function of α_B, the solid line in Figure 3.1, and the consumer surplus with algorithmic targeting (CS^{A}) as a function of α_B, the dashed line in Figure 3.1. (In Figure 3.1, we assume $\delta\gamma < 1$.)

2. Underestimation

In a world with big data and sophisticated algorithms, Seller can distinguish between the biased and unbiased consumers, offering P1 to the unbiased consumers and P2 to the biased consumers.[84] In our example, the algorithm offers the hybrid vehicle to the unbiased consumers, at a price of $p_1 = \gamma b_1$. At the same time, the algorithm offers the low-fuel-efficiency car to consumers who are identified as suffering from present bias, namely, to myopic consumers who fail to account for the significant long-term cost saving that the hybrid vehicle promises; these consumers will be charged $p_2 = \gamma b_2$. Seller's overall profit, in an algorithmic world, is $\pi^A = \alpha_U (p_1 - c) + \alpha_B (p_2 - c) = \alpha_U (\gamma b_1 - c) + \alpha_B (\gamma b_2 - c)$, and the overall consumer surplus is $CS^A = \alpha_U (b_1 - p_1) + \alpha_B (b_2 - p_2) = \alpha_U (1 - \gamma) b_1 + \alpha_B (1 - \gamma) b_2$.

To appreciate the potential algorithmic harm in such cases, we must compare the algorithmic targeting outcome to the no-differentiation benchmark. What would car sellers do in a pre-algorithmic world, where they cannot distinguish the present-biased consumers from the unbiased consumers? Unable to discriminate, the sellers would offer the same car to all consumers. But which car will they offer? Will they offer the hybrid (P1) or the gas guzzler (P2)? And what price will they set? The answer depends on market conditions—on the aggregate demand for each model, which depends on the number of biased versus unbiased consumers.[85]

Which product will Seller offer—P1 or P2? If Seller offers P2, then misperception doesn't play a role (since only the benefit from P1 is underestimated). Seller sets a price of $p_2 = \gamma b_2$ and earns a profit of $\pi_2^{PA} = \gamma b_2 - c$. Note that all consumers buy P2. If Seller offers P1, then she must choose which consumers she wants to serve. If Seller wants to serve all consumers, specifically if she wants to keep the underestimators, she will set a price of $p_{1B} = \gamma \delta b_1$ and earn a profit of $\pi_{1B}^{PA} = \gamma \delta b_1 - c$. Alternatively, Seller could forgo the business generated by the biased consumers and set a higher price, $p_1 = \gamma b_1$, at which only unbiased consumers will make the purchase. Seller's profit will then be $\pi_1^{PA} = \alpha_U (\gamma b_1 - c)$, reflecting a higher per-unit profit but a smaller number of units sold.

Note that, since $\pi_2^{PA} > \pi_{1B}^{PA}$, Seller will never offer P1 at a price that will attract all consumers. Intuitively, in order to sell the hybrid to all consumers, Seller would have to reduce the price to a level that even present-biased consumers would be willing to pay. But if such a low price is needed to capture the entire market with a hybrid, it is more profitable for Seller to capture the entire market with the gas guzzler that can fetch a higher price. Therefore, in a pre-algorithmic world:

(i) Seller will offer P2, the gas guzzler, to all consumers, if the profit that Seller can make from offering the gas guzzler to all consumers exceeds the profit that she can make from offering the hybrid only to unbiased consumers, that is, if $\pi_2^{PA} > \pi_1^{PA}$. In this case, consumer surplus will be $CS_2^{PA} = (1 - \gamma) b_2$.

(ii) Seller will offer P1, the hybrid, at a price that will attract only unbiased consumers, if the profit that Seller can make from offering the hybrid to these unbiased consumers exceeds the profit that she can make from offering the gas guzzler to all consumers, that is, if $\pi_1^{PA} > \pi_2^{PA}$. In this case, consumer surplus will be $CS_1^{PA} = \alpha_U (1 - \gamma) b_1$.

And since $\pi_2^{PA} > \pi_1^{PA}$ is equivalent to $\gamma b_2 - c > \alpha_U (\gamma b_1 - c)$, there exists a threshold $\hat{\alpha}_U = \frac{\gamma b_2 - c}{\gamma b_1 - c}$, such that P2 will be offered to all consumers when $\alpha_U < \hat{\alpha}_U$ and P1 will be offered only to unbiased consumers when $\alpha_U > \hat{\alpha}_U$. Equivalently, there exists a threshold $\hat{\alpha}_B = 1 - \hat{\alpha}_U$, such that P2 will be offered to all consumers when $\alpha_B > \hat{\alpha}_B$ and P1 will be offered only to unbiased consumers when $\alpha_B < \hat{\alpha}_B$. We can thus write:

$$CS^{PA} = \begin{cases} CS_2^{PA} = (1 - \gamma) b_2 & , \quad \alpha_U < \hat{\alpha}_U \\ CS_1^{PA} = \alpha_U (1 - \gamma) b_1 & , \quad \alpha_U > \hat{\alpha}_U \end{cases}$$

or:

$$CS^{PA} = \begin{cases} CS_1^{PA} = \alpha_U (1 - \gamma) b_1 & , \quad \alpha_B < \hat{\alpha}_B \\ CS_2^{PA} = (1 - \gamma) b_2 & , \quad \alpha_B > \hat{\alpha}_B \end{cases}$$

To assess the welfare effects of algorithmic targeting, we compare the pre- and post-algorithmic worlds. In case (i), when $\alpha_B > \hat{\alpha}_B$, algorithmic targeting helps consumers, since $CS^A > CS_2^{PA}$. In a pre-algorithmic world, all consumers get the inferior product (the gas guzzler), P2, whereas in the post-algorithmic world, the unbiased consumers get the better product (the hybrid), P1. Also in case (ii), when $\alpha_B < \hat{\alpha}_B$, algorithmic targeting helps consumers, since $CS^A > CS_1^{PA}$. In a pre-algorithmic world, biased consumers are left out of the market, whereas in the post-algorithmic world, they at least get P2 (which still provides a positive benefit). To conclude, when the misperception takes the form of *under*estimation (of product benefits), algorithmic targeting always helps consumers, relative to the no-differentiation benchmark.

Chapter 4
Algorithmically Enhanced Misperceptions

Thus far we have assumed that consumers, or some of them, "come with" certain information or rationality deficits and that the AI-powered algorithm exploits these existing misperceptions—setting higher prices for, or offering inferior products to, consumers who overestimate the benefit from a product or service. In this chapter we relax the exogenous misperceptions assumption and consider the case where AI-powered algorithms create or exacerbate the information or rationality deficits. They might, for example, provide misleading or even false information to certain people, and they might work to inculcate present bias or unrealistic optimism in other people. It is easily imaginable that AI would know which consumers are most likely to be susceptible to interventions of this kind.

Here is another way to put the point. We might think of people as having fixed amounts of information and fixed levels of bias. But how much information they have might be a function of, or endogenous to, what they are told. If people are told that a product is likely to last for five years, they might believe it. Something similar can be said about behavioral biases. Unrealistic optimism can be induced, and the same is true for present bias. Of course it is true that skeptical consumers, pessimistic consumers, and future-focused consumers might be resistant to any efforts to induce the relevant biases. The only point is that an algorithm might be able to increase the biases that people have or produce biases that people do not have.

We are entering an era when AI-powered large language models like ChatGPT, AI Studios, and Synthesia design the communications—text-based, audio, or video—that flow from seller to consumer. Given the enhanced profits that sellers stand to make when consumers suffer from information and rationality deficits (as laid out in the previous chapters), an algorithm that is programmed to maximize profits could be expected to design communications that would effectively misinform consumers or trigger misperceptions unless legal (or extralegal) constraints are put in place. This chapter offers a series of examples illustrating how AI-powered algorithms might create or exacerbate misperceptions among the seller's potential customers.

Algorithmic Harm. Oren Bar-Gill and Cass R. Sunstein, Oxford University Press. © Oren Bar-Gill and Cass R. Sunstein (2025). DOI: 10.1093/oso/9780197778197.003.0005

The harms from these misperceptions are the same harms that we studied in previous chapters. When algorithms create misperceptions, they transform an S market into a U market, with the algorithmic harms such a market entails. And when algorithms exacerbate misperceptions, they amplify the harms from algorithmic price discrimination or algorithmic targeting. (We can assume that after one algorithm creates or exacerbates misperceptions, another algorithm—or even the same algorithm—will engage in price discrimination or product targeting.)[86]

A. Algorithmic Infidelity

Ashley Madison defines itself as a "discreet ... dating community." The website's trademarked byline reads, "Life is short. Have an affair" (Ashley Madison n.d.). In 2015, Ashley Madison was hacked and the company's source code, member database, and internal communications were made public. Beyond the horrible consequences of this privacy breach (at least one person committed suicide; see Baraniuk 2015; McPhate 2016), the information revealed that Ashley Madison was defrauding its customers. It was, at the time, a new kind of fraud. Users—mostly men, but not only—were having intimate communications on the Ashley Madison platform with fembots, and not with actual potential female partners. These fembots convinced guests to become paying members, as membership was necessary to engage with the bot, presenting as a potential partner, who was initiating contact. And even members were paying to send messages to a bot. According to one account, "[A]verage paying customers of Ashley Madison had a 35 percent chance of paying to send a message to a bot. And 80 percent of men paid to join after messaging with a bot, too."[87] In December 2016, an FTC investigation of Ashley Madison concluded with a Stipulated Order for Permanent Injunction and Other Equitable Relief, which, among other things, required Ashley Madison to stop the fembot con.[88]

The Ashley Madison fembots were pretty basic, but more sophisticated AI-powered chatbots, in the sex industry and beyond, are already here, their algorithms learning how to optimize messaging to make money for their corporate masters (Debuk 2015). The Ashley Madison chatbots were designed to create misperceptions—to make users believe that they were communicating with a potential female partner. Using the analytical framework that we developed in previous chapters, these bots caused consumers to overestimate the benefit from the service that Ashley Madison offered. Because of this overestimated benefit, Ashley Madison was able to convert more nonpaying guests into paying members and also to retain paying members for longer periods, probably while paying higher prices. (In the Ashley Madison example, there is no evidence that AI-powered algorithms engaged in price discrimination or targeting.)

The specific type of AI-induced misperception is worth emphasizing. It is a misperception about the identity of a counterparty: a bot masquerading as a human being. And AI is getting really good at simulating human agents.[89] Moreover, with the advent of "deepfakes," the algorithmic manipulation is reaching far beyond text to voice and video, making it very easy to present as a human, even a specific human. If consumers trust a certain celebrity's opinion about the value of a product, sellers can easily deep-fake an endorsement by this celebrity. The misperception about the identity of the endorser could easily result in misperception about the product's value.[90]

B. Algorithmically Prioritized Disclosures

Many consumer products—packaged foods, big-ticket items, financial products—are complex and multidimensional, such that it is often impractical to effectively communicate to buyers the quality of each dimension. Of course, sellers disclose information about their products—in advertising, on product packaging, and so on—but consumers cannot realistically be informed of all the product's qualities. Hence sellers, and their algorithms, need to choose what information, on which product attribute, to prioritize. In a recent article, one of us (Bar-Gill) and a co-author analyzed how sellers strategically prioritize disclosure in a way that can harm consumers (Bar-Gill & Ben-Shahar 2023). We draw on that analysis here.

Consider the following example:

> A food product has various quality dimensions, each of which can be regarded by buyers as good or bad. These dimensions may include taste, nutritional aspects like sugar or fat content, health effects, or production qualities (organic, fair trade). Consumers care about some or all of these dimensions but cannot fully examine them for each product in a shopping cart. When disclosing information, the seller could refer to all of the aspects equally, for example in a list that expands on the familiar nutrition data disclosure. Alternatively, through advertising or package design, the seller

> may highlight only the good dimensions (low fat or naturally flavored) and remain silent about the bad dimensions, present them in a less salient manner, or otherwise make it more costly for buyers to learn about them. Because buyers can review only some of the information, how sellers prioritize the different dimensions . . . affect[s] buyers' valuation of the product and the choices they make. (Bar-Gill & Ben-Shahar 2023, 306–307)[91]

Importantly, strategic prioritization of information does not require lying. The seller can disclose everything, just in a way that highlights the good product attributes and de-emphasizes the bad ones. The seller can even overload consumers so as to manipulate them not to pay attention to certain attributes. Or, to put it differently, sellers can be expected to prioritize product disclosures in a way that maximizes their profits, not in the way that maximizes consumer welfare. And AI-powered algorithms can be used to optimize the prioritization of product disclosures—the mode, place, time, and context of presentation of each piece of product-related information. Optimize in terms of seller profits, of course, not in terms of consumer surplus. Without regulation, algorithms might well prioritize information to create or exacerbate consumer misperceptions—to maximize the overestimation of benefits (and underestimation of cost or risk), such that the seller, or its price-setting algorithm, can charge the highest possible price. Moreover, the AI can be expected to choose different prioritizations for different consumers—the "organic" attribute for one consumer and the "low fat" attribute for another.

It is true, of course, that market pressures might help. If a company is known to use AI to reduce consumer welfare, it might be hurt in the marketplace. Other companies might assert that they are using AI to help consumers, not hurt them. But there are reasons to think that competitive pressures will not work in this context (Bar-Gill, Sunstein, & Talgam-Cohen 2023; Akerlof & Shiller 2015). Indeed, companies that play it straight, so to speak, and do not use AI in a way that increases profits while reducing consumer welfare might find themselves at a competitive disadvantage. Market pressures might be the problem, not the solution.

C. What Did the Chatbot Say?

Sellers increasingly communicate with consumers via customer-service bots (Spherical Insights LLP 2024; MarketsandMarkets 2024; McCarthy 2019).

These AI-powered bots might learn to manipulate consumers and cause misperceptions about the seller's product or service.[92] Consider the following real-life story: Jake's grandmother died. He visited Air Canada's website to book a flight from Vancouver to Toronto to attend the funeral. Unsure of how Air Canada's bereavement rates worked, Jake asked Air Canada's chatbot to explain. The chatbot wrote:

> If you need to travel immediately or have already travelled and would like to submit your ticket for a reduced bereavement rate, kindly do so within 90 days of the date your ticket was issued by completing our Ticket Refund Application form.

Jake bought a ticket, flew to Toronto, and later submitted a Ticket Refund Application form (as suggested by the chatbot).

Air Canada refused to issue a refund, citing their bereavement travel policy, which explicitly states that the airline will not provide refunds for bereavement travel after the flight is booked. It should be noted that the bereavement policy was available on Air Canada's website. Indeed, the chatbot's earlier response linked to a webpage with the airline's bereavement travel policy. But Jake was messaging with Air Canada's chatbot, and he relied on the chatbot's answers. A Canadian court sided with Jake and forced Air Canada to pay up (Belanger 2024).

The Air Canada chatbot was successful in getting Jake to buy a ticket. Indeed, the bot was probably programmed to maximize conversion rates. In this story, the chatbot invented a new service feature—an option to receive a refund ex post (rather than only an ex ante discount). This may be an extreme example. In most cases, we would not expect the bots to invent new features but rather to highlight existing attractive features while de-emphasizing less attractive ones (see also Section B above). Or we would expect the bots to figure out how to communicate with a specific customer in a way that most effectively triggers this customer's biases or emotions. But at the end of the day, the result is the same: the AI-powered bot learns to communicate in a way that creates a misperception—an overestimation of the product's value.

D. Algorithmic Advertising

AI-powered algorithms can now create video clips from scratch, based on a simple text prompt (OpenAI n.d.; Deepbrain AI n.d.; Eaton 2024). It would be surprising if such algorithms do not play an increasing role in the creation of advertising and other consumer-facing promotional materials. We also expect that the algorithm will learn how to design such materials in a way that triggers cognitive biases and emotional responses.

For example, an algorithm may emphasize the many things that you could buy right now with money from a loan—a credit card loan, a home equity line of credit, a payday loan—so as to trigger present bias. "Just imagine what you could do with the money, if you could have it now!" Or an algorithm may create a video clip that invokes consumers' patriotic feelings before offering made-in-the-USA products. Such a clip could easily be emotionally engaging and lead people to feel that if they do not purchase such products, they will be acting in a way that hurts their own country. (To be sure, engaging such feelings may or may not involve a bias.) Or an algorithm might produce a video that appeals to optimistic bias by brightly painting a picture of what could happen to property values after one buys a small piece of real estate in some remote area.[93]

Of course, humans have been creating advertising that triggers bias and emotion for a long time, way before the AI era. Our claim, based on current trends, is that the AI-powered algorithm will eventually do a far better job in triggering these cognitive biases and emotional responses. Beyond that, and following the argument from segmentation and personalization that we developed in earlier chapters, AI will design different promotional materials for different consumers: an ad that triggers present bias for a consumer in whom such bias is more easily invoked, and a tear-jerking ad for a consumer who is susceptible to emotional manipulation.[94]

Chapter 5
Algorithmic Coordination

Thus far, we have focused on algorithmic harm that results when AI-powered algorithms meet the information and rationality deficits that afflict many consumers. We now turn to another category of algorithmic harm: harm that algorithms can inflict on consumers regardless of their rationality or sophistication. This is the harm from implicit coordination among algorithms employed by competing sellers. Imagine two hotels in a small resort town that compete over the patronage of tourists. Competition has forced the hotel prices down. After all, if one hotel tries to raise prices, all the tourists would flock to the competing hotel. Of course, both hotels could increase their revenues and profits by colluding and agreeing on higher, supracompetitive prices, but that would be an antitrust violation.[95]

Now imagine that the two hotels, each acting independently, decide to delegate their pricing decisions to an algorithm (or algorithms). The algorithm receives as input dynamic, real-time information about room availability, demand for hotel rooms, and the cost of serving more or fewer customers. The algorithm also receives information about prices charged by the competing hotel. Each of the two hotel owners specifies a straightforward objective for their respective algorithm: set prices to maximize profits. No further instructions are given. (Indeed, the machine-learning algorithms are normally designed to attain a specified objective, and develop, or learn, how to do so optimally on their own.)

It is possible that the algorithms will compete with one another, driving prices down, as in the pre-algorithmic equilibrium. But it is also possible that the algorithms will learn that coordination, that is, keeping prices high as long as the other hotel follows suit, more effectively attains their profit-maximization objective. The result is a new algorithmic equilibrium that is decidedly anticompetitive, where consumers are harmed by the high prices.[96] To be clear, no one told the algorithms to coordinate, and, clearly, the algorithms could not have reached an actual agreement to keep prices high. And herein lies the legal challenge: Can antitrust law police algorithmic coordination? At the very least, it is clear that policymakers, not to mention

Algorithmic Harm. Oren Bar-Gill and Cass R. Sunstein, Oxford University Press. © Oren Bar-Gill and Cass R. Sunstein (2025). DOI: 10.1093/oso/9780197778197.003.0006

legal scholars, are increasingly concerned about the prospect of algorithmic coordination.[97]

While algorithmic coordination does not depend on consumer sophistication, or lack thereof, the harm from algorithmic coordination is a function of consumer misperception. Specifically, if consumers overestimate the benefit from the product or service, the supracompetitive price that the algorithms will coordinate on will be higher.

We begin, in Section A, with evidence of algorithmic coordination. In Section B, we turn to the doctrinal questions implicated by algorithmic coordination.

A. Evidence of Algorithmic Coordination

Sellers are increasingly using machine-learning algorithms to set prices (Ezrachi & Stucke 2016b). And there is evidence that these algorithms could coordinate, and perhaps already are coordinating, among themselves to raise prices. Evidence of algorithmic coordination comes from empirical analysis of real-world pricing data and from experiments that simulate the interaction between pricing algorithms employed by competing sellers. Starting with real-world pricing data, the leading study is by Stephanie Assad, Robert Clark, Daniel Ershov, and Lei Xu (2024). Looking at the German retail gasoline market, these researchers show that adoption of pricing algorithms led to higher prices through increased coordination. Other real-world evidence is anecdotal. Any account will quickly go out of date, but in the real-estate rental market, one algorithm, YieldStar by the Texas-based company RealPage, has dominated the market, guiding some of the country's largest property management companies in setting rent amounts for their properties. Reportedly, RealPage executives touted YieldStar's success in raising rents. It is telling that the YieldStar algorithm uses data on the rents that competitors are charging when generating a recommended rental price for its landlord clients.[98] We expect that the problem is likely to get worse over time.

Additional evidence comes from simulation studies that examine the behavior of pricing algorithms in the lab. The leading study, by Emilio Calvano, Giacomo Calzolari, Vincenzo Denicolò, and Sergio Pastorello (2020), found that "reinforcement learning algorithms generate supra-competitive prices and that these higher prices are the result of tacit autonomous algorithmic collusion."[99] It should be noted that, in these simulation studies, a coordination outcome is not inevitable and, depending on various specifications of the algorithm, may not even be the most likely outcome. For example, it matters whether the algorithm is programmed to maximize current-period profits or the long-term aggregate stream of profits; the nature of the algorithm's learning protocol also matters.[100] But even the more skeptical voices concede that "[c]onstructing well-performing pricing algorithms that learn to collude should certainly be possible, given the many algorithmic techniques that in the last decade have been developed in the dynamic-pricing-and-learning literature within Operations Research" (den Boer, Meylahn, & Schinkel 2022).

Pricing algorithms facilitate collusion by helping competitors meet the conditions for coordination.[101] Specifically, the employment of algorithmic software can "facilitate collusion through increased ease of monitoring and speed of detection and through punishment of possible deviations" (Assad et al. 2024, 724). Indeed, the simulation studies described above observe punishment of competitors who deviate from the high-price equilibrium.[102] Perhaps the most damning evidence comes from the sales pitch used by some vendors of pricing algorithms, such as Kantify, that "promote their products by suggesting that they optimize for long-term revenues and avoid price wars" (Assad et al. 2021, 461).

B. Doctrinal Questions

Algorithmic coordination can arise even when the algorithms are not told to coordinate and keep prices high. The AI-powered algorithms just learn that coordination is the best way to attain the programmed objective: to maximize profits. This scenario poses challenging questions about the doctrinal reach of competition law. In the United States, the main doctrinal requirement for liability is the "agreement" requirement in §1 of the Sherman Act. Algorithmic coordination does not entail actual agreement, in the sense of two parties meeting, discussing pricing, and agreeing to keep their prices at a high, supracompetitive level. But the law does not require such an express agreement. "Agreement," which is not clearly defined or consistently applied, is a doctrinal term of art (Kaplow 2011). Accordingly, there is no consensus on whether algorithmic coordination violates the antitrust laws. In our view, such a consensus should emerge, and in short order.[103]

Since tacit collusion, understood as the mere fact of competitors setting similarly high prices, is not a violation of competition law (Ezrachi & Stucke 2016b, 56–58, 66), some commentators have concluded that algorithmic coordination is not unlawful under current doctrine.[104] Other commentators think that, in some cases, the use of algorithms should count as a "plus factor," which under current doctrine can overcome the liability exemption for tacit collusion.[105] In our view, the doctrinal requirement of "agreement" can and should be understood broadly to encompass algorithmic coordination. It can and should count as an "agreement" when two CEOs actively choose to deploy pricing algorithms with predictable consequences.[106] The reason is that the use of such algorithms is not the same as tacit collusion; it is not a "mere fact" that competitors set similarly high prices. On the contrary, the algorithms are working together, and doing so in the interest of maximizing profits, just as if company heads made an agreement to do so in a hotel room. For markets, algorithmic coordination, as understood here, is equivalent to human coordination. It is an a fortiori case, and hence an easy one, if a vendor sells a common algorithm to competitors, and the competitors know that they are all buying the same "playbook."[107]

C. Summary

In the antitrust context, algorithmic coordination has emerged as a major source of concern, and rightly so. While there is ongoing debate about the conditions under which algorithms are likely to coordinate and set supra-competitive prices, there is little doubt that AI-powered algorithms will soon be able to meet even the more stringent conditions. Competition authorities are right to be concerned about algorithmic coordination, and antitrust law should be interpreted and applied to cover the delegation of pricing decisions to price-coordinating algorithms. While algorithmic coordination has been the focus of antitrust scholars and policymakers who consider the potential harm from algorithmic decision-making, it is not the only potential harm. AI-powered algorithms can also help sellers gain, maintain, and exploit market power, thus harming consumers.[108]

Chapter 6
Race and Sex Discrimination

We now turn to an issue that is receiving a great deal of attention: algorithmic discrimination on the basis of race and sex.[109] The central concern is simple. Human beings discriminate on those grounds. Algorithms might not make the situation better; they might make it worse.

Algorithms might discriminate for specific reasons, and those reasons need to be distinguished. For example, they might be trained on data that reflects human discrimination. In the employment context, companies and their algorithms might learn, for example, that women are more likely than men to leave the workforce to take care of young children. Under plausible assumptions, the algorithm might give a preference to men for that reason. Alternatively, algorithms might learn something true about who most wants what. They might learn that women or members of a minority group are especially likely to want certain products, and they might offer higher prices, or special kinds of targeting, to women or to members of the minority group. For example, there have been widespread concerns that cigarette companies advertise menthol cigarettes to Black people. We could easily imagine a form of AI-powered targeting that would exploit an absence of information or unrealistic optimism among members of protected groups. Or algorithms might learn that members of some racial groups (say, Whites) are willing to pay more for healthcare than are members of other groups (say, Blacks), and might allocate more attention and resources to the former groups for that reason, wrongly using willingness to pay as a proxy for serious health problems.

Outside of the context of race and sex, algorithms might know that people who suffer from mental health challenges (depression, anxiety) are vulnerable to certain forms of marketing or to automatic enrollment, and they might target people accordingly, perhaps in violation of law forbidding discrimination on the basis of disability. Or algorithms might know that people over the age of eighty can be induced to purchase certain products, even though those products are essentially worthless, producing what might be a violation of law forbidding age discrimination.

Algorithmic Harm. Oren Bar-Gill and Cass R. Sunstein, Oxford University Press. © Oren Bar-Gill and Cass R. Sunstein (2025). DOI: 10.1093/oso/9780197778197.003.0007

In cases of this kind, algorithms might perpetuate existing discrimination or produce new forms of discrimination. If their operations are not transparent, and if they are taken to be neutral and objective, they might make things worse than they now are. We could easily imagine similar concerns for discrimination on many bases, including religion, citizenship, and sexual orientation.

We share these concerns, and we will aim to explain why. But in our view, the likely effects of AI-powered algorithms on discrimination are more interesting, complicated, and nuanced than is generally appreciated. To be sure, there are scenarios where algorithms discriminate or exacerbate the problem of discrimination. But there are also scenarios where the shift from human decision-making to algorithmic decision-making can help reduce discrimination based on race and sex or other grounds. On the one hand, algorithms programmed to maximize profits are less likely to engage in statistical discrimination or taste-based discrimination (to be explained in short order). In addition, they are most unlikely to suffer from the unconscious bias that afflicts many human decision-makers.[110] Algorithms do not have an unconscious!

On the other hand, decisions made by AI-powered algorithms might introduce new forms of discrimination. Consider an online retailer who is unaware of the race or sex of its customers (because the retailer never interacts with these customers in person) and thus cannot discriminate on the basis of race or sex. If this retailer delegates pricing or targeting decisions to an AI-powered algorithm, the algorithm will likely have access to reams of data. It might have access, for example, to the customer's IP address and the customer's history of online purchases across multiple retailers, and these might be correlated with race or sex. Thus the algorithm's pricing or targeting decisions that are calculated to maximize profits might turn out to have harmful effects on racial minorities or women. For example, the algorithm might charge women more than men, knowing that women are more likely to be willing to pay a lot for the product (perhaps because of their preferences, perhaps because of a behavioral bias). If discrimination of this kind is forbidden, we might be especially concerned about the use of algorithms, because they might be able to discriminate in circumstances in which human beings could not.

Similarly, the AI-powered algorithm might circumvent legal prohibitions on race- and sex-based discrimination in ways that are unavailable to a human decision-maker. Suppose that a human retailer could in fact observe the customer's race or sex. Even so, the retailer may well be deterred by antidiscrimination laws from discriminating based on these observed characteristics. An AI decision-maker may or may not be programmed to disregard direct information on a customer's race or sex. Suppose that it is programmed to disregard that information. Even so, its profit-maximizing algorithm might rely on other variables (or combinations of variables) that correlate with race or sex; a human decision-maker might not be able to identify the correlations or even have access to the underlying information.

For these and other reasons, AI-based decision-making might circumvent legal prohibitions on race- and sex-based discrimination, at least if those prohibitions are inadequately enforced. At the same time, the shift from human to algorithmic decision-making can actually make it easier to police discriminatory conduct. Even black-box machine-learning algorithms can be audited and inspected. Their training data and their operations can be subjected to quantitative scrutiny, which cannot be applied to a human decision-maker. Indeed, the human mind is perhaps the ultimate black box. Who knows what is inside it? Even introspection might not provide a full answer. It can be easier to peek inside the algorithmic black box, relative to the human one. In short, and this is the good news, it will often be easier to detect discrimination by algorithms than discrimination by human decision-makers if the law appropriately adjusts to the rise of algorithms. We discuss such adjustment in Part II below.

For these reasons, we argue for a broadening of focus—supplementing attention to algorithmic discrimination based on race and sex with algorithmic discrimination based on information and rationality deficits, as manifested in the algorithmic harms that we analyzed in the preceding chapters.

After providing some background on antidiscrimination law in Section A, we explain in Section B how algorithms used in consumer markets might make discriminatory decisions. A particular problem, to which we draw attention, is the use of proxies—"proxy bias," as it is sometimes called. In Section C, we elaborate on the benefits that algorithms present in the context of race-based and sex-based discrimination. While we argue that algorithms may reduce the incidence of discrimination, we emphasize that algorithms may sometimes discriminate on the basis of race and sex (and other grounds). In Section D, we discuss precisely when such discrimination is most likely to occur.

Note that while we focus on discrimination on the basis of race and sex, we do so simply for convenience and simplicity of exposition. As some of the examples above suggest, a similar analysis could be applied to discrimination on the basis of (for example) religion, nationality, age, sexual orientation, and disability. Indeed some of these grounds for discrimination deserve special attention in the context of algorithms; we would single out age and disability as important domains, especially in the consumer context.

An algorithm might be programmed, for example, to take account of age, in which case it will discriminate on that ground, perhaps by giving weight to information deficits and behavioral biases typically shown by people who are young or people who are old. It might target people known to be suffering from cognitive decline, such as Alzheimer's disease. Or an algorithm might use proxies for old age or youth, and might discriminate against old or young people because of its use of such proxies. If an algorithm knows that certain people suffer from some kind of disability, it might target them; targeting people with depression or anxiety disorders could be highly beneficial or devastatingly damaging, depending on what the targeting entails. We do not discuss these issues in detail here, but the analysis is similar to that for race and sex, and in the context of age and disability, we think the problem of algorithmic harm merits extended analysis.

A. Background: Antidiscrimination Law

To understand the challenges introduced by AI-powered algorithms, it is important to lay out the legal fundamentals, which differ from nation to nation, but which tend to show similar patterns. We focus on U.S. law, which adresses two different problems. The first is disparate treatment; the second is disparate impact (Barocas & Selbst 2016, 694). If we are concerned about the possibility that algorithms might promote discrimination or on the contrary reduce it, we need to distinguish sharply between the two. The U.S. Constitution, and all civil rights laws, forbid disparate treatment.[111] The U.S. Constitution does not concern itself with disparate impact,[112] but some civil rights statutes do.[113]

The prohibition on disparate treatment reflects a commitment to a kind of neutrality. When the prohibition is in place, it is essentially impermissible to favor men over women or Whites over Blacks. If a company charges higher prices to women than to men, it is engaged in disparate treatment, and so too if it sells certain products to Blacks but not to Whites. When disparate treatment occurs, it might be a product of "taste," "prejudice," or "animus." A seller might prefer, personally, not to hire or to sell to Blacks. A seller might hate Blacks or dislike Blacks, or might simply prefer Whites. A seller might prefer to run an all-White or all-male company, or at least a mostly White or mostly male company. Or a seller might have no particular racial preference but might believe, or know, that her employees prefer not to work with Hispanics or to sell to Blacks. In that case, a seller would be deferring to the preferences of the relevant employees. Or a seller might have no particular gender preference but might know that her customers prefer to work with or buy from men. Male or female customers might be more likely to buy a house from a male real estate agent; male or female customers might prefer to have a massage from a female masseuse. In that case, a seller would be deferring to the preferences of the relevant customers, probably because the goal is to maximize profits. Taste-based discrimination might be driven by the tastes of employers, coworkers, or customers. In any event, it is generally unlawful in North America and Europe.

Alternatively, disparate treatment might be a product of something very different: statistical discrimination. Sellers and employers might have no discriminatory taste at all; they might simply want to make money. Even so, they might find that the best way to make money is to discriminate on some ground. For example, a seller might believe that on average, women are more likely to be willing to pay more for certain products than men are. Or an employer might believe that on average, men are more likely to stay in a job for a longer time than women are. The seller or employer might have statistical evidence to that effect or might be making an inference from observation and reality. Or a lender might believe that Blacks are more likely to default on their loans as compared to Whites. The lender might have statistical support for that belief or might be making a statistical generalization based on experience. In any of these cases, a seller, employer, or lender might discriminate even though it has no "animus," is not racist or sexist, and has no taste or preference for discrimination.

Statistical discrimination might be fully rational, in the sense that those who engage in it might be acting on the basis of accurate information. It might be the case that some statistical difference between groups, relevant to a company's decisions, is real and large. Alternatively, statistical discrimination might be some kind of mistake, based on false inferences (say, from anecdotes or a small sample of cases). There is frequently a question whether statistical discrimination is too *crude*, in the sense that statistical discriminators would do better to rely on other, nondiscriminatory grounds for making the relevant judgments. For example, an employer or seller might make more specific inquiries into individuals and their circumstances rather than rely on generalizations about men and women. In any case, statistical discrimination is counted as a form of disparate treatment, and in North America and Europe it is generally unlawful. We will explore some of the complexities below. For now, notice that disparate treatment is broadly forbidden, whether it is based on prejudice or "taste" or instead on statistical generalization.

The prohibition on disparate impact is very different. It does not involve bigotry, preferences, animus, or tastes. Nor does it involve statistical discrimination. To many people, it seems more innocuous. It means, in brief, that if some requirement or practice has a disproportionate adverse *effect* on members of specified groups (Blacks, women), the requirement or practice must be shown to be adequately justified.[114] Suppose, for example, that a police department establishes a height requirement for its employees. If this practice has a disproportionate adverse effect on women (because they are shorter than men on average), the practice will be invalidated unless the department can show that the practice is justified by "business necessity."[115] For example, the department might argue that the height requirement is an essential filter for police department employees, given the nature of the job. Or suppose that an employer imposes some requirement of educational attainment (say, college graduation) on applicants. If that requirement has a disproportionate negative impact on Hispanics, the employer will be required to show that the requirement has a strong business justification.

The best justification of the disparate impact standard is widely disputed, and the existence of the standard raises fundamental questions about the nature and scope of the antidiscrimination principle (Strauss 1989; Rutherglen 2006). The standard can be defended in two different ways (Strauss 1989; Perry 1991). First, it might be seen as a way of ferreting out some kind of illegitimate motive—and might therefore be essentially equivalent, at the level of basic principle, to the disparate treatment standard. Lacking the tools to uncover bad motives, the legal system might ask: Does the manager have a sufficiently neutral justification for adopting a practice that has adverse effects on (say) women? Does a seller have a sufficiently neutral reason for adopting a practice that ends up hurting female consumers? If not, we might suspect that some kind of discriminatory motive is really at work.

An alternative defense of the disparate impact standard would not speak of motivation at all (Fiss 1976; Sunstein 1993). It would insist that if a practice has disproportionate adverse effects on (say) women, it should be struck down, unless it has a strong independent justification (Fiss 1976; Colker 1986). On this view, the motivation of the decision-maker is not relevant. What matters is the elimination of practices that keep some groups below others – of social subordination of certain groups or something like a caste system (Carle 2011). The disparate impact standard does not, of course, go nearly that far (Ayres & Siegelman 1996). But by requiring a strong justification for practices with discriminatory effects, it tends in that direction. These points obviously bear on current concerns about algorithmic discrimination.

B. Algorithms and Discrimination in Consumer Markets

How might AI-powered algorithms discriminate? There are many possible answers. In consumer markets, a standard concern has been that women are being, and will be, charged higher prices. Suppose that a seller does in fact set higher prices for women because they are women; suppose that for one or another reason, algorithms do that and are designed to do that. That would be a form of disparate treatment; it would involve discrimination against women as such. We could design the case so that it involves discriminatory tastes explicitly incorporated in an algorithm; perhaps the seller prefers to sell to men, or perhaps the seller does not like women or perhaps the seller knows that its customers prefer to buy from men, and perhaps the algorithm has been designed to include that taste. Or we could design the case so that it involves statistical discrimination; perhaps the algorithm "knows" that women have a higher WTP for a product. In either case, disparate treatment is involved, and the practice is unlawful.

Now assume that a seller uses an algorithm that is programmed simply to maximize profits, and that algorithm ends up setting higher prices for women (because that is how profits are maximized). Suppose that the company that uses the algorithm did not ask for this result or seek to program it. Is this just another example of disparate treatment? Or should we think of the seller's delegation of price-setting decisions to an algorithm as a practice that has a disproportionate adverse effect on women and is therefore subject to challenge under the disparate impact doctrine?

The answers to these questions are not especially complicated. Suppose that the algorithm is treating women differently from men; it gives men a benefit that it does not give women, or it treats women worse because they are women. If so, we surely have a case of disparate treatment: a seller is discriminating against women, even if an algorithm, and not a seller, designed the discriminatory practice. If a seller does not know about the discrimination, we might be tempted to say that it is innocent. It has simply attempted to maximize profits, and the algorithm might be, to the seller, a kind of black box. There are two answers to this suggestion. The first is that the seller might well know, in fact, that there is discrimination. Someone will probably draw the discrimination to the seller's attention. But suppose that has not happened. The second answer is that if a seller treats women differently than men, it is engaged in disparate treatment, even if it is relying on an algorithm rather than its own judgment. If a seller delegated certain decisions to an independent contractor, and if that contractor engaged in disparate treatment, the seller would be held responsible, even if it did not know what the contactor was doing.

This conclusion has broad implications. If a company's decisions are made by algorithm, it will be engaging in disparate treatment and violating the civil rights laws if it is drawing lines between men and women or White people and Black people.

Alternatively, an algorithm might not be producing disparate treatment, but its actions might produce disparate impact. Suppose, for example, that an algorithm suggests that it would be valuable to use a test of physical strength for employment, and that men are more likely to pass the test than women. If an employer uses such a test, the fact that an algorithm recommended or generated it is no defense. Or suppose that an algorithm requires all consumers to fill out complex forms before making certain purchases, and that the complex forms screen out some groups more than others. If disparate impact is prohibited in this context, seemingly neutral form-filling requirements might run afoul of the prohibition.

C. Algorithmic Benefits

Notwithstanding these points, it remains true that algorithms are less likely than human beings to engage in taste-based discrimination, and for a simple reason: algorithms do not have tastes. If they are programmed to maximize sales or profits, it is most unlikely that they will be showing taste-based discrimination (except, perhaps, if they are incorporating the tastes of coworkers or customers). It also remains true and important that algorithms will not suffer from the unconscious bias that afflicts many human decision-makers; they do not have an unconscious or implicit biases in the way that people do. And as explained in more detail below, whereas human decision-makers often engage in statistical discrimination, using race or sex as proxies for WTP or profitability, algorithms that have access to direct, accurate information about WTP or profitability are less likely to rely on such crude proxies. Why rely on a crude proxy when more fine-grained information is available?

In a world without algorithms, we might well observe a significant amount of racism and sexism, reflecting and producing taste-based discrimination. In many times and places, that is, of course, exactly what we observe. In a world without algorithms, we might also observe a significant amount of statistical discrimination, in which race and sex are used as proxies for relevant characteristics, such as WTP, ability to repay, and so forth. In many times and places, that is also what we observe. Finally, in a world without algorithms, in many times and places, we observe a significant amount of unconscious bias. One goal of civil rights laws is to forbid these forms of discrimination, but let us stipulate that those laws are imperfectly enforced, which means that taste-based discrimination, statistical discrimination, and unconscious bias will occur.

Now, compare this pre-algorithmic world to a world where algorithms make pricing and targeting decisions. We start with the case of statistical discrimination. Let us suppose that algorithms are able to make fine-grained judgments, based on rich data, about who is willing or able to pay more for a product or service and who is more or less likely to repay a loan. If so, algorithms that are programmed to maximize profits should not be expected to engage in race- or sex-based statistical discrimination. The reason is that if they can make fine-grained judgments, they would not need to rely on proxies, which are likely to be unnecessarily coarse.

Suppose, for example, that women are less likely to repay loans than men are, and that human decision-makers take that point into account in deciding on interest rates for loans. Algorithms ought to be able to use far less crude approaches; they should not use sex as a proxy.[116] There are no guarantees here, but crude proxies of that kind are unlikely to be excellent predictors, and algorithms should be expected to use excellent predictors. For example, an algorithm tasked with predicting the likelihood of loan repayment would use data on borrowers' past loans, rent payments, utility payments, and a host of other factors that are statistically correlated with repayment patterns.

Similarly, the use of algorithms will eliminate the effects of unconscious bias. The preceding example assumed that the borrower's sex is in fact correlated with repayment probability. But it may well be that there is no such correlation; only the lender who suffers from unconscious bias mistakenly believes that a correlation exists. A shift to algorithmic loan pricing would avoid the adverse implications of the unconscious bias.

The case of taste-based discrimination can be analyzed similarly. Algorithms will focus on the relevant characteristics of consumers. If John has a credit record identical to Joan's, John and Joan will be treated similarly, and if existing evidence suggests that John is willing to pay more than Joan, it will not matter that John is male and that Joan is female. Once again: algorithms do not have tastes, and they will not show taste-based discrimination unless they have been programmed to do so or they learn that considering the discriminatory tastes of some group helps to maximize their assigned objective (e.g., profit maximization). For this reason, we could easily imagine situations in which the use of algorithms is likely to have particular benefits for (say) women and people of color, as compared to a situation in which decisions are made by human beings (Kleinberg et al. 2018, 114).

Since algorithms are less likely to engage in taste-based or statistical discrimination and should not display unconscious bias, the rise of algorithms in consumer markets may be highly beneficial from the perspective of those who seek to reduce or eliminate race- and sex-based discrimination.[117] (Something similar can be said with respect to other forms of discrimination, such as discrimination on the basis of age or sexual orientation.) This does not mean that algorithms will never discriminate on the basis of race and sex. Indeed, as explained below, there are circumstances where algorithms might exacerbate discrimination on the basis of race and sex.

D. Algorithmic Harm and Algorithmic Discrimination

Thus far, then, the problem of race- and sex-based discrimination seems more serious for human beings than for algorithms. But that conclusion is far too simple, and in important contexts it might be wrong. Suppose, for example, that the data on which algorithms are trained reflects human bias. Suppose that loan performance records reflect human judgments that are themselves discriminatory; suppose that loan officers are more likely to target people of color, and less likely to give them a degree of flexibility with respect to payments. If so, algorithms that take account of such records will discriminate. Biased training data can produce discrimination.[118] Or suppose that arrest records reflect discriminatory (human) judgments about whom to arrest; suppose that people of color are more likely to be arrested, not because they have done anything wrong, but because the police are more likely to arrest them. If so, an algorithm that relies on arrest records will perpetuate and extend discrimination. This, then, is an important category of cases in which use of algorithms can promote disparate treatment.

There is also the question of disparate impact. Even if the algorithm is programmed to exclude race and sex data, the algorithm might pick up other variables (or combinations of other variables) that are closely correlated with race or sex. Suppose, for example, that people of color are less likely to have graduated from college than are White people, or that people of color are less likely to have good credit ratings than are White people. If an algorithm that is programmed to maximize profits identifies a correlation between these variables and profits, and treats consumers in accordance with them, it might well produce a disparate impact on people of color (Slaughter 2021, 20). It might be challenging, of course, to know whether there is a disparate impact and to test the question whether it might be justified under prevailing standards. Moreover, when there is disparate impact, it is not always clear that it is harmful; if, for example, race is correlated with income, people of color may be offered lower prices.

Proxy bias, sometimes called "label bias," occurs when an algorithm uses some seemingly reasonable proxy, such as expenses devoted to health problems, to measure some characteristic, such as medical need.[119] Proxy bias is an exceedingly important problem for AI-powered algorithms and indeed for AI of all kinds. Since Black people are less likely to obtain access to medical services, this proxy turns out to produce discrimination. Expenses devoted to medical problems are a poor proxy for medical need; in fact they are a discriminatory proxy. If we allocate resources to those who are most likely to spend most, we will end up discriminating on the basis of race. In numerous consumer markets, disparate impact might be a product of proxy bias in a world in which AI-powered algorithms are in widespread use. Such algorithms might use a proxy that effectively produces discrimination (consider height or weight, or care for young children, in the context of sex discrimination).

In some circumstances, algorithms might produce disparate treatment or disparate impact *even though neither would occur in a pre-algorithmic world.* The reason is that algorithms might well have access to information that human beings lack. For example, in a pre-algorithmic world, when a consumer makes a purchase by phone or online, the seller would not know whether the consumer is White or African American. But an algorithm, armed with endless data linking the consumer's phone number or IP address to a host of traits and past behaviors, might pick up variables (or combinations of variables) that are correlated with race. And even if a human decision-maker observes the consumer's race, she might not know that race is correlated with a higher WTP or with a lower ability to repay, and thus might offer the same price or interest rate to both Black and White consumers. An algorithmic decision-maker, on the other hand, will learn these correlations and might well set prices in a way that discriminates between Black and White consumers.

For the same reason, the AI algorithm might circumvent legal prohibitions on race- and sex-based discrimination in ways that are unavailable to a human decision-maker. Even if she observes the customer's race or sex, a human retailer might not discriminate whether or not she is inclined to do so, knowing that a lawsuit would quickly follow. An AI decision-maker might also disregard direct information on a customer's race or sex, because the algorithm's designer would face a lawsuit. But the profit-maximizing algorithm might rely on other variables (or combinations of variables) that correlate with race or sex, resulting in (almost) equivalent discrimination, albeit discrimination that is much harder to detect.[120] (A human decision-maker would not be able to identify the correlations or even have access to the underlying information.) As noted above, there are enforcement advantages when the decision-maker is an AI, which may outweigh this concern about circumvention. We return to these advantages in Part II below.

With respect to our focus on the distinction between S markets and U markets, the harms and benefits from algorithmic decision-making, in terms of discrimination based on race and sex, apply in both S and U markets. In S markets, the algorithm might discriminate when WTP or ability to repay is correlated with race or sex. In U markets, there is an additional concern that the misperception component of the WTP might be correlated with race or sex. Members of traditionally disadvantaged groups might be especially vulnerable to imperfect information and imperfect rationality. In other words, we cannot neglect the possibility that in some markets, consumer sophistication may itself be correlated with race or sex. For example, past discrimination might have resulted in limited access to information and to mechanisms, such as expert advice, that can mitigate bias. If that is so, the particular harms identified in Chapters 1–4 would disproportionally fall on traditionally disadvantaged groups (cf. Paterson et al. 2021, 8–9). We might end up with cases of disparate impact.

And while our focus has been on discrimination on the basis of race and sex, we could see illuminating variations in other cases of discrimination. Suppose, plausibly, that certain kinds of disability are associated with greater deficits in terms of information or rationality; certain mental health conditions might be associated with both. Consider depression or anxiety. If so, the conditions are ripe for algorithmic harm. Elderly people might also be overrepresented in U markets. If so, we might expect to see disparate impact in terms of age as well as disability. That is a serious problem, and it is likely to get worse over time. It is essential to identify ways to handle it.

Chapter 7
Consumer-Side Algorithms

Our focus has been on AI-powered algorithms deployed by sellers and service providers and the harm they might impose on consumers. But consumers are not alone in this fight. AI can help consumers, not only harm them. (And government is also there to help, sometimes wielding its own AI. More on this in Part II.) There are consumer-side algorithms that can help consumers make better choices and thus mitigate the algorithmic harms that we have identified. "Digital butlers" like Alexa, Siri, and Google Assistant can help consumers make purchasing decisions, and more specialized apps can compare prices and help identify attractive options (Gal 2017, 330; Lippi et al. 2020). Much more is inevitably on the way. In this chapter, we describe these consumer-side algorithms and how they can help consumers. We also highlight the limits of the consumer-side algorithms. Because of structural asymmetries between sellers and buyers, these algorithms can reduce the harms that we identified, but they are unlikely to eliminate them.

A. Algorithms in the Service of Consumers

Consumers have long used algorithms to help them make more informed purchasing decisions—to find lower prices or higher-quality products. With the help of price-comparison websites, many consumers can and do avoid overpaying for products. And there are platforms that allow users to screen for lower-priced products or products with higher user ratings (Ezrachi & Stucke 2016b, 5, 9, 27–28). An example is Honey (by PayPal), an app or browser add-on that searches for online coupons and thus reduces the prices that Honey users pay for different products. In an important article, Michal Gal and Niva Elkin-Koren (2017) describe a world where consumers delegate many purchasing decisions—from buying dog food to laundry detergent—to algorithms. They argue that this better world is just around the corner.

Algorithmic Harm. Oren Bar-Gill and Cass R. Sunstein, Oxford University Press. © Oren Bar-Gill and Cass R. Sunstein (2025). DOI: 10.1093/oso/9780197778197.003.0008

These consumer-side algorithms can be exceedingly helpful. In particular, they can mitigate consumers' information and rationality deficits. For instance, an algorithm may easily obtain access to and compare thousands of quality-price combinations. And an algorithm will not be confused by a complex, multidimensional pricing scheme, and will not let unrealistic optimism or present bias guide its choices (Gal & Elkin-Corren 2017, 321).

In consumer markets and beyond, algorithms can serve as "choice engines" (to borrow a term that one of us developed in other work: Sunstein 2024). These algorithmic choice engines can help consumers make better decisions in myriad contexts, including the choice of retirement savings plans, dogs, laptops, mystery novels, cell phones, shavers, shoes, tennis racquets, and ties. (See, e.g., Purina n.d.) The algorithm can take different roles, from less active to more active. Consider retirement savings. The algorithm might simply present the different options to the employee. Or to help the imperfectly rational employee who will struggle choosing among many options, the algorithm could present only a subset of options that the algorithm predicts would be most suited for and attractive to that employee (see, e.g., Fidelity n.d.). It could also provide employees with simple information by which to choose among these curated options.

A more active algorithmic choice engine could select a default option and automatically enroll the employee into a specific retirement savings plan, probably a diversified, passively managed index fund, and ask the employee if she wants to opt out and choose a different plan. A moderately paternalistic choice engine might impose nontrivial barriers to those who seek certain kinds of plans (e.g., plans with high fees). The barriers might take the form of information provision, "Are you sure you want to?" queries, and requirements of multiple clicks. An even more active, or more paternalistic, choice engine might forbid employees from selecting any plan other than the one that it deems (knows) to be in their interest, or might make it exceedingly difficult for employees to do that. Once again, the main point is that the algorithmic choice engine might work to overcome an absence of information or behavioral biases.[121]

Returning to the consumer context, consider this question: What kind of car would you like to buy? Would you like to buy a fuel-efficient car that will cost you \$800 more up front than the alternative but that would save you \$2,000 over the next 10 years? Would you like to buy an energy-efficient refrigerator that would cost you \$X today but save you 10 times \$X over the next 10 years? What characteristics of a car, or a refrigerator, matter most to you? Do you need a large car? Do you like hybrids? Are you excited about electric cars, or not so much?

We have noted that many consumers suffer from "present bias."[122] For present-biased consumers, current costs and benefits loom large; future costs and benefits do not. For many of us, the short term is what most matters, and the long term is a foreign country. The future is Laterland, a country that we are not sure we will ever visit. This is so with respect to choices that involve money, health, safety, and more.[123] Such present bias might prevent consumers from choosing the best car or the best refrigerator.

An algorithmic, AI-powered choice engine need not suffer from present bias.[124] Imagine that you consult this choice engine and ask it what kind of car you should buy. Imagine too that you discover that you are, or might be, present-biased, in the sense that you prefer a car that is not (according to the AI) the one that you should get. What then? We could easily imagine choice engines for motor vehicle purchases in which different consumers provide relevant information about their practices, their preferences, and their values, and the choice engine immediately provides a set of options—say, Good, Better, and Best, with verbal descriptions explaining the ranking. Or a choice engine might simply say Best For You. It might do so while allowing you to see other options if you indicate that you wish to do so. If you want to display present bias, you might be able to do so. A choice engine may or may not be paternalistic or come with guardrails designed to protect consumers against serious mistakes.[125]

To conclude: consumer-side algorithms can help consumers make better purchasing decisions. Whereas seller-side algorithms seek to exploit consumers' information and rationality deficits, consumer-side algorithms can mitigate the adverse consequences of such deficits.

B. Limits of Consumer-Side Algorithms

Consumer-side algorithms, or choice engines, can be very helpful, but they are no silver bullet. Design is crucial. To start, it is not clear that consumer-side algorithms will be sufficiently informed about the consumer's tastes, values, and constraints. If the algorithmic recommendations, or the choice architecture that the algorithm creates, are coarse, if they use a few simple cues (such as age and income), they might not have the expected or hoped-for welfare benefits. They might make recommendations that are inadequately suited to the situations or values of particular consumers. The consumer-side algorithm will be similarly limited if it is insufficiently informed about the range of options—products and prices—in the market.[126] We can hope that these challenges will be overcome in time, but there is a risk that even a well-motivated choice engine will not steer consumers in the right direction.

In addition, it is not obvious that consumer-side algorithms are a solution to consumers' behavioral biases. The algorithm might suffer from its own biases. An algorithm trained on biased data will produce biased results.[127] In general, of course, an algorithm should not show a cognitive bias if it is trained on real-world data and asked to predict an outcome given the presence of specified factors. In those circumstances, it should be able to handle prediction problems, free from cognitive biases. But if, for example, consumers in a relevant data set suffer from present bias, an algorithm that uses a "what choosers like you choose" heuristic will promote biased choices. So too if consumers in a relevant data set show optimistic bias and an algorithm is asked to predict "what consumers like you" will choose. In addition, LLMs are importantly different from other AI algorithms. There is evidence that LLMs can show some of the biases, racial, cognitive, and otherwise, that human beings do.[128]

Perhaps the main risk is that the algorithm designer might be self-interested or malevolent. Recall that some of the most prominent digital butlers—Alexa, Siri, and Google Assistant—that allegedly implement, or could implement, consumer-side algorithms are produced by firms that are also sellers or work with sellers. Given this conflict of interests, can we trust that the algorithm will help consumers? Would it correct the absence of information or behavioral biases, or *exploit* them? Indeed, we know that Alexa works only with Prime-eligible products that are sold or fulfilled by Amazon and that Google Assistant originally permitted consumers to shop only from participating Google Express retailers.[129] Consumers get the products that are affiliated with the algorithm's corporate master, not necessarily the best or cheapest products. There is also a real concern that, even within the subset of Amazon Prime or Google Express products, the algorithm might steer consumers to the products that maximize Amazon's or Google's profits rather than those that maximize consumer welfare, perhaps by exploiting consumers' information and rationality deficits.

What if unconflicted algorithm designers enter the market? This could be a real improvement, but there are also significant obstacles. These unconflicted, consumer-side algorithms will have to compete with the likes of Amazon, Apple, and Google on two fronts. First, they will have to convince consumers to use unconflicted algorithms rather than the tech giants' algorithms. Despite the advantage of an unconflicted algorithm, it is not clear that enough consumers will ditch the brand names of Amazon, Apple, and Google. And it is not just the name; the immense resources that the tech giants control—in terms of both money and data—may allow them to create attractive buyer-side algorithms, despite their conflict of interests.

Second, if consumers adopt the unconflicted algorithms, these consumer-side algorithms will face an algorithmic battle against the seller-side algorithms on which we have focused in previous chapters. In theory, the buyer-side algorithm can mitigate many of the harms caused by seller-side algorithms. For example, the buyer-side algorithm can reveal and even undo demand-inflating misperceptions and thus reduce prices, and it can protect consumers who are targeted with inferior products. But once again, there is a real concern that the seller-side algorithm will have a decisive advantage—in terms of both money and data—in this algorithmic battle. Simply put, the seller-side algorithms that seek to manipulate consumers and exploit their information and rationality deficits might turn out to be more powerful than the buyer-side algorithms that try to protect consumers against such manipulation and exploitation.

* * *

To conclude: consumer-side algorithms are increasingly prevalent, and they can mitigate the harms caused by seller-side algorithms. And yet, for the reasons discussed above, it is unlikely that consumer-side algorithms will be able to eliminate the harms on which we have focused, at least not in the foreseeable future.

PART II
POLICY AND LAW

To reduce algorithmic harm in consumer markets, we consider three sets of legal reforms. The first would use, and expand on, current initiatives in three domains. Policymakers can attempt to increase information and to reduce the impact of behavioral biases, with an understanding that the rise of AI-powered algorithms imposes fresh threats to consumer welfare from the exploitation of information and rationality deficits. In addition, policymakers can seek to increase privacy and data security in an attempt to choke off the data fueling AI-powered algorithms. Finally, policymakers can use antitrust law to limit market power, since many instances of algorithmic harms—specifically, algorithmic price discrimination and product differentiation—require some degree of market power.

As we shall see, the argument for increasing information and reducing the impact of behavioral biases is significantly strengthened by an appreciation of the algorithmic harms that we have explored. Those reforms have increased importance. At the same time, the case for expanded privacy protections and for enhanced antitrust enforcement is not necessarily bolstered by the rise of algorithmic decision-making. In the latter contexts, intuitions turn out to be misleading.

The second set of reforms would involve *a right to algorithmic transparency*, designed to ensure that consumers (and others) can know about the nature, uses, and consequences of algorithms. The central idea here is that sunlight might serve as a disinfectant, reducing the incidence and magnitude of algorithmic harm.[130] In principle, the argument for transparency is exceedingly strong. In practice, things are more complicated. If we focus on AI-powered machine-learning algorithms, the challenge is the black-box nature of these algorithms. Indeed, with these black-box algorithms, the process of manipulating inputs to generate outputs is opaque, even to the programmer. With machine-learning algorithms, the challenge is in opening the black box, that is, creating previously unavailable knowledge about how algorithmic decisions are made. Only then can we talk about the transparent sharing of this knowledge. We describe, without attempting to resolve, the ongoing debate within the computer science community about whether meaningful transparency is even possible with machine-learning algorithms.

The broader point is that, when feasible, transparency about how algorithmic decisions are made may trigger a public or market reaction, one that might operate as a corrective to the problems we have identified.[131] Transparency may also trigger regulatory scrutiny. Specifically, by forcing firms to learn how their algorithms actually work, this reform would open the door to liability under legal doctrines that require knowledge or intent.

The third category of reforms involves more direct intervention in the design and implementation of algorithms that are used in consumer markets, either through ex post policing or through ex ante regulation. We begin by proposing an expansion of disparate impact review. Developed under antidiscrimination law, the disparate impact doctrine has been used to combat discrimination based on race, sex, and other protected characteristics. We propose to use disparate impact analysis to identify and police discriminatory behavior that targets imperfectly informed and imperfectly rational consumers. Disparate impact analysis focuses on outcomes—for example, whether men and women are subjected to different outcomes (lower wages for women, higher prices for women, worse product offers for women)-and thus helps overcome the difficulty of proving discriminatory intent. In the algorithmic context, disparate impact overcomes the challenge of opening the algorithmic black box. It does not matter how the algorithm manipulated inputs to create outputs. It matters only that it creates different outputs for men and women, or for more and less sophisticated consumers.

Next, we propose the regulatory imposition of nondiscrimination constraints into the algorithm's code. In contrast to the ex post disparate impact review, this approach involves the ex ante policing of the algorithm's design, ensuring that equal treatment of more and less sophisticated consumers is an integral component of the algorithm. (We note that an effective ex post disparate impact review could provide incentives for sellers and algorithm designers to insert equal-treatment constraints on their own, such that the practical effect of the two approaches could be quite similar.) Also, in appropriate cases, regulators should consider prohibitions and bans on the use of algorithms, or on the use of black-box algorithms, when such use is likely to harm consumers in the ways that we have discussed.

The proposed reforms are designed to address the algorithmic harms that we identified in Part I. We have shown that algorithmic harm is more likely in U markets, and we thus urge policymakers to focus on such markets. But there is more. We have argued that, among U markets, policymakers should focus on markets where consumers are likely to overestimate, rather than underestimate, the benefits from the product or service. And we have argued that policymakers should be less worried about algorithmic price discrimination when it is cost-based (or risk-based) rather than benefit-based. These insights should help policymakers to prioritize their limited enforcement budgets.[132]

Before we begin, it is important to address the following concern about the regulation of algorithmic decision-making: *How will regulators ever be able to police the algorithms that are used to price and target millions of products and services, especially when these algorithms change rapidly over time*? First, note that the actual number of algorithms is not all that large. The big tech firms (e.g., Amazon, Apple) employ their own algorithms—the same algorithm for many products—and a small number of developers provide algorithms for smaller sellers. Second, and more important still, policymakers can and should develop policing algorithms that will monitor the sellers' algorithms. Major components of the reform proposals discussed below should be automated and performed by the regulators' own algorithm.[133] Third, regulatory approaches should be developed in a way that reduces the risk that they will become obsolete with technological improvements. Of course, that risk cannot be eliminated. If it materializes, new regulations will be in order.

Chapter 8
Regulating Preconditions for Algorithmic Harm

The analysis in Part I identified several preconditions for algorithmic harm. We begin by considering policies that target these preconditions. First and foremost, we saw that algorithmic harm is especially prevalent in U markets, where most consumers suffer from information and rationality deficits. It is therefeore natural to consider policies that attempt to increase information and to reduce the impact of behavioral biases. Second, AI-powered algorithms need a lot of data to engage in the harmful activities that we described, such as price discrimination and product targeting. Policies that seek to increase privacy and data security can thus reduce algorithmic harm. Finally, algorithmic harm (for example, price discrimination or enhanced product targeting and differentiation) often requires a certain degree of market power. Policies that limit market power, as in the domain of antitrust law, can reduce algorithmic harm.

A. From U to S

Because algorithmic harm is, in large part, a product of people's limited sophistication in U markets, the most obvious remedies involve consumer protection in the form of information disclosure and debiasing, designed to increase sophistication and transform U markets into S markets. Suppose, for example, that people are given clear information about the performance of certain products (say, refrigerators, microwave ovens, or clothes washers). The information might be designed to protect against simple ignorance. It might be intended to counteract unrealistic optimism or limited attention. If disclosure works, it might turn U markets into S markets, or at least ensure that many consumers are informed or free from behavioral biases.

In federal law, of course, disclosure policies are pervasive, and the need for those policies increases to the extent that algorithms can be used to exploit

Algorithmic Harm. Oren Bar-Gill and Cass R. Sunstein, Oxford University Press. © Oren Bar-Gill and Cass R. Sunstein (2025). DOI: 10.1093/oso/9780197778197.003.0009

a lack of knowledge and behavioral biases. Many existing disclosure policies are explicitly meant to overcome such biases (U.S. Department of Transportation 2019). To an increasing degree, such policies are behaviorally informed, in the sense that they are based on an understanding of specific biases and attempt to design a remedy that will reduce the risk that some seller (human or algorithmic) will exploit them. Such efforts might be built directly on an understanding of how to counteract biases, as by increasing salience (and producing what are sometimes called "salience shocks" [Sarin 2019]).

For example, many disclosure policies are directed against hidden fees and hence are meant to counteract limited attention (Agarwal et al. 2014, S240). When formerly hidden fees are no longer hidden, people are more likely to pay attention to them. Other disclosure policies, such as graphic health warnings, can be seen as intentional efforts to counteract unrealistic optimism.[134] Because they are graphic, such warnings should combat complacency. Present bias can be a special problem in the context of both health and savings (Wang & Sloan 2018, 178), and with disclosure policies. Creative efforts have been made to overcome that bias on the part of savers by training people's attention on their older selves (Hershfield 2011, 31).

When will behaviorally informed disclosure policies succeed? There is no simple answer. (For a catalog, see Sunstein 2020.) They do show promise in some contexts. After all, GPS devices work. A clear warning, informing people that certain foods contain allergens (such as peanuts or shrimp), is likely to promote public health. There is reason to think that Nutrition Facts panels do some good, and the same might well turn out to be true for the "Nutrition Facts" panels for internet services, adopted in the United States in 2024. But their efficacy in other contexts is quite limited (Agarwal et al. 2015; Ben-Shahar & Schneider 2014). Disclosure requirements will not promote their intended goals if people do not pay attention to them or if the relevant information is hidden or so complicated that people cannot understand it. We know an increasing amount about where and when such requirements work and how they can be designed to be as effective as possible (Sunstein 2020). The central point is that behaviorally informed disclosure policies, seeking to counteract biases, will have increasing importance to the extent that algorithms, employed in consumer markets, can exploit these biases.[135]

A related approach for transforming U markets into S markets is through policy that supports consumer-side algorithms. We reviewed the promise, and the limits, of such algorithms in Chapter 7. Policymakers can help to mitigate the shortcomings of consumer-side algorithms. Specifically, many existing consumer-side algorithms are offered by firms that are affiliated with the sell-side of the market and thus may or may not have the consumers' best interests "in mind." (Think again of Amazon's Alexa, Google Home, or Apple's Siri.) Policymakers can reduce this problem by subsidizing the development of consumer-side algorithms by firms that are not affiliated with the sell-side of the market. To ensure that the algorithms are faithful agents of the consumer, the subsidy should be conditioned on a business model that avoids any conflict of interests. For example, an ad-based model, where the algorithm designer's revenues come from sellers, would be suspect. In contrast, a subscription model, where revenues come from consumers, should be preferred, and perhaps even subsidized.

In addition to avoiding conflicts of interest, policymakers could work to minimize the informational disadvantage that consumer-side algorithms face. In the "battle of the algorithms" between seller-side algorithms and consumer-side algorithms, data is ammunition. One central category of data includes information on consumers' past purchases and search histories. Sellers, and the tech platforms that support them, have much more ammunition. A policy that mandates the transfer of data from the seller-side algorithms to the consumer-side algorithms would help level the playing field.[136]

Thus far we have focused on policies that support consumer-side algorithms developed by the private sector. Policymakers should also consider creating government-run platforms that feature consumer-side algorithms. Indeed, governments already run web-based tools that help consumers to make more informed and more rational choices. In the United States, the Consumer Financial Protection Bureau website hosts a tool that provides information on available mortgage rates as a function of the borrower's credit score, geographic location, loan type, and so forth; this tool also calculates total financing costs for different mortgage types and rates.[137] Such tools can be supercharged with more personalized, consumer-specific data and AI-powered algorithms.[138] There is much room for further work here. Our central point is that insofar as algorithms might take advantage of information deficits and behavioral biases, it is all the more important to reduce both of these. We should see remedies of this kind as "no regrets" policies—and as the first line of defense.

B. Privacy and Data Security

A precondition for algorithmic harm, indeed for any algorithmic decision-making, is data, especially data about consumers: their preferences, their financial situation, and their biases and misperceptions. We can think of data as the "fuel" on which the algorithm drives. If we limit the algorithm's access to this fuel, then we will also reduce algorithmic harms. Policies designed to increase privacy protections and data security measures can thus reduce algorithmic harm.[139] The problem is that, as we have seen, algorithmic decision-making—both algorithmic price discrimination and algorithmic targeting—are not always harmful. Indeed, they can provide significant benefits to consumers, especially in S markets. Therefore, it is not clear whether choking off the flow of information would provide a net gain for consumers.

In theory, it would be good to choke off information in U markets while allowing the flow of information in S markets. But in practice, the same information flows in both types of markets. (As we noted, most markets include both more and less sophisticated consumers.) In theory, it would be good to choke off information about consumers' biases and misperceptions while still allowing the flow of information about preferences and budget constraints. But it is questionable whether privacy law can be fine-tuned in this way. Moreover, it is likely that the information that sellers collect is not neatly divided into preferences, budget constraints, and misperceptions. Rather, sellers seek information about consumers' WTP, which implicitly aggregates both "good" information (about preferences and budget constraints) and "bad" information (about biases and misperceptions).

A related and more modest suggestion would be to establish a "Do Not Profile Me" registry (inspired by the existing "Do Not Call" registry) and allow consumers to opt out of algorithmic differentiation. At first glance, the creation of such a registry would seem to be a good idea, but the matter is not simple. One problem is that some people might forbid profiling even if they would benefit from it; their fears might be misplaced. Another problem is that the people who most stand to lose from profiling might not bother to forbid it. Finally, there is a concern that sellers could draw inferences from the decision to opt out. This could limit the benefits of the "Do Not Profile Me" registry. It might even cause harm, as the decision by some consumers to opt out would indirectly provide sellers with additional information about the remaining consumers who did not opt out. For example, if it is known that the more sophisticated consumers opt out, sellers will infer that the consumers who allow profiling are less sophisticated.

C. Competition

Another precondition for algorithmic harm is a minimal degree of market power. Absent such market power, sellers could not engage in price discrimination—with or without algorithms (Stole 2007). Similarly, product differentiation and targeting require some degree of market power.[140] Accordingly, a robust competition law, focusing on curbing market power or preventing the acquisition of market power, would reduce algorithmic harms. But once again, policymakers must exercise caution: since algorithmic price discrimination and targeting can be beneficial, at least in S markets, attacking a precondition for such price discrimination and targeting may prove harmful. Of course, there are good reasons to promote competition and limit firms' market power; it is just not clear that the rise of algorithmic decision-making strengthens the case for such policies.

A stronger case for legal policies that curb market power can be made when the relevant harm comes from algorithmic coordination. Coordinating on higher prices would be more difficult in a more competitive market, even for an algorithm.[141] It follows that the risk of algorithmic coordination provides a new reason to invigorate our competition laws. And as we argued in Chapter 5, competition law should be interpreted, or revised, in a way that bans algorithmic coordination.

Chapter 9
The Right to Algorithmic Transparency

It would be unrealistic to think that efforts to provide information and to counteract behavioral biases can entirely eliminate algorithmic harm. A more targeted disclosure policy would require transparency *with respect to the nature, the uses, and the consequences of algorithms in the relevant markets* (cf. Paterson et al. 2021). In various areas of regulatory law, transparency of certain kinds is mandatory,[142] largely on the theory that sunlight can be a kind of disinfectant, helping consumers to make better choices and potentially deterring certain practices.[143] Can we design a "right to algorithmic transparency" that would uncover and mitigate the kinds of practices that concern us here?

In countless contexts, the law requires transparency (Sunstein 2020). To a substantial degree, regulatory law consists of disclosure requirements. In the United States, for example, companies must disclose their emissions of toxic substances, and also their greenhouse gas emissions. When credit is denied, the consumer is entitled to an explanation, and many states impose transparency requirements on insurance companies that use algorithms.[144] The analysis in this chapter is designed to provide guidance for the design and implementation of laws of this kind.

A. The Promise of Algorithmic Transparency

Start with algorithmic price discrimination. Suppose, for example, that a seller's algorithm divides consumers into four categories corresponding to their income and wealth; suppose too that wealthier consumers are charged higher prices. Companies might have to disclose that (not particularly alarming) fact. Or suppose that an algorithm uses data on a consumer's borrowing and saving behavior to identify myopic consumers (who tend to borrow more and save less) and then offer such consumers low introductory prices and high long-term prices.[145] Or suppose that the algorithm learns to identify consumers who would likely overestimate the benefit from the firm's

Algorithmic Harm. Oren Bar-Gill and Cass R. Sunstein, Oxford University Press. © Oren Bar-Gill and Cass R. Sunstein (2025). DOI: 10.1093/oso/9780197778197.003.0010

product, and then sets higher prices for these consumers. A transparency requirement, if implementable (more on this below), would force firms to disclose that their algorithms are searching for myopic consumers or for consumers who suffer from an overestimation bias, and offering different prices to these consumers. It is easily imaginable that transparency could deter some of the practices on which we have focused here.[146] The requirement of disclosure of toxic substance emissions has led to significant reductions in such emissions (Hamilton 2005), and something similar can be said about greenhouse gas emissions (Yang, Muller, & Liang 2021). It is reasonable to think that a disclosure requirement could have a significant effect here.

Next, consider algorithmic targeting. Suppose that companies use algorithms to identify less sophisticated consumers and offer them inferior products. Or to elaborate on the prior example, suppose that an algorithm is told to identify myopic consumers and then offer these consumers products and prices with immediate benefits and deferred costs, such as a gas-guzzling car, an appliance that is not energy-efficient, or a cheap printer with expensive ink.[147] Transparency could deter such harmful targeting. Similarly, transparency could deter the use of algorithms to enhance misperceptions. For example, pending legislation would require labeling of any AI-generated content.[148] Transparency could also hinder attempts to coordinate on high, supracompetitive prices.

Finally, consider the case of discrimination on the basis of race or sex. Antidiscrimination law clearly prohibits algorithms that are designed to identify women or racial minorities and single them out for disparate treatment. A transparency requirement could help enforce this prohibition. Such a requirement could also deter attempts to skirt the antidiscrimination law. Suppose that a seller, in an attempt to avoid liability, designs the algorithm to ignore direct data on a consumer's sex, but that the algorithm learns to use the consumer's height instead (as height is correlated with sex). If the seller is forced to disclose the role that height plays in its algorithmic decision-making, then the seller, and the algorithm designer, will be incentivized to avoid what might be indirect sex-based discrimination.[149]

Indeed, transparency could show if algorithms are displaying "proxy bias" or "label bias," which is said to occur whenever they use a proxy that embeds race or sex discrimination (or discrimination on some other prohibited ground). Suppose, for example, that an algorithm uses predicted health-care costs as a proxy for predicted health needs; suppose too that unequal access to care means that we spend less money caring for Black patients than for White patients (Obermeyer et al. 2019). Transparency about the use of predicted health care costs would be both necessary and sufficient to demonstrate a form of discrimination. If algorithms can be made transparent, in the sense that their inputs are knowable, discrimination of this kind can be ferreted out.

A right to algorithmic transparency can serve different policy goals. First, by enhancing transparency about algorithmic harms, it can facilitate public scrutiny and market discipline. If, for example, algorithms are taking advantage of an absence of information or behavioral biases, the public might learn about that—and the practices might stop. There is some reason to believe that a public outcry about relevant practices could change corporate behavior (Yang, Muller, & Liang 2021, 2; Fung & O'Rourke 2000).[150]

Second, transparency can serve as a basis for a more aggressive regulatory response when it reveals harm beyond a certain threshold. At the same time, introducing the proposed transparency reforms might show that any consumer harm falls below a certain threshold and thus belong in a safe harbor against regulatory scrutiny.

Third, a transparency requirement can buttress legal doctrines that require knowledge or intent as a condition for liability. When it comes to AI-powered algorithms, it could be difficult to prove knowledge or intent, since even the algorithm's designer right not know precisely how it works. For example, the designer might not know that the algorithm is differentiating based on the consumer's sex or sophistication (more on this below). A transparency requirement can force the creation of knowledge and thus eliminate the "I didn't know" defense.

B. Transparency Protocols

Computer scientists have been developing methods that allow us to peer into the algorithmic black box.[151] We call these methods "transparency protocols." While it is impossible (in many cases) to attain a full understanding of how a black-box machine-learning algorithm operates, these transparency protocols may allow us to identify the main decision drivers, that is, the variables that significantly affect the algorithm's decisions. For example, the transparency protocol might reveal that a consumer's height significantly influences the price that the consumer is charged. (The Appendix describes some of the transparency protocols that have been developed by computer scientists.)

It is worth emphasizing that what we have in mind goes beyond the usual scope of transparency regulation. In most cases, such regulation is straightforward, at least in theory: a party, perhaps a seller, knows something, and the regulator forces that party to disclose this information. That is also true for many algorithms. But with black-box, AI-powered algorithms, policymakers need to mandate the creation of information before they can require its disclosure. This broader right to algorithmic transparency may well be necessary given the growing use of black-box algorithms.[152] To achieve algorithmic transparency in these contexts, we need the transparency protocols.[153]

C. The Challenge of Algorithmic Transparency

We have alluded to the main challenge of algorithmic transparency: with AI-powered algorithms, it is not at all clear that the seller, or even the algorithm designer, has access to the relevant information. It may be hard to figure out what an AI-powered algorithm is doing. Return to the example of an algorithm that engages in sex-based discrimination. We may be able to figure out that the consumer's sex has a major effect on the algorithm's pricing or targeting decisions (e.g., the algorithm may be offering certain products to men but not to women).[154] We may even be able to figure out that the consumer's height has a major effect on the algorithm's pricing or targeting decisions, in lieu of sex.

But what if the algorithm implicitly identifies the consumer's sex based on hundreds of different data points, including past purchases, search history, income, credit score, health history, current and previous employment, and so forth? Could we be (sufficiently) confident that the algorithm is offering coding classes to male consumers rather than to consumers who have expressed interest in STEM topics and are between jobs? The challenge becomes even greater when the algorithm finds proxies for consumer ignorance and imperfect rationality rather than for race or sex, and uses these proxies to discriminate against vulnerable consumers.

With these black-box machine-learning algorithms, the process of manipulating inputs to generate outputs is opaque, even to the programmer. There is an ongoing debate within the computer science community about whether an AI-powered algorithm can be made transparent in a meaningful way. We have noted that computer scientists have been developing transparency protocols—methods to "open" the black box and "explain" the algorithm's decision-making process. And yet the success of these methods is being questioned. Even if it can be shown that the consumer's height influenced the algorithm's decision, is this a meaningful description of the algorithm's decision-making process? Perhaps for the next (male) consumer the same algorithm would use search history rather than height. Perhaps for another (male) consumer it would use some combination of 100 different variables that similarly correlate with the consumer's sex (Rudin 2019; Babic et al. 2021).

A major problem with the available transparency protocols is their lack of consistency: different protocols can yield different sets of important, decision-affecting variables.[155] Even when utilizing a single transparency protocol, we may get different sets of important, decision-affecting variables. The underlying reason for this problem is the correlations among the different variables (Blattner & Spiess 2022; Blattner, Nelson, & Spiess 2021; Babic et al. 2021).[156] One response to these limitations is to use multiple transparency protocols and, with each protocol, to consider multiple outcomes (i.e., multiple sets of important, decision-affecting variables) (Fisher, Rudin, & Dominici 2019).[157]

We do not presume to resolve this debate. Our more modest goal in this chapter is to present the view that algorithmic transparency is attainable. In the following chapters, we will consider alternative policy responses to algorithmic harm—responses that do not depend on the (questionable) ability to "open" the black box of the AI-powered algorithm.

D. Applying the Transparency Protocols

We now explain how policymakers can use transparency protocols to mitigate algorithmic harms. There are (at least) two possible approaches for applying the transparency protocols, depending on whether the regulator has access to an identifiable "protected characteristic."

Without an identifiable "protected characteristic": look for suspicious characteristics. The idea behind this approach is straightforward: apply a transparency protocol to identify the consumer characteristics that exert significant influence over the algorithm's decision-making process, and promote scrutiny—either market scrutiny or regulatory scrutiny—toward "suspicious characteristics." For example, the regulator might observe that height plays an important role in the decision-making process: shorter consumers are offered higher prices, perhaps because height is correlated with gender. Or the regulator might observe that consumers with little savings and a lot of debt are offered treadmills or gym subscriptions, perhaps because limited savings and significant debt are correlated with present bias.[158] The role played by such seemingly irrelevant, suspicious characteristics could trigger regulatory scrutiny, or it could be made public and trigger a market reaction.

We recognize, of course, that what counts as a *suspicious* characteristic might not be obvious. Still, there will be cases, as in the examples we offered, where it is clear that the weight placed by the algorithm on a consumer characteristic can be explained only by that characteristic's correlation with the consumer's race, sex, or bias.[159] Moreover, any concern about the identification of the suspicious-characteristic criterion should be mitigated to the extent that the transparency exercise is designed to trigger a market reaction. Then the market, rather than a regulator, would decide whether the firm has a convincing reason to set higher prices for shorter consumers, for instance.

Does an identifiable "protected characteristic" emerge as a key decision driver? With this approach, the regulator would again apply a transparency protocol to identify the consumer characteristics that exert significant influence over the algorithm's decision-making process. But now the question is not whether one of the influential characteristics is suspicious. Rather the question is whether one of the influential characteristics is a previously identified "protected characteristic." If the protected characteristic emerges as a key decision driver, then regulatory or market scrutiny should follow.

It is straightforward to identify race or sex as a protected characteristic and see whether either emerges as a influential decision driver when applying a transparency protocol. But as explained above, one of our main concerns is about a different protected characteristic: the consumer's information or rationality deficit. And it is more challenging to identify a protected characteristic variable that distinguishes between informed and uninformed consumers or between biased and unbiased consumers. Can this category of less sophisticated, imperfectly rational consumers be identified in advance? We suggest that, at least in some cases, the answer is yes.

Specifically, biases, misperceptions, and other deviations from perfect rationality can be measured using survey evidence. For example, in the health insurance context, Baillon et al. (2022) used survey evidence to measure (i) overestimation of risk (of incurring medical expenses) and (ii) the shape of the consumer's Prospect Theory utility function.[160] And in the consumer credit context, Meier and Sprenger (2010) used incentivized choice experiments to measure subjects' level of present bias.[161] Assuming that generally administered surveys (like the Survey of Consumer Finances) provide data on a sufficiently large subset of a seller's customer base, and that such surveys could be amended to include bias-measuring questions, we think that these surveys can be used to define, in advance, a protected class of biased or imperfectly rational consumers. Alternatively, regulators may be able to use measures of, or proxies for, sophistication, such as the consumer's level of education or experience in the relevant context,[162] and then treat these proxies for limited sophistication as a protected characteristic.

In the context of algorithmic coordination, we can think of a competitor's pricing behavior as akin to a "protected characteristic." Antitrust regulators should want to employ a transparency protocol that can reveal whether Seller A's algorithm sets prices based on what Seller B is charging and punishes Seller B for any price reduction below the high oligopoly price (e.g., by shifting to below-cost pricing).[163]

In implementing this approach, we should be cognizant of possible correlations between the protected-characteristic variable and other variables. For example, if present bias is highly correlated with limited retirement savings, then the transparency protocol would yield either the present-bias variable or the retirement savings variable. A possible response to this concern is to employ several transparency protocols (and, with each protocol, to consider multiple outcomes, i.e., multiple sets of important, decision-affecting variables) and see whether the larger set of decision drivers that comes out of these protocols includes the protected characteristic.

In the previous approach, we did not have a protected-characteristic variable, and so the search for influential characteristics could produce only suspicious variables that correlate with the protected characteristic. Now we have a protected-characteristic variable, and the question is whether the search for influential characteristics will identify this variable as influential. The "suspicious characteristics" approach has an important advantage: the regulator is not required to define, in advance, a protected characteristic. The crux of that approach was identifying the characteristics that exerted the most influence on the algorithm's decision-making process, relying on ex post "suspiciousness" scrutiny by the regulator or by the market. When we have an identifiable "protected characteristic," we can avoid the "suspiciousness" criterion but, of course, the regulator must be able to define, in advance, what the protected characteristic is, and there must be an objective way to identify or measure this protected characteristic.

E. Global versus Local Approaches

The transparency protocols can be applied both globally and locally. As mentioned above, global approaches give us a general sense of what drives the algorithm's decisions for all relevant consumers (e.g., prices that the algorithm will set for all consumers). Regulators will often be interested in such a global assessment of a seller's algorithm, especially if they need to approve an algorithm before it is put to use, but also if they need to scrutinize an algorithm after it is put to use. For example, regulators should like to know if consumer biases significantly influence the algorithm's decisions across the entire consumer group.

Regulators may also be interested in local approaches that focus on specific decisions or clusters of decisions made by the algorithm. Suppose, for example, that the regulator receives complaints from consumers (e.g., through the complaints database of the Consumer Financial Protection Bureau). If so, the regulator may want to perform a local analysis of the decisions that consumers complain about to ascertain the main variables that affected those decisions. A local analysis may reveal that consumer biases significantly influence the algorithm's decisions for a subset of vulnerable consumers, whereas a global analysis—one that uses a much larger set of algorithmic decisions for a much larger group of consumers—might not identify these consumer biases as a (globally) important decision driver.

Local approaches can also be used to support individualized transparency. If an algorithm identifies a biased consumer and sets a higher price for that consumer or offers that consumer a lower-quality product, then perhaps the seller should be required to inform that consumer why he is being charged the higher price or receiving the inferior product.[164]

F. Less Opacity

AI-powered black-box algorithms are infamously opaque. The question is whether they can be made transparent. We have described recent work by computer scientists that develops transparency protocols to peek inside the black box. We have also acknowledged the limits of these transparency protocols. Indeed, many computer scientists believe that it is impossible to identify the key variables affecting the algorithm's decision-making. The core issue is the large number of variables and the correlations among them. Whenever a transparency protocol points to variable X as influential in the algorithm's decision-making, another transparency protocol, or even the same protocol, might point to Y (or to some combination of Y1, Y2, and Y3) that is correlated with X as the influential variable.[165]

If transparency protocols evolve to overcome these powerful critiques, they could become an important regulatory tool. Regulators could require that companies implement these methods to identify algorithmic harm—from price discrimination, product targeting, algorithmic coordination, and discrimination based on race and sex. The regulator would need to define the transparency-generating methods to be used by firms. Alternatively, firms could be required to disclose their code and their data, and the regulator itself would then implement these methods. It is important to reiterate that while AI-powered algorithms can be opaque, human decision-making is often far less transparent. Indeed, the human mind is perhaps the ultimate black box. Algorithmic decision-making has the potential to be more transparent.

Finally, we should acknowledge alternatives to black-box algorithms. There are white-box algorithms, namely, algorithms that implement a set of instructions specified by the firm—by the seller or by the firm that wrote the algorithm. Computer scientists have also been developing AI-powered machine-learning models that are inherently interpretable, that is, simple enough that a human being, including a regulator, could understand them.[166] With these algorithms, transparency is easy. Indeed, if algorithmic transparency is sufficiently important, and black-box algorithms cannot be made transparent in a meaningful way, then policymakers may consider regulation that restricts sellers to using only white-box or interpretable algorithms.

Appendix

In this Appendix we describe several transparency protocols that have been developed by computer scientists. We focus on protocols that are model-agnostic and post hoc, namely protocols that can be applied to any machine learning model after it has been trained. We consider both global protocols, which provide information about the model's overall behavior, and local protocols, which provide information about specific (local) decisions.[167]

Teacher-Student. In this global protocol, the main black-box algorithm, referred to as the "Teacher" algorithm, trains a simpler, interpretable "Student" algorithm.[168] Specifically, the regulator defines the structure and complexity of the Student. For example, the regulator can specify that the Student will be an easily interpretable decision-tree algorithm with a depth of three layers. The protocol would then search for the three-layer tree that most closely approximates the decisions made by the Teacher algorithm. For example, in the context of algorithmic price discrimination, the regulator could apply the protocol and observe the consumer characteristics that drive pricing decisions in the best Student algorithm (i.e., in the best three-layer tree).

Linear Model. This protocol seeks out a linear model that most closely approximates the global decisions made by the black-box algorithm. Using standard linear-regression techniques, this method searches for a linear combination of consumer characteristics that most closely predicts the outcomes—such as prices and product offers—produced by the black-box algorithm. A challenge with this method is that the resulting linear model would include a very large number of characteristics, limiting the model's interpretability. This challenge is met by utilizing sparsity-creating methods, like LASSO ("least absolute shrinkage and selection operator"), to limit the number of characteristics, such that the linear model includes only those characteristics that have the largest effect on the outcome (Molnar 2022, §5.1). (It should be noted that linear models might be too "weak" to provide a sufficiently close approximation of nonlinear machine-learning models, which allow for complex interactions among the different variables.)

Permutation Importance. This protocol measures the global importance of a variable using a sensitivity analysis. Consider a pricing algorithm that receives as inputs the consumers' income levels and education levels. The protocol would shuffle income levels across consumers, such that a high-income consumer may be presented to the black-box algorithm as a low-income consumer (and a low-income consumer may be presented as a high-income consumer), and see how this affects the algorithm's pricing decisions. This shuffling process would then be performed for education levels, and for other input variables (Breiman 2001; Fisher,

Rudin, & Dominici 2019).[169] When the shuffling of a variable leads to larger changes in the algorithm's pricing decisions (relative to the original, non-shuffled baseline), this variable is more important in driving the algorithmic decisions.

Local Surrogate (LIME). The three previous protocols can be viewed as global surrogate protocols. A local surrogate protocol starts with a specific decision made by the black-box algorithm, such as a price that is set for a specific consumer (the "original" consumer). It then considers a number of "similar" consumers and finds an interpretable model that provides the best possible approximation of the black-box algorithm's decisions (for example, pricing decisions) for the set of original and similar consumers.[170] For example, the protocol may fit a linear model to this "local" set of consumers.[171] We thus learn the key, decision-driving variables for this group of consumers. The LIME protocol then repeats this local analysis for multiple algorithmic decisions—choosing different "original" consumers, identifying sets of consumers who are "similar" to these "original" consumers, and fitting interpretable models for these "local" sets of consumers. Finally, the results from the multiple "local" analyses are aggregated to identify globally important decision variables.[172]

SHapley Additive exPlanations (SHAP). In this protocol, the importance of a variable is measured by its "Shapley values," a concept from cooperative game theory. Intuitively, this value represents the contribution of a variable to a specific (local) algorithmic decision. The protocol considers the decisions that the algorithm would make when different subsets of variables are excluded (and replaced with background data). Then, averaging across different subsets of included and excluded variables, the protocol calculates the marginal impact of each variable on the algorithmic decision.

Consider a pricing algorithm that receives as inputs the consumers' income levels, education levels, and credit scores. For a specific consumer, the SHAP protocol would simulate the decision (for example, the price that would be set), by the black-box algorithm, if it knows (i) only income and education, (ii) only income and credit score, (iii) only education and credit score, (iv) only income, (v) only education, and (vi) only credit score. By comparing these pricing decisions to the price that the algorithm set when it knew all three variables, SHAP can derive the impact of each variable. As with LIME, this local process is repeated for multiple algorithmic decisions, and the results are aggregated to identify globally important decision variables (Lundberg & Lee 2017).[173]

Counterfactual (Contrastive) Explanations. Counterfactual explanations interpret specific (local) algorithmic decisions by describing the minimal changes to the input variables that would have resulted in a different decision. For example, if the algorithm decided to deny credit to a certain consumer, what would it take to reverse the decision? A counterfactual explanation would say, "If your income was 10% higher, you would have been approved." Or "If your credit score was 30 points higher, you would have been approved." When a small change in the value of a certain input variable flips the algorithmic decision, we know that this variable is a locally important variable. And when a small change in the value of this variable flips many algorithmic decisions, we know that this variable is a globally important decision driver. A main shortcoming of counterfactual explanations is that they are often not unique: there might be many, equally convincing counterfactual explanations (e.g., the decision would flip if either your income was higher, your credit score was higher, your total debt was lower, etc.).

Chapter 10

Ex Post Policing and Ex Ante Regulation

We have thus far considered (i) regulating the preconditions for algorithmic harm, especially with regulations designed to reduce the effects of behavioral biases and lack of information on the part of consumers and (ii) vindicating a right to algorithmic transparency. We now turn to policies that directly target the design and implementation of AI-powered algorithms—either through ex post policing of algorithmic outcomes or through ex ante regulation of the algorithm's code.

A. Ex Post Policing: Disparate Impact Review

Algorithmic transparency depends on the technical ability to open the black box of AI-powered, machine-learning algorithms and assess whether the algorithm is discriminating against certain groups of consumers—minorities, women, or less sophisticated consumers (our major emphasis)—in a harmful way. But as we have seen, the technical ability to peer inside the black box is limited. In many cases, we cannot identify the algorithms' key decision drivers in a meaningful way. Stated differently, we cannot observe the algorithmic inputs. And so, if we cannot identify the inputs, let us focus on the outputs. It may be possible to identify the harm caused by the algorithm, that is, the algorithm's outputs, even without fully understanding how the black-box algorithm generated those harmful outputs. And when harmful outputs are identified, some form of regulatory scrutiny and enforcement can follow.[174]

This output-based approach follows closely in the footsteps of disparate impact doctrine. As we have seen, that aspect of antidiscrimination law allows courts to focus on outcomes—worse outcomes for women or minorities—without conditioning liability on a showing of discriminatory intent (as a decision-making input). In the algorithmic context, the idea is to evaluate the algorithm's decisions, or outcomes, and target scrutiny toward cases where consumers with a protected characteristic are treated differently.

Algorithmic Harm. Oren Bar-Gill and Cass R. Sunstein, Oxford University Press. © Oren Bar-Gill and Cass R. Sunstein (2025). DOI: 10.1093/oso/9780197778197.003.0011

Recall once more that this disparate-impact approach has been developed in the context of discrimination based on race or sex as protected characteristics.[175] Aware that the proposal is adventurous, we suggest that the approach might be extended to discrimination based on imperfect information or imperfect rationality as protected characteristics.[176]

Of course, to implement any such disparate impact approach, the regulator must specify, in advance, what the protected characteristic is. Consistent with our emphasis here, the regulator must identify the group of unsophisticated consumers. It is much harder to identify the group of consumers who suffer from information and rationality deficits than it is to identify the group of female consumers or consumers from a minority group. But as we suggested in Chapter 9, it is possible, at least in some cases, to pre-identify the group of unsophisticated consumers. In particular, generally administered surveys can be used to identify consumers who likely suffer from relevant biases and misperceptions. Alternatively, more easily measurable proxies for sophistication, like education or experience, can be used. If, for example, an AI-powered algorithm is treating people without college education differently from people with college education, we have a red flag. Or if such an algorithm is treating people under the age of twenty-one, or over the age of seventy, differently from people in other age groups, we might have reason to suspect that it is targeting behavioral biases. (Of course there might be legitimate reasons to distinguish between people with different levels of education or of different ages.)

Another challenge for any disparate impact analysis is that consumers with a protected characteristic may be treated differently because the protected characteristic is correlated with other relevant (and not protected) characteristics. For example, imperfect information or imperfect rationality may be correlated with income or preferences. In the case of discrimination based on race or sex, the doctrinal question is whether "similarly situated" consumers were treated differently.[177] The same question should be asked when the protected characteristic is bias or misperception: whether biased consumers were treated differently from "similarly situated" unbiased consumers.

Regulators can address this challenge by using a linear-regression model to evaluate how different consumer characteristics affect the algorithm's decisions. The model would include the protected-characteristic variable, say, a measure of consumer sophistication, and the coefficient assigned to that variable would measure the effect of sophistication on the outcome.

The model would also include other relevant (not protected) characteristics, such as income. By including these other control variables, regulators can make comparisons between similarly situated consumers. In our example, the coefficient assigned to the sophistication variable would measure the effect of sophistication on the outcome for consumers with the same income level. If this effect is significant, then regulatory scrutiny should follow. (Market scrutiny could also follow. For example, consumers might refuse to buy from sellers who are known to exploit the unsophisticated.)

How do we select the set of control variables? Put differently, how do we define what counts as "similarly situated"? Should we include only income? Should we add the consumer's wealth? Credit rating? Zip code? The appropriate control variables are context dependent.[178] The regulator can use its subject-matter expertise to select these variables. Or we can use sparsity-creating methods, like LASSO ("least absolute shrinkage and selection operator"), to select the control variables, or consumer characteristics, with the largest effect on the outcome.[179]

A related approach would assess the disparate impact of the algorithm, relative to the pre-algorithm baseline. To implement this approach, the regulator would need data on outcome decisions, such as pricing decisions, before and after the black-box pricing algorithm was adopted. The regulator would then run the regression model with the same explanatory variables—the same protected-characteristic variable and the same control variables—on pre- and post-algorithm outcome data. If the coefficient assigned to the protected-characteristic variable is larger when the algorithm sets prices, then the disparate impact on the protected group was made worse by the algorithm (compare Gillis 2022).

A related approach emphasizes the least discriminatory alternative prong of the disparate impact doctrine. Computer scientists and economists have been developing tools that can assess whether there is an alternative to the seller's algorithm that is less discriminatory (Gillis, Meursault, & Ustun 2024). There are even start-up companies that purport to help sellers to "tune [their] models to be fairer while preserving or enhancing accuracy."[180] Regulatory or market scrutiny should be applied to sellers who do not employ the least-discriminatory algorithm.

Finally, we note that ex post policing, based on a finding of disparate impact, can be implemented through litigation, perhaps looking to tort law. Courts can police especially harmful algorithms under a model of liability for defective products.[181]

B. Ex Ante Regulation: Constraining the Algorithm's Code

We now turn to what is perhaps the most direct attack on algorithmic harm: ex ante regulation of the design and implementation of AI-powered algorithms.[182] The development of AI-powered algorithms includes a critical training stage. This is the stage where the machine-learning algorithm does the learning. If the algorithm is trained on bad data, such as data that is already biased against certain groups (perhaps because the data incorporates prior decisions of biased human decision-makers), then it would not be surprising if the algorithm learns to make bad decisions. If human decision-makers are biased against racial minorities and their past decisions are part of the training data, then decisions made by an algorithm that was trained on these bad data might well be biased against racial minorities. Similarly, if pricing decisions made by human sellers are biased against unsophisticated consumers and these decisions are part of the training data, then an algorithm trained on these data might set higher prices for unsophisticated consumers. Regulators could impose requirements on the data that are used to train machine-learning algorithms, most obviously by excluding data that is biased in a relevant sense (FTC 2016).[183]

In addition, regulators might require that algorithms be programmed with certain constraints. For example, computer scientists and others have explored different mathematical formulations of fairness or equality constraints that can be imposed on the algorithm.[184] Specifically, Cohen, Elmachtoub, and Lei (2022, 8537) propose four definitions of "fairness," the most relevant being "price fairness," that is, that "prices offered to the two groups are nearly equal." To date, this work has generally focused on race and sex, requiring that men and women be offered nearly equal prices, or that Whites and Blacks be offered nearly equal prices. But it could be applied to consumer bias or misperception if they can be defined and measured (as explained above). Regulators could then require that biased and unbiased consumers are charged (nearly) the same prices or offered the same products.[185,186]

Another regulatory option, already suggested in Chapter 9, is to allow only white-box algorithms. This option may be attractive if we are concerned that black-box algorithms might learn to discriminate against consumers who show behavioral biases. A white-box algorithm, with its preset, transparent directives, avoids this risk. Of course, there are good reasons why sellers prefer black-box algorithms. In S markets, they can benefit consumers and increase social welfare, as, for example, by finding a better-matching product or by setting lower prices for poorer consumers. It follows that regulators should exercise caution before they ban black-box algorithms and allow only white-box algorithms.

At the extreme, would it be desirable to prohibit certain uses of algorithms? For reasons we have sketched, there is no sufficient justification for doing so in S markets, except perhaps if sex-based or race-based discrimination is identified or if there is a significant risk of algorithmic coordination. But in U markets, there is a real question whether it might be appropriate to forbid the use of algorithms to make distinctions with respect to prices and product characteristics. In principle, such a prohibition could benefit consumers in the circumstances we have discussed. If regulators could devise a finely tailored intervention and apply it only in those circumstances, that intervention would by hypothesis increase consumer welfare.[187]

Such prohibitions could be viewed as the continuation, in the algorithmic context, of behaviorally informed policies forbidding practices that exploit behavioral biases. Consider the CARD Act of 2010, which imposes regulatory restrictions on late fees and overuse fees, which are not transparent to consumers. Those restrictions are best understood as an effort to respond to consumer harm in U markets, which have been particularly pronounced among people with poor credit ratings (Sarin 2019, 1524–1525). In these circumstances, regulatory restrictions—in this case in the form of price caps—could be taken as a response to a kind of behavioral market failure, and they should be effective if companies are not, in fact, competing over the relevant product characteristics. Indeed, the evidence suggests that consumers have gained almost $12 billion annually as a result of the restrictions, with particular benefits for people who are struggling economically (Agarwal et al. 2015, 113). To the extent that consumers suffer algorithmic harm in U markets, the argument for restrictions of that kind gains force.[188]

To be sure, there are serious problems of administrability. As we have emphasized, regulators do not deal with binary cases of S versus U markets. They deal with heterogeneous populations, with complex mixes of information and rationality. If regulators were themselves perfectly informed, they would be able to make a judgment about the net benefits of any ban. They would be able to identify the circumstances in which algorithms would, on balance, do more harm than good (and perhaps hurt people at the bottom of the economic ladder). Lacking perfect information, they might do best to keep prohibitions in the toolkit but reserve them for the most obvious or egregious cases.

Finally, in a less extreme step than outright prohibition, policymakers can tax the extra profits generated by harmful algorithms. We have seen that in U markets, algorithmic price discrimination allows firms to increase their profits by setting prices that track consumers' overestimated WTP. A targeted tax would reduce firms' incentives to engage in such harmful algorithmic pricing.[189]

Chapter 11
Applying the Reforms to the Different Harm Categories

The preceding discussion offered examples of algorithmic harms that our proposed reforms were designed to address. We now offer a more systematic exploration of how those reforms can reduce or eliminate the main categories of algorithmic harm to consumers.

A. Algorithmic Price Discrimination

One of our main concerns has been algorithmic pricing that targets consumers' biases and misperceptions. For those who seek to implement the proposed reforms, a main challenge involves identifying instances of such targeting, especially when sellers employ AI-powered black-box pricing algorithms. Our discussion of algorithmic transparency suggested several ways to meet this challenge.

First, regulators can use, or force sellers to use, transparency protocols—to identify variables that exert significant influence over the algorithm's pricing decisions. If any of these variables is "suspicious," that is, if its influence can be explained only as a proxy for consumer bias or misperception, then regulatory or market scrutiny should follow. Suppose, for example, that the pricing algorithm used by a credit card issuer places significant weight on the consumer's retirement savings. That may well be considered suspicious—especially if low savings trigger offers with low introductory interest rates and high long-term rates, perhaps because the algorithm associates low savings with present bias. Second, suppose that a specific bias or misperception can be measured – for example, through generally administered surveys. If so, regulators could use transparency protocols and see if the measured bias or misperception emerges as one of the key decision drivers. Third, regulatory scrutiny should follow if a predefined proxy for sophistication, such as education or relevant experience, emerges as a key decision driver.

Algorithmic Harm. Oren Bar-Gill and Cass R. Sunstein, Oxford University Press. © Oren Bar-Gill and Cass R. Sunstein (2025). DOI: 10.1093/oso/9780197778197.003.0012

Now suppose that the transparency regulations reveal bias-based price discrimination. If so, there could potentially be liability under relevant law—in the United States, for example, under Section 5 of the Federal Trade Commission Act, which prohibits unfair practices, or similar state UDAP (unfair, deceptive, or abusive practices) statutes. In the consumer credit context, where the prohibition extends also to abusive practices, it would be even easier to impose liability.[190] And as mentioned above, the transparency reforms, which force an opening of the algorithmic black box, would prevent sellers from claiming that they did not know that their algorithms were discriminating. To be clear, it is not our purpose here conclusively to identify a specific doctrinal source of liability. This would require a full analysis of legal and policy considerations for and against using a specific doctrine to police algorithmic harms. We relegate such analysis to future work. The conceptual point is that algorithmic transparency can help make the case for imposing liability.

Next consider the disparate impact approach. This regulatory approach can be implemented when a specific bias or misperception can be identified and measured. At the ex post stage, courts or regulators can test for special harm on those who suffer from such a bias or misperception: Are consumers with high bias levels charged higher prices than consumers with low bias levels who are otherwise similarly situated? If a disparate impact of the relevant kind is identified, consumer protection laws can be triggered, as discussed above. At the ex ante stage, policymakers can regulate the design and implementation of pricing algorithms to reduce the risk of bias-based pricing. Specifically, regulators can force sellers and algorithm designers to include a no-discrimination constraint in the algorithm's code—to ensure that consumers who show behavioral biases are charged (nearly) the same price as consumers who do not show such biases.

B. Algorithmic Targeting

While this category of harm is distinct from the previous category, the proposed legal reforms apply in a similar way. The main difference is that regulators now need to ask what affects the algorithm's product-targeting decisions rather than pricing decisions, and, relatedly, whether biased consumers are offered inferior products. For example, it would be suspicious if a consumer's low rate of retirement savings significantly influences the algorithm's decision to offer the consumer a gas guzzler rather than a hybrid car. It would also be suspicious if the low rate of retirement savings causes a lender's algorithm to offer credit products with low introductory rates and high long-term rates. Alternatively, if the level of consumers' present bias can be measured, does this bias variable play an important role in the algorithm's targeting decisions? If so, there is reason for suspicion.

Under the disparate impact approach, regulators would want to know if biased consumers are more likely to be offered (for example) credit products with back-loaded pricing, or appliances that are not energy-efficient, as compared to unbiased consumers who are similarly situated. If the transparency regulations or the disparate impact review reveal bias-based targeting, liability might be triggered for unfair or abusive practices. Finally, at the ex ante stage, regulators can force sellers and algorithm designers to include a no-discrimination constraint in the algorithm's code—to ensure that a consumer's bias level does not affect the type of appliance (or credit product) that this consumer is offered.

C. Algorithmically Enhanced Misperceptions

In Chapter 4, we argued that AI-powered algorithms not only exploit existing misperceptions but might also create or enhance misperceptions. This possibility significantly strengthens the case for the legal reforms discussed above. In addition, policymakers should consider reforms that specifically target the concerns that we identified in Chapter 4. For example, policymakers should require sellers and algorithm designers to disclose whether content is generated by AI, as in the chatbot and deepfake contexts.[191]

D. Algorithmic Coordination

The application of the proposed reforms in the context of algorithmic coordination is distinctive. Here the concern is not about discrimination between different groups of consumers. Rather, the concern is that all consumers will pay higher prices because the algorithms learn to coordinate and set a high, oligopolistic price. (In addition, whereas in prior categories of harm the focus was on the decision-making process of a single algorithm, here the concern is about the strategic interaction between several pricing algorithms.) Transparency mandates can help regulators evaluate whether the algorithm's pricing decisions are influenced by a competitor's pricing strategy. Also, by exposing the algorithmic coordination, the transparency requirement will "force" upon the competing sellers knowledge of the coordinated pricing and may thus help to overcome antitrust law's reluctance to police naked tacit collusion or parallel behavior (e.g., antitrust law might not impose liability when competing sellers charge similarly high prices, without evidence of actual collusion; the transparency mandates could provide the necessary evidence).[192]

There is also an interesting analog to the disparate impact approach. The crux of this approach is to focus on outputs rather than on inputs. Regulators could require competing sellers to submit their algorithms and data and simulate a strategic interaction between the algorithms.[193] If the simulation produces coordination on a high, supracompetitive price (and especially if the algorithms punish deviation from this high price), then antitrust enforcement could follow. Finally, consider more direct regulation of the algorithm's design. As explained in Chapter 5, certain types of machine-learning algorithms are more likely to learn to coordinate on high prices. Regulators could consider restrictions on the use of such algorithms.

E. Algorithmic Discrimination Based on Race and Sex

Policing algorithmic discrimination on the basis of race and sex is, in some sense, easier than policing discrimination between more and less sophisticated consumers. As explained above, some of the proposed reforms can be applied only if the protected characteristic is identifiable or measurable. This condition is more easily met with discrimination that is based on race and sex, as many data sets that are used by algorithms in consumer markets include information on the consumers' race and sex. Therefore, it would be easier to know whether race or sex had a significant influence in the algorithm's decision-making process (suggesting the presence of disparate treatment). And it would be easier to identify disparate impact—in terms of pricing or product targeting—on women and minorities. Finally, it would be easier to force sellers and algorithm designers to include a no-discrimination constraint in the algorithm's code.[194]

The proposed reforms could be applied even if the algorithms are denied access to information about the consumer's race or sex, perhaps in an attempt to comply with antidiscrimination laws. As a preliminary matter, and as we explained above, removing this information from the data might well fail to prevent discrimination (even in the sense of disparate treatment), as the algorithm could find other variables that correlate with race or sex. In terms of the proposed reforms, the regulator can require submission of the full data, including the race and sex variables, if the regulator itself wants to apply the transparency protocols. Or it could force the seller to apply the transparency protocols using the full data.

Similarly, and going beyond disparate treatment, the regulator could conduct a disparate impact review (on the basis of race or sex, or other protected characteristic) using the full data. And the regulator could force sellers and algorithm designers to include a no-discrimination constraint in the algorithm's code, using the full data, and specifically the race and sex variables, to implement the constraint.

PART III
BEYOND CONSUMER MARKETS

We have thus far focused on consumer markets—on the potential harms of AI-powered algorithms that sellers are increasingly using in such markets (Part I) and on the potential legal policy responses to these algorithmic harms (Part II). But much of what we have said can be applied beyond consumer markets. In this part, we briefly sketch two such applications—to labor markets (Chapter 12) and to political markets (Chapter 13). We intend the brief sketches to be suggestive rather than definitive. The basic theme is that our account of potential harms has implications for those domains, and that legal responses are very much in order there as well.

Chapter 12
Labor Markets

Labor markets share many of the key features that raise concern about algorithmic harm in consumer markets. In important labor markets (although not in all), a sophisticated party, the employer, wields big data, LLMs, and AI-powered algorithms to maximize profits from interaction with less sophisticated parties, the employees.[195] And as in consumer markets, there is a concern that algorithmic price discrimination, where the price is the wage paid to employees, and algorithmic targeting of jobs to applicants would harm employees. Again as in consumer markets, there is concern about algorithmically enhanced misperceptions, about algorithmic coordination, and about discrimination based on race or sex. Note that, unlike in consumer markets, here the less sophisticated party, the employee, is the seller (selling labor), and the more sophisticated party, the employer, is the buyer.

This is our central argument in highly compressed form. In Section A, we elaborate on these potential algorithmic harms in labor markets. In Section B, we turn to legal policy. We argue that many of the reforms and regulatory tools that we developed in Part II for consumer markets turn out to be relevant in the labor market context.

A. Algorithmic Harm in Labor Markets

As with consumer markets, labor markets can be divided into S markets and U markets. And as with consumer markets, we are much less concerned about algorithmic harm in S markets. If the relevant employees are sophisticated—for example, highly paid software engineers—it is far less concerning when firms use AI-powered algorithms to predict the employee's willingness to accept (WTA) and set wages accordingly. Similarly, with such a sophisticated pool of potential employees, it is far less concerning when firms use AI-powered algorithms to target job offers to particular candidates. If such algorithms offer various opportunities and benefits plans to candidates who particularly value them, there is no reason to object. As

Algorithmic Harm. Oren Bar-Gill and Cass R. Sunstein, Oxford University Press. © Oren Bar-Gill and Cass R. Sunstein (2025). DOI: 10.1093/oso/9780197778197.003.0013

with S consumer markets, the use of algorithms in S labor markets will have a wide range of benefits, including benefits to workers. Accordingly, for the types of algorithmic harms that concern us—price discrimination and targeting—our focus will be on U markets.

In our discussion of consumer markets, where consumers are subject to significant information and rationality deficits, we highlighted the harm that can be caused when AI-powered algorithms set individualized prices that track consumers' inflated WTP. In the labor context, the concern is different: unsophisticated employees will have a *deflated* WTA, namely, they will accept low wages. They might not realize how low the wages are when the compensation package is complex. They might overestimate the value of other employer-provided benefits (such as retirement benefits). They might underestimate certain risks, such as safety risks, associated with the particular workplace. And they might underestimate the value of outside options. Indeed, evidence suggests that workers—especially workers at low-paying firms—systematically underestimate the wages that they can earn at other firms (Jäger et al. 2023). Algorithms that allow employers to identify and target such misperceptions can significantly harm workers.[196]

The central problem is that to an increasing degree, AI-powered algorithms will know precisely what compensation packages to offer, given the fact that unsophisticated employees will take worse offers than they should. Exploitation of a lack of information and of behavioral biases might ensure that employees end up with (for example) less safety, worse healthcare, worse retirement packages, and lower salaries than they should. Focus in particular on safety: if an algorithm knows that employees are unrealistically optimistic, it might offer a job with serious risks for which little or no compensation is paid.[197]

There is also a risk of harmful targeting. In consumer markets, the concern is about the targeting of inferior products to unsophisticated consumers. In labor markets, the concern is about the targeting of inferior job offers to unsophisticated employees. In consumer markets, we are worried about particular, identifiable consumers overestimating the benefits from these inferior products and overpaying for them. In labor markets, we are worried that particular, identifiable employees will overestimate the benefits from an inferior job or underestimate the costs in terms of the employment environment (how nice the boss and coworkers are, how good the coffee is), promotion opportunities, proximity to public transportation or to after-hours food and entertainment, and again health and safety—and thus accept a low wage or a subpar compensation package. An algorithm might know that particular employees will not much worry about safety risks associated with work and might be able to attract people who demand little or no compensation for running those risks. Note in this regard that while some employees appear to be compensated for facing mortality risks, other employees appear to receive no such compensation.

The incidence and magnitude of harm—from algorithmic pricing and algorithmic targeting—depend on additional factors, as detailed in Part I. Some misperceptions are not particularly harmful; other misperceptions are very harmful indeed. Starting with price or wage discrimination, *under*estimation of a product's value can increase the consumer surplus. And in labor markets, misperception that increases, rather than decreases, employees' WTA can be beneficial because it can lead to higher wages (unless the employer decides not to make an offer). With algorithmic targeting, the concern is about overestimation of a product's benefits or of the benefits from an employment opportunity; *under*estimation of such benefits produces mistaken decisions, but it does not lead to harmful targeting.

Another important distinction is between benefit-based and cost-based price discrimination. We saw that the concern about algorithmic price discrimination in consumer markets arises mainly when the price discrimination is benefit-based; cost-based pricing is less harmful. Similarly in labor markets, algorithmic wage discrimination is particularly harmful when the wage varies with employees' (misperceived) WTA. It is less troubling if the employer sets different wages based on the cost, to the employer, of hiring the specific employee; for example, it should be fine to pay lower wages to an employee whom the algorithm identifies as being less productive or less trustworthy.[198] Of course, some cost-based wage discrimination is unlawful; for instance, an employer cannot set a lower wage for a disabled employee who requires costly accommodations or for a pregnant employee who will soon require parental leave.[199]

As we have seen, the harm from algorithmic pricing and algorithmic targeting arises from the exploitation of information and rationality deficits that consumers, or employees, already have. As we have also seen, AI-powered algorithms can be used to create or exacerbate such deficits—to create or exacerbate misperceptions. In labor markets, we should be worried that LLM-generated, targeted job offers would deceive potential employees into thinking that the job is more attractive than it really is. This could be done by outright lying. But it could also be done by playing into existing biases or by manipulatively prioritizing the good things about the job and de-prioritizing the bad. Imagine, for example, that LLMs or AI-powered algorithms are able to identify people who are subject to present bias. They might well exploit that bias by emphasizing (for example) a hiring bonus. Or imagine that LLMs or AI-powered algorithms are able to identify people who have limited attention. They might well exploit that bias by hiding certain terms, such as waivers of various sorts and noncompete clauses. In the United States, the FTC has shown intense concern with hidden terms for consumers and workers alike.[200] It is easy to imagine a situation in which LLMs or AI-powered algorithms target workers who are particularly likely not to attend to such terms.

While our focus has been on the harms that are caused when LLMs or AI-powered algorithms interact with biases and misperceptions, we have also described categories of harm that exist even if all consumers, or employees, are fully informed and rational. In the consumer context, we discussed the risk of algorithmic coordination that can result in supracompetitive prices. The same is true in labor markets, where such coordination can result in wage levels below what a competitive market would offer.

Finally, concern about algorithmic race- and sex-based discrimination is probably even greater in labor markets than in most consumer markets. Such discrimination could manifest itself in lower wages for women or minorities, in the targeting of women or minorities for lower-level jobs, or in discriminatory employment termination decisions.[201] As we emphasized in Part I, while concern about race- and sex-based discrimination is of paramount importance, it is not immediately obvious whether shifting decisions—about hiring, firing, and wages—from human beings to algorithms would increase or instead decrease discriminatory outcomes. But where the result is to increase discrimination, there is reason for serious attention. Return to proxy or label bias, arising when an algorithm uses some seemingly reasonable proxy to measure something important. We offered the example of using expenses devoted to health problems to measure medical need. We noted that because Black people are less likely than White people to obtain access to medical services, this proxy turns out to produce discrimination.[202] Employment discrimination might be a product of proxy bias in a world in which AI-powered algorithms are in widespread use.

B. Policy and Law

In Part II, we considered a series of legal policy responses to algorithmic harm in consumer markets. Many of these responses can also help to address algorithmic harm in labor markets.[203] Starting with the preconditions for algorithmic harm, we argued for behaviorally informed, disclosure-type interventions designed to reduce the information and rationality deficits that algorithms exploit. Similar interventions can mitigate algorithmic harm in labor markets. For example, our analysis supports regulation that forces effective communication of varied characteristics of an offered employment opportunity, and of the benefits and costs of those characteristics. Disclosure of safety risks is an obvious example; in the United States, the Occupational Safety and Health Administration has devoted a great deal of effort to disclosure requirements. In the fullness of time, we might be able to imagine a Worker Opportunity Label, akin to the Nutrition Facts label, adopted by the U.S. Food and Drug Administration, and the Broadband label adopted by the Federal Communications Commission. Such a Label might describe, in a clear and simple manner, all relevant features of a job opportunity.

Next, consider the right to algorithmic transparency. The idea is to open the algorithmic black box and see whether the algorithm is relying on signs of bias and misperception in setting wages or targeting job offers. Transparency protocols—protocols that open the black box and identify the key variables driving the algorithm's decision—can be useful both in triggering a market reaction and in facilitating further enforcement actions. It would be essential to know, for example, that an algorithm is offering jobs that entail health or mortality risks to applicants whom the algorithm predicts will underestimate such risks.[204] Here, as in the consumer context, questions remain about whether, in what circumstances, and for which class of algorithms such transparency protocols can be effectively implemented. Even at this stage, however, a degree of transparency should be possible, and we think it should be mandated.

A third category of policy responses is centered around an expansion of the disparate impact doctrine. If we cannot see into the black box, given the limits of the transparency protocols, then we should focus on what comes out of the box. Disparate impact analysis considers outcomes—prices, wages, job offers—and asks whether the outcome you experience significantly depends on your group affiliation. Traditionally, disparate impact doctrine, as part of antidiscrimination law, protected women and minority groups who experienced systematically worse outcomes, often in the employment context.[205] Our suggestion, which applies with equal force in labor markets as in consumer markets, is to test for systematically inferior outcomes experienced by the group of less sophisticated employees—those suffering from significant information and rationality deficits. Are these employees being offered inferior jobs? Or lower wages? (Of course, as emphasized in Part II, this approach depends on our ability to identify, objectively and in advance, this group of less sophisticated employees.)

The disparate impact methodology could be applied ex post—as part of a regulatory review or enforcement process (or even litigation). It can also be applied ex ante: as a legal mandate to encode equal treatment as a hard constraint in the algorithm's optimization problem. Once again, we can require equal treatment between men and women and between members of majority and minority groups. And focusing on the main concern developed here, we can require equal treatment between more and less sophisticated employees.[206]

Chapter 13
Political Markets

We now venture into the worlds of politics and democratic theory. It might seem that these worlds have nothing to do with the market contexts—consumer markets and labor markets—on which we have focused thus far. There are indeed major differences. Still, it is useful to think about a market for votes and a market for political contributions. More fundamentally, the algorithmic harms that we have identified appear in these political markets, with potentially severe and even devastating consequences for democracy. In Section A, we discuss these algorithmic harms. In Section B, we consider possible responses from the standpoint of policy and law. Our treatment will be brisk and suggestive rather than full and authoritative. Our main goal is to suggest that our treatment of algorithmic harm has close parallels in political markets, and that the same kinds of harms are occurring, and will likely get worse, in those markets. The remedies we have sketched might well have parallels there as well. Those remedies, and potential alternatives, deserve serious attention in a period in which algorithmic harm poses severe threats to the enterprise of self-government.

A. Algorithmic Harm in Political Markets

Suppose that a candidate for public office seeks campaign donations. Call him John Jones. Suppose that an AI-powered algorithm identifies, with real precision, a population of people who are especially likely to donate to Jones's campaign. The population includes people who are willing to give their money to political campaigns and who are likely, according to the algorithm, to be favorably disposed toward Jones and what he has to offer. That population includes (1) some people who are very careful with their money and attentive to all relevant details and (2) some people who are not very careful with their money and not attentive to all relevant details. Those in category (1) can be counted as S types, while those in category (2) can be counted as U types.

Algorithmic Harm. Oren Bar-Gill and Cass R. Sunstein, Oxford University Press. © Oren Bar-Gill and Cass R. Sunstein (2025). DOI: 10.1093/oso/9780197778197.003.0014

Now suppose that an algorithm is able to specify, with considerable accuracy, the kinds of solicitations that will maximize donations to Jones. It can do so because it can target and personalize. The algorithm knows that, for some people, it would be most effective to emphasize Jones's military background. For others, the algorithm knows that it would be most effective to emphasize Jones's record on civil rights. For still others, it would be most effective to emphasize Jones's personal life, above all his love for his wife and children. The algorithm is able to target people by specifying the candidate's characteristics that are most likely to appeal to them. On these counts, the algorithm can be very precise. It can also be manipulative or deceptive. It might be able to get people to be very excited about Jones, perhaps even thrilled by him. It might be able to get people to be very worried about Jones's opponents, perhaps even terrified by them.

The algorithm can also design contribution forms that are likely to produce high levels of donations. It might know, for example, that a form that calls for recurring monthly contributions will be highly effective, and that a form with a prechecked box for such contributions will be even more effective. It might also be able to identify the particular subpopulations with which one or another form will be especially effective. It might be able to send such forms to those subpopulations. Some forms will work best with S types; others will work best with U types. For example, a form with a prechecked box might work well with U types because they will not be attentive to the fact that they will be making recurring contributions; they would not make such contributions if they were, in fact, attentive to what they were doing.

There is nothing hypothetical about such scenarios. Before the 2020 U.S. election, for example, one political campaign used choice architecture to excellent effect (Posner et al. 2023). In fact it included prechecked boxes, which made all donations into weekly contributions. Unless people deleted the checks, such donations would automatically take that form. The result, it has been found, was to increase contributions by a staggering $43 million over what they would have been without the prechecked boxes. Notably, many donors eventually noticed that they were giving money every week—and they sought millions of dollars in refunds. So far as we are aware, this approach was not personalized or targeted; it was quite general. And so far as we are aware, the approach was not a product of an algorithm; it was based on a judgment, informed by behavioral economics, that prechecked boxes would produce continuing donations. That judgment turned out to be correct. There is every reason to think that a personalized approach, powered by AI, would be even more successful and perhaps far more successful.

Analytically, the use of algorithms to solicit campaign contributions is similar to the use of algorithms to influence consumers. More broadly, we can think of a political campaign as "selling" a candidate, a party, an agenda a policy. If voters or donors are S types, then all would appear to be well. If a campaign uses an algorithm to identify likely donors, nothing seems to be amiss. And if a campaign uses an algorithm to identify truthful messages that would appeal to such donors, there would be no problem. But now suppose that voters or donors are U types, and the algorithm is able to target them. It might, for example, use prechecked boxes with the expectation that U types will not pay attention to them. As we have seen, these donors might be harmed; they might well donate more than they would absent the misperception.

Now expand the viewscreen. AI-powered algorithms or large language models (LLMs) might craft and distribute skewed or misleading information. If so, people might vote for a candidate whom they would not support absent the misperception. These voters or donors would be very much like consumers who end up purchasing a product because of a lack of information or a behavioral bias. And as in consumer markets, the AI-powered algorithm or LLM can both exploit existing misperceptions and create misperceptions where none existed before.

Of course nothing is entirely new under the sun. It is true that politicians have crafted and distributed skewed or misleading information for a very long time. As in the context of consumer markets, we are dealing with a new set of tools, not a new practice. But these new tools allow for greater differentiation in the practice of crafting and distributing skewed or misleading information. And as in the context of consumer markets, greater differentiation magnifies the relevant risks. To say the least, the impact of those magnified risks on democracy would not be good (and to the nontrivial extent that all of this is now happening, is not good). Candidates would receive (and are receiving) funds or votes not because people wanted to support them, all things considered, but because algorithms succeeded in exploiting gaps in knowledge, behavioral biases, or limited attention in order to get them to part with their money or to cast their vote. Ultimately, the result could well be a destructive form of competition in which different campaigns enlist state-of-the-art AI-powered algorithms to see which is best at that kind of exploitation.

Consider in this regard the Cambridge Analytica scandal of 2018. To be sure, 2018 might seem like ancient history, but the scandal tells us a great deal about current and coming risks. Cambridge Analytica obtained the personal data of about 87 million Facebook users. It did so by using its app, called "This Is Your Digital Life." The app asked users a set of questions designed to learn something about their personality. By using the app, people gave Cambridge Analytica not only those answers but also permission to access millions of independent data points, based on their use of the internet. In other words, those who answered the relevant questions "agreed" to allow Cambridge Analytica to track their online behavior. Far more broadly, they gave the company access to a large number of data points *involving the online behavior of all of the users' friends on Facebook.*

With these data, Cambridge Analytica had the capacity to engage in "psychological targeting." It used people's online behavior to develop psychological profiles, and then sought to influence their behavior, their attitudes, and their emotions through psychologically informed interventions. Through those interventions, Cambridge Analytica believed that it could affect people's political choices.

Let us bracket the details and the question whether Cambridge Analytica did in fact have that capacity. It seems clear that current and coming AI-powered algorithms, armed with information about voters and potential donors, should be in a terrific position to devise strategies for producing the desired political behavior, whether it involves voting, donating, or attending events. AI-powered algorithms should know which people are most likely to lack information or to have misperceptions perhaps based on behavioral biases.

Perhaps even more troubling, AI-powered algorithms are getting really good at simulating human agents. They can produce deepfakes of political figures and use them to enhance the influence of misleading messages or to discredit political figures.[207] AI-powered algorithms can create and exploit misperceptions to the detriment of voters and donors and to the detriment of democratic processes.[208] In our view, these are exceedingly serious problems.

B. Policy and Law

What is the proper policy response? The answer is not at all obvious, especially in nations that are committed to freedom of speech. We should begin by building on the response that we have sketched in the context of consumers. Happily, the analogies are pretty good. Regrettably, the analogies are highly imperfect.

As we have seen, many policy initiatives are designed to counteract a lack of information and behavioral biases on the part of consumers. In democratic processes, no government official has the responsibility, or should have the responsibility, of ordaining "the truth" with respect to contested issues. To be sure, many nations have institutions that police certain practices. In the United States, the Federal Election Commission has relevant responsibilities, and both national and state officials have roles to play in combating fraud and certain kinds of misinformation. But those roles are constrained and relatively narrow.[209]

We suggest that the initial response, and one well-suited to current risks, is consideration of an ambitious proposal: in politics, as in consumer markets, there should be a right to algorithmic transparency. Campaigns should be required to disclose their own practices, and people should be entitled to see what political algorithms are doing. If campaigns are using algorithms to target particular voters, voters should be entitled to see that that is what they are doing. Here, as in the context of consumer protection, sunlight is a potential disinfectant. Indeed we are hopeful that it might be a significant ex ante deterrent and ex post corrective to the most troublesome uses of AI-powered algorithms and AI more generally in politics.

It is true that free speech principles have special importance in the context of political campaigns, and those principles impose restrictions on what governments may do. But there should be no barrier to efforts to require candidates and campaigns to disclose the uses of AI-powered algorithms by which they target voters and donors. A requirement of that sort promotes the purposes of free speech guarantees, such as the First Amendment to the U.S. Constitution; it does not compromise them. And even if forcing the disclosure of the algorithm's inner workings is legally problematic or technically infeasible (see our discussion about the limits of transparency protocols in Chapter 9), it would still be beneficial to disclose the mere fact that algorithmic targeting is taking place or that tailored campaign messaging is being crafted by an AI-powered algorithm.

What about regulation? That is a singularly challenging question. Candidates manipulate people; they deceive people; they lie. They might lie to populations that are particularly susceptible to those manipulations, deceptions, and lies. They might use AI-powered algorithms to make manipulation, deception, and lying especially effective. Can that be prohibited?

In a remarkable decision in 2012, the Supreme Court of the United States has held that intentional falsehoods are protected by the First Amendment in the political context. The case involved Xavier Alvarez, an inveterate liar who falsely claimed, among other things, that he had been a Vietnam veteran, a police officer, married to an actress from Mexico, and a professional hockey player for the Detroit Red Wings. But he got into trouble with the law when serving as a member of the Three Valley Water District Board, a governmental entity with headquarters in Claremont, California. He said this: "I'm a retired marine of 25 years. I retired in the year 2001. Back in 1987, I was awarded the Congressional Medal of Honor. I got wounded many times by the same guy."[210]

None of that was true. One part of it was also illegal. His claim to have received the Medal of Honor violated the Stolen Valor Act, which makes that particular lie a crime. Nonetheless, the Supreme Court ruled that the lie was protected by the First Amendment. Among other things, the justices who agreed with the result emphasized that punishing false speech would deter free debate and that less restrictive alternatives, including counterspeech, could promote the state's legitimate interests (such as not diluting the effect of actual receipt of the Congressional Medal of Honor). In a crucial passage, highly relevant to potential uses of AI in the political context, the Court's plurality said this:

> Permitting the government to decree this speech to be a criminal offense, whether shouted from the rooftops or made in a barely audible whisper, would endorse government authority to compile a list of subjects about which false statements are punishable. That governmental power has no clear limiting principle. Our constitutional tradition stands against the idea that we need Oceania's Ministry of Truth. Were this law to be sustained, there could be an endless list of subjects the National Government or the States could single out.[211]

It is clear that the Supreme Court does not like the idea of a Ministry of Truth, even if the government is seeking to protect the democratic process against the adverse effects of falsehoods. We do not like the idea of a Ministry of Truth, either. In free nations, any effort to forbid political communications, even false or deceptive ones produced with the help of AI-powered algorithms, would run into serious legal challenges. Still, a great deal might be done to address our concerns here. The central ideas should involve *autonomy* and *consent*. Nothing in free speech principles or the First Amendment should be taken to forbid governments from policing efforts to exploit limited attention by automatically enrolling people in a program of weekly donations; government might well prohibit use of algorithms to target susceptible populations with that approach.

Nor should anything in free speech principles or the First Amendment forbid government from requiring political campaigns to disclose their use of targeting algorithms, or from disclosing how, exactly, they are targeting voters. We have offered only a brisk and suggestive treatment here, meant to flag the problem rather than to resolve it, but we think that steps of this kind should indeed be required. They should be the first steps toward a series of efforts to police political campaigns to reduce the risk of algorithmic harm.

Conclusion

In an era of extraordinary technological change, it seems hard to get a grip. With respect to AI, large questions loom: Will the economy change in fundamental ways, so that it will not be recognizable one or two decades hence? When, if at all, will AI obtain general intelligence, and so surpass people? With artificial general intelligence, will humanity be at risk? Or might AI find a cure for cancer? Might it be able to help us discover energy sources that are inexpensive and that do not contribute to climate change?

In 1921, Frank Knight (1933, 19–20) wrote, "Uncertainty must be taken in a sense radically distinct from the familiar notion of Risk, from which it has never been properly separated. . . . The essential fact is that 'risk' means in some cases a quantity susceptible of measurement, while at other times it is something distinctly not of this character; and there are far-reaching and crucial differences in the bearings of the phenomena depending on which of the two is really present and operating." Knight argued that it is sometimes impossible to assign probabilities to various outcomes. Also writing in 1921, John Maynard Keynes (1921, 214) pointed to "uncertain" knowledge, about which "there is no scientific basis on which to form any calculable probability whatever. We simply do not know." There is a reasonable argument that with respect to some of the outcomes plausibly associated with AI, we are dealing with uncertainty rather than risk. It is not possible to assign probabilities to those outcomes. We simply do not know.

Our aim here has been to focus on a set of enduring problems—problems that, we think, will last for a very long time and that are put in sharp relief by the rise of AI-powered algorithms. With respect to those problems, there is a great deal that we know.

As long as there have been transactions, sellers have attempted to learn something about the information, preferences, and biases of buyers, and to act on what they learn. A sucker may or may not be born every minute, but countless people are vulnerable to savvy sellers who are eager to prey on human vulnerabilities, and in particular on people's hopes and fears. Federal and state regulators have worked to prevent fraud, deception, and unfairness. When buyers are sophisticated, of course, there are no suckers, and in that respect, at least, competitive markets are likely to work well.

Algorithmic Harm. Oren Bar-Gill and Cass R. Sunstein, Oxford University Press. © Oren Bar-Gill and Cass R. Sunstein (2025). DOI: 10.1093/oso/9780197778197.003.0015

In many consumer markets, however, many (most?) buyers are unsophisticated. They are prone to make mistakes. Recall that whether buyers should be counted as unsophisticated depends not only on what they know and on whether they show biases, but also on the nature of the good or service in question; with complicated products, most of us might be unsophisticated. Our real topic is consumer error.

Long before algorithms, of course, many sellers could find ways to single out the suckers. For example, motor vehicles are typically sold through a process of negotiation, and sharp motor vehicle sellers, working on the lot, are able to distinguish quickly among buyers, and to obtain large profits from those who know less or who suffer from one or another bias. But AI-powered algorithms have greatly upped the ante. Armed with such algorithms, sellers have unprecedented ability to identify the particular misperception or bias from which specific buyers suffer, and to exploit consumers in a much more personalized, and thus more effective, way. Personalized pricing and personalized product offerings are the wave of the present, and even more of the future.

In S markets, the shift toward use of AI-powered algorithms and hence toward more in the way of personalization is nothing to deplore. In general, it should be celebrated. In U markets, however, we should hold the applause. Consumers in such markets are likely to be hurt. Exploitation of a lack of knowledge, and of behavioral biases, will be especially harmful when algorithms are in a position to target people with knowledge of where they are most vulnerable. Consumers might be led to purchase products that have little or no value for them. Algorithms might use what they know about people's optimism bias, present bias, or availability bias to lead them to welfare-reducing choices. Indeed, algorithms might be able to heighten or even to inculcate optimism bias, present bias, or availability bias.

We have suggested three sets of remedies. *First*, it is more important than ever before to increase the likelihood that consumers will be sophisticated, or at least to increase the likelihood that their information deficits, and their biases, will not lead them to make welfare-reducing choices. Clear, simple disclosure policies can provide information, counteract biases, and increase consumers' potential for agency.

Second, algorithms should be made transparent, at least to the extent feasible. If an algorithm is offering higher prices to some consumers and lower prices to others, people should be made aware of that fact. (Recall that price discrimination is not always objectionable; for example, universities often offer lower tuition to poor students than to wealthy ones, and sometimes require no tuition at all.) We think that regulators should embrace a right to algorithmic transparency.

Third, more aggressive approaches, including a disparate impact test, deserve serious consideration. It should be unlawful for AI-powered algorithms to exploit people's lack of information, and so to harm identifiable categories of consumers. The same is true if such algorithms exploit behavioral biases—as, for example, by automatically enrolling consumers in a monthly payment scheme for some good from which they do not benefit. With respect to race and discrimination, *proxy bias* is a particular concern; it should be unlawful.

Labor markets and political markets present similar problems. Of these, the former is more tractable. If employees lack information or suffer from (for example) unrealistic optimism or present bias, employers might be able to convince them to enter into agreements that are not in their interest. Our three sets of remedies deserve serious consideration here as well. In some ways, political markets are the most fundamental of all, and we share the widespread concern that campaigns are now able, and will be increasingly able, to use algorithms to exploit ignorance or biases to obtain votes or money. We have argued in favor of adapting the remedies in the consumer context to the political context, emphasizing that transparency is essential and that certain practices, which amount to or which verge on deception, should be forbidden.

It is far too soon, of course, to answer the largest questions about the effects of AI. But it is not too soon to address an assortment of large problems that are here right now. Solving those problems would produce significant gains in terms of human welfare.

Notes

Introduction

1. See Chapters 1 and 3. See also Hogan (2018), describing how retailers use algorithms to tailor pricing and promotions, to customize search results, to personalize content, and more. Popular culture offers some complicated tales of personalization and individuation, with particular reference to algorithmic harm, such as the films *Her* (Annapurna Pictures 2013) and *I'm You're Man* (Letterbox Filmproduktion 2021).
2. AI algorithms dubbed "recommender systems" perform tasks such as suggesting which Netflix show you may want to watch next or which grocery item you may want to add to your Amazon Fresh cart. See Burke, Felfernig, and Göker (2011, 13–14); Hardesty (2019); Assad et al. (2021, 460–461); Netflix Research (n.d.). As noted by Assad et al. (2021, 461), "[Algorithms] can . . . exploit consumer information, providing potentially highly personalized offers that could increase allocative efficiency." See also FTC (2016), listing beneficial uses of big data and algorithms.
3. The general problem is discussed in Akerlof and Shiller (2015) without reference to algorithms and algorithmic harm. It is worth noting that, in certain cases, the implications of imperfect information and imperfect rationality may differ. In parts of our analysis we allow for search costs, and thus for imperfect information, even in S markets. And in U markets, we emphasize misperception and imperfect rationality; if consumers were imperfectly informed but fully rational, they might not be willing to pay systematically higher prices (although consumers could sometimes overestimate and sometimes underestimate, and the algorithms would identify the direction of the mistake). We also note that, in some parts of our analysis (e.g., Chapter 3), we study markets with both sophisticated and unsophisticated consumers. Finally, since the S versus U distinction is really about the likelihood of mistakes, we note that such mistakes are more likely in markets where the opportunities for learning (or feedback) are limited. Related: the S versus U distinction can be, to some extent, endogenous to the degree of algorithmic exploitation of unsophisticated consumers. If mistakes are very costly, then consumers will have strong incentives to avoid mistakes—to become more sophisticated.
4. We focus throughout on algorithms that learn from online behavior, which suggests a relevant distinction between (1) people who have a significant online presence and (2) people who do not. For reasons that will emerge, algorithms might know very little about those in category (2), which would in important respects be unfortunate for them, and in important respects be a safeguard for them.
5. Or by more accurately identifying an individual's high willingness to pay (WTP), even if the algorithm does not know that the high WTP is driven by information and rationality deficits. The increased risk of harm from differentiation that targets information and rationality deficits justifies the focus on regulation of AI-based decision-making. The benefit from the regulation, that is, the reduction in the harm from such differentiation, would be greater, relative to similar, but smaller, harms in the pre-AI age. And the cost of the regulation may be smaller, since it is often easier to police algorithmic decision-making than it is to police human decision-making. See Part II. Of course, even in the pre-AI world a cost-benefit analysis would justify certain regulatory interventions.
6 See Chapter 6 for references that focus on algorithmic discrimination based on race and sex in consumer markets. More prominently, the literature has focused on algorithmic discrimination based on race and sex, when algorithms make decisions in the criminal justice system about bail and sentencing (Mayson 2019; Huq 2019; Wisser 2019). The reference to discrimination on the basis of race and sex in consumer markets is meant to be merely illustrative; there are of course other forms of discrimination, as we will note below. Algorithmic decision-making might be especially likely to harm members of other disadvantaged groups, including

people who are suffering from certain disabilities (such as mental health problems) and people who are elderly.

7. See, for example, Gal (2017, 330); Lippi (2020); Steele (2022). We note that it might be difficult to trust the pro-consumer intentions of algorithms like Alexa and Siri that are developed by major sellers. Cf. Van Loo (2019a, 839–840), who notes that "[p]ersonal and general information laws may prove determinative of AIs' ability to help consumers by making it less likely that informer AIs either lose out to marketplace AIs like Amazon or are coopted by sellers to gain data access."
8. We acknowledge that when parties are imperfectly rational, normative evaluation can be challenging, since we cannot rely on revealed preferences. On the challenges of behavioral welfare economics, see Goldin (2015); Bernheim and Rangel (2009); Bernheim (2016).
9. Department of Treasury et al. (2021, 16837). The request notes concerns that the "use of AI can also create or heighten consumer protection risks, such as risks of unlawful discrimination, unfair, deceptive, or abusive acts or practices" (16839).
10. Office of Management and Budget, *Memorandum for the Heads of Executive Departments and Agencies: Guidance for Regulation of Artificial Intelligence Applications*, by Russell T. Vought, M-21-06, Washington, D.C.: (2020), https://www.whitehouse.gov/wp-content/uploads/2020/11/M-21-06.pdf, which directs executive agencies to "carefully consider the full societal costs, benefits, and distributional effects," including effects on "decisions . . . made by consumers" when regulating algorithmic decision-making.
11. For example, the Algorithmic Accountability Act of 2023, "[d]irects the Federal Trade Commission to require impact assessments of automated decision systems and augmented critical decision processes"; Digital Platform Commission Act of 2023, S. 1671, 118th. Cong. (2023), establishing a "new federal body to provide reasonable oversight and regulation of digital platforms to avoid the development of increasingly powerful algorithmic processes." The Commission's prerogative includes competition and consumer protection. Section 8 empowers the Commission to propose "voluntary or enforceable behavioral codes, technical standards, or other policies . . . with respect to transparency and accountability for algorithmic processes." Algorithmic Accountability Act of 2023, H.R. 5628, 118th Cong. (2023). See also Graham and Warren (2023), describing their bill, the Digital Consumer Protection Commission Act.
12. See also Kahn (2023), who notes that "the A.I. tools that firms use to set prices for everything from laundry detergent to bowling lane reservations can facilitate collusive behavior that unfairly inflates prices—as well as forms of precisely targeted price discrimination."
13. See European Parliament legislative resolution of March 13, 2024, on the proposal for a regulation of the European Parliament and of the Council on laying down harmonized rules on AI (Artificial Intelligence Act) and amending certain Union Legislative Acts. (COM(2021)0206—C9-0146/2021–2021/0106(COD)), https://eur-lex.europa.eu/legal-content/EN/TXT/?uri=EP%3AP9_TA%282024%290138. The European Union has also passed recent laws meant to regulate the power of large tech companies to engage in algorithmic decision-making; see Regulation (EU) 2022/1925 of the European Parliament and of the Council of September 14, 2022, on contestable and fair markets in the digital sector and amending Directives (EU) 2019/1937 and (EU) 2020/1828 (Digital Markets Act), 2022 O.J. (L 265) 1; Regulation (EU) 2022/2065 of the European Parliament and of the Council of October 19, 2022, on a Single Market for Digital Services and amending Directive 2000/31/EC (Digital Services Act), 2022 O.J. (L 277) 1. In addition, the European Commission has established the European Centre for Algorithmic Transparency. See European Centre for Algorithmic Transparency (n.d.).
14. See Law Commission of Ontario (2023).
15. See, for example, Lei No. 13.709, de 14 de Agosto de 2018, Diário Oficial da União, 59 de 15.8.2018 (Braz.), regulating automated and algorithmic decision-making to benefit "free competition" and "consumer relations"; Tobin (2023); Ministry of Electronics and Information Technology, Proposed Digital India Act, 2023, https://www.meity.gov.in/writereaddata/files/DIA_Presentation%2009.03.2023%20Final.pdf.
16. Compare Restatement (First) of Consumer Contracts § 1 (Am. L. Inst. 2024), which states that the principles of the Restatement apply also to employment contracts.
17. See Benkler, Faris, and Roberts (2018), discussing the "epistemic crisis" in American politics.

Chapter 1

18. The analysis in this chapter is based on Bar-Gill (2019).
19. We should emphasize that price discrimination and personalized pricing are generally legal in the United States. See OECD Directorate for Financial and Enterprise Affairs Competition Committee (2018).
20. Assad et al. (2021, 460) describe how Amazon emphasizes "the possibility and the benefits of pricing automation in its marketplace with a Selling Partners API service," and observes that "[t]here is a growing new industry of software intermediaries offering automated pricing services, from turnkey options that even small sellers can afford to fully customized pricing software for large companies. Many of these repricing companies, such as Kalibrate.com, a2i.com, and Kantify, explicitly rely on AI as a key characteristic of their algorithms." OECD Directorate for Financial and Enterprise Affairs Competition Committee (2018) documents personalized pricing in a wide range of industries, including retailing, travel, and personal finance. Stucke and Ezrachi (2017, 1264) note that United Kingdom regulators have found evidence that "price discrimination [has become] more prevalent online" due to algorithms that use data collected from digital assistants. Chen, Mislove, and Wilson (2016) find that 543 out of 1,641 Amazon merchants of best-selling products likely used algorithmic pricing strategies. Thomas (2014) describes B&Q's testing of in-store electronic price tags that alter the price of an item based on the profile of the customer. Valentino-DeVries, Singer Vinc, and Soltani (2012) report on evidence that retailers like Staples and Home Depot were personalizing prices on their websites, based on a consumer's browsing history and distance from a competitor's store. See also Ipsos, London Economics, and Deloitte Consortium (2018), Wallheimer (2018); Ezrachi and Stucke (2016b, 89–96). Firms try to hide their price discrimination strategy. For example, they offer personalized digital coupons or discounts (Skrovan 2017; Reimers & Shiller 2019; Rossi, McCulloch, & Allenby 1996; Shiller 2020). Firms also use personalized rank-sorting algorithms, which promote more expensive items to price-insensitive consumers (Hannak et al. 2014, 305; Mikians et al. 2012).
21. Insurance companies also engage in cost-based (or risk-based) price discrimination. On the distinction between cost-based pricing and pricing that is based on the consumer's willingness to pay, see Chapter 2, Section D.
22. The differentiation is not only between individuals but also within a single individual; for example, the algorithm may learn that a person has a higher WTP when watching a baseball game or during certain times of the day or when the weather is bad.
23. See, for example, Kahn (2023), who noted that "the A.I. tools that firms use to set prices for everything from laundry detergent to bowling lane reservations can facilitate . . . forms of precisely targeted price discrimination." Already in 2014, the FTC was concerned about data brokers peddling in information that is indicative of consumers' level of sophistication (FTC 2014, 117): information traded between data brokers and suppliers includes lists of "financially challenged" consumers.
24. See, for instance, Stole 2007). Stole notes, "It is well known that price discrimination is only feasible under certain conditions: (i) firms have short-run market power, (ii) consumers can be segmented either directly or indirectly, and (iii) arbitrage across differently priced goods is infeasible" (2226). As Stole observes, price discrimination cannot be sustained if arbitrage is feasible (e.g., if consumer A who is offered a low price can then resell the product to consumer B, for whom the algorithm would set a high price). We note that in many markets arbitrage is infeasible, difficult, or costly. Moreover, sellers can deliberately increase the cost of arbitrage (e.g., by adding personal, nontransferable warranties). Another precondition for price discrimination is weak fairness constraints. In some markets, consumers will rebel against price discrimination that they view as unfair. And yet fairness constraints, while limiting the extent of feasible price differentiation, need not prevent it entirely. The AI-powered algorithm may learn to adjust pricing to reduce the risk of consumer backlash. Also, fairness concerns can be viewed as another component of the consumer's WTP. The algorithm will set a lower price for a consumer whose WTP is reduced by fairness concerns.
25. This assumption is relaxed in Chapter 2, Section E and in Bar-Gill (2020).
26. See, for instance, Mas-Colell, Whinston, & Green (2012, 316–322); Varian (2010, 292–294).
27. See, for instance, Mas-Colell, Whinston, and Green (2012, 384–386); Varian (2010, 441–443).

28. Rhodes and Zhou (2024) similarly focus on the "full differentiation" case: "[W]e focus on the limit case of perfect, or first-degree, price discrimination; as firms gain access to richer data and more sophisticated AI, this type of very fine-tuned personalization is likely to become increasingly feasible." Partial differentiation, or imperfect price discrimination, is considered below.
29. There are additional distributional implications for the consumer side of the market. Consumers with a higher WTP, who would have purchased the product at the (no-discrimination) monopoly price, suffer an affirmative loss, as they pay more for the same product. Consumers with a lower WTP are not affected—without price discrimination they would have been priced out of the market, and with price discrimination they still get a zero (net) surplus.
30. Welfare effects can be non-monotonic in the degree of differentiation, such that consumers (especially poor consumers) benefit from a move from no differentiation to partial differentiation but are then harmed by a move from partial differentiation to full differentiation. Dube and Misra (2023) find, in a field experiment, that while personalized pricing reduces the overall consumer surplus, many consumers, with lower WTP, benefit from lower prices. More generally, the economics literature, which has been focused on S markets, shows that the effect of price discrimination on consumer welfare is ambiguous. Mauring (2022) finds that, with rational consumers and WTP based on preferences and budget constraints (but not misperceptions), regulation that limits price discrimination can help consumers, but only if it is strict enough. Aguirre, Cowan, and Vickers (2010, 1611) find that although "[i]n many cases [price] discrimination reduces welfare," the "conditions for [price] discrimination to raise welfare are not implausible." And Nalebuff (2009) identifies cases in which imperfect price discrimination leads to ambiguous effects on consumer welfare.
31. The overestimation inflates demand and thus increases the quantity sold. The higher price somewhat tempers this quantity-increasing effect, but cannot reverse it.
32. When the misperception is even stronger and the perceived demand curve shifts even higher above the actual demand curve, the quantity, Q_M', can be larger than Q_C. In this case, the black triangle disappears entirely, and the problem of insufficient purchases is replaced with a problem of excessive purchases. Specifically, consumers in the $[Q_C, Q_M']$ range inefficiently purchase the product. Misperception can either increase or decrease overall efficiency in this market, depending on the relative magnitudes of the insufficient purchases problem (without misperception) and the excessive purchases problem (with misperception).
33. There are additional distributional implications for the consumer side of the market, especially if we add budget constraints and wealth effects: consumers with a high WTP, who would have purchased the product and gained a positive surplus in the absence of price discrimination, lose that positive surplus and more; consumers with a low WTP, who would have been priced out of the market in the absence of price discrimination, now purchase the product and pay a price equal to their full WTP, including both the preference-based and misperception-based components.
34. When the misperception is stronger such that Q_M' is larger than Q_C, price discrimination definitely decreases efficiency. In this case, there is an excessive quantity problem even in the absence of price discrimination, and price discrimination only exacerbates this problem.
35. See, for example, Bar-Gill (2021). Relaxing the linear-demand assumption can lead to more nuanced results.
36. Our analysis in this chapter focused on a single market. How would the analysis change when the same consumer participates in many markets (buying food, a car, a laptop, a vacation package, etc.), as is common? For some consumers, purchasing many products and services across multiple markets will strain their financial resources, such that the budget constraint will have a larger effect on the consumer's WTP, leaving less room for overestimation to influence the consumer's WTP.
37. In some cases, the algorithm may learn that a consumer suffers from a particular bias or misperception; for example, the algorithm may observe that a consumer saves too little for retirement and infer that this consumer suffers from present bias. The algorithm could then use this information about the consumer's bias in predicting the consumer's WTP.

Chapter 2

38. The correlation between consumers' bias levels and their preference-based WTP will be positive when bias is proportional to (actual) value. The correlation between consumers' bias

levels and their preference-based WTP will be negative when bias is negatively correlated with wealth. It is not that poor people are more prone to bias; rather, rich people can afford to hire expert advisors—human or virtual—that mitigate bias and misperception. And so, if preference-based WTP is positively correlated with wealth, and wealth is negatively correlated with bias levels, then the preference-based WTP will be negatively correlated with bias levels (Bar-Gill 2019, 246).

39. The underestimation deflates demand and thus decreases the quantity sold. The lower price somewhat tempers this quantity-decreasing effect, but cannot reverse it.
40. Consumers who purchase the product despite the misperception enjoy a larger surplus, thanks to the lower price.
41. The analysis of this extension draws on the excellent discussion in Porat (2024). In the appendix to this chapter, we provide a formal analysis of algorithmic BBP and derive its implications for both total surplus and consumer surplus (including implications for different subgroups of consumers) in S markets and in U markets. Here we provide an informal summary of this analysis.
42. Recent work has begun to develop algorithms that anticipate strategic responses and are robust to such responses (Björkegren, Blumenstock, & Knight 2020). These algorithms would be expected to increase sellers' profits and reduce the consumer surplus in S markets (i.e., where sophisticated consumers are likely to respond strategically to BBP).
43. Amazon stopped these experiments when consumers found out about them and expressed their unhappiness (CNNMoney 2000).
44. Yang (2022, 1365) observed that "data companies such as Acxiom and Datalogix gather and sell personal information including government records, financial activities, online activities, and medical records to retailers." Martin (2016, 57) notes that "[b]road data aggregators summarize information across diverse contexts into profiles and sell aggregated information to companies looking for a specific, target market." And the FTC (2014, 23) found that "data brokers obtain detailed, transaction-specific data about purchases from retailers and catalog companies" and turn them into marketing products that "enable the data brokers' clients to create tailored marketing messages to consumers."
45. In S markets, BBP helps consumers and harms sellers. Therefore, in the early period, sellers would prefer to commit to refraining from using BBP, if they can. But such a commitment may well prove impossible: in the later period, armed with reams of data and the algorithms to analyze it, sellers will have a strong incentive to engage in BBP, and sophisticated consumers will anticipate this in the early period and respond accordingly.
46. See, for example, Lessmann et al. (2015, 124); Thomas (2009, 25–26); Yap, Ong, and Husain (2011, 13274); and Jin et al. (2021, 143593). More specifically, Ma et al. (2018) study machine-learning algorithms used to assess default risk in p2p lending; Kvamme et al. (2018) and Chen, Guo, and Zhao (2021) study machine-learning algorithms used to assess default risk in mortgage lending; Butaru et al. (2016) study machine-learning algorithms used to assess default risk in credit card lending. We emphasize that, while cost-based or risk-based price discrimination is common in consumer credit markets, the benefit-based or WTP-based price discrimination that we focused on in Chapter 2 is also prevalent in many consumer credit markets (Gillis 2024).
47. A similar analysis applies in insurance markets. Some insurance markets rely on pooling between high-risk and low-risk insureds, which occurs in the pre-algorithmic world when both groups of consumers face the same insurance premium. Algorithmic price discrimination might be harmful in such markets if it prevents the pooling and the socially desirable cross-subsidization that comes with it. However, as with credit, it is possible that, without price discrimination, the low-risk insureds would exit the market. Algorithmic price discrimination would then be socially desirable, as it extends the insurance coverage to low-risk insureds (assuming that each of the two insurance pools—the one with only high-risk insureds and the one with only low-risk insureds—is independently viable).
48. See, for example, Gao, Yi, and Zhang (2023) and Langenbucher (2022).
49. Similarly, if consumers were imperfectly informed but fully rational, they would not make systematic mistakes; for example, their WTP would not be systematically inflated. Still, such consumers could sometimes overestimate and sometimes underestimate the benefit from a product, and the algorithms would identify the direction of the particular mistake and set prices, or target product offers, accordingly.

50. See Sunstein and Thaler (2008) and Kamenica, Mullainathan, and Thaler (2011, 417–418).
51. The oligopoly case is analyzed in Bar-Gill (2020). The industrial organization literature has largely focused on S markets and did not explore the implications of consumer misperceptions. The classic article in this literature found that price discrimination helps consumers. Thisse and Vives (1988) find that in a linear Hotelling model, personalized pricing, that is, offering each consumer a different price based on their location on the Hotelling line, leads to a reduction in the price paid by every consumer. Intuitively, each firm tries to poach consumers on its rival's "turf" with low prices, which then forces the rival to lower prices. More recent work suggests that price discrimination can be either good or bad for consumers, depending on market conditions (Rhodes & Zhou 2024).
52. Consumers will have a higher WTP if they do not have attractive outside options. Consumers will also have a higher WTP if they are less likely to shop around and explore their outside options, perhaps because they are very busy or less savvy. Once again, algorithms will identify such consumers and charge them a higher price. Kahn-Lang (2022) studies price discrimination in the residential electricity market, where sellers set different prices for consumers with different levels of search frictions.
53. For example, half of all consumers get a value of $\frac{V}{2}$ or less from the product, that is, $F\left(\frac{V}{2}\right) = \frac{V/2}{V} = \frac{1}{2}$.
54. The monopolist sets a price that solves $\max_p \pi(p)$.
55. As long as $p_2^H \geq p_1$. This condition is satisfied (as we show below).
56. The price that maximizes $\pi_2^H(p_2^H)$ in an unrestricted domain is $\frac{V}{2}$. Since $p_1 > \frac{V}{2}$ (as we show below) and the domain of the high-value segment is $v \in [p_1, V]$, we have a corner solution: $p_2^H = p_1$.
57. This is the price that maximizes $\pi_2^L(p_2^L)$.
58. The seller sets a price that solves $\max_{p_1} \left\{\pi_1(p_1) + \pi_2^H(p_1) + \pi_2^L\left(\frac{p_1}{2}\right)\right\}$.
59. The result that BBP increases overall efficiency depends on the uniform distribution assumption.
60. If richer consumers are more likely to be aware of the seller's BBP strategy and thus less likely to be harmed by BBP (see Appendix Section B below), then we should be less concerned about BBP.
61. From the preceding paragraph, we know that $\pi_1(p_1) = p_1 \cdot [1 - F(\tilde{v}_1(p_1))] = p_1 \cdot [1 - F(2p_1)]$, $\pi_2^H(p_2^H(p_1)) = p_2^H(p_1) \cdot [1 - F(p_2^H(p_1))] = 2p_1 \cdot [1 - F(2p_1)]$, and $\pi_2^L(p_2^L(p_1)) = p_2^L(p_1) \cdot [F(\tilde{v}_1(p_1)) - F(p_2^L(p_1))] = p_1 \cdot [F(2p_1) - F(p_1)]$. The seller sets a price that solves $\max_{p_1} \left\{\pi_1(p_1) + \pi_2^H(p_2^H(p_1)) + \pi_2^L(p_2^L(p_1))\right\}$.

Chapter 3

62. To be precise, our analysis covers targeted advertising, assuming a sufficiently high conversion rate (from ads to purchases). With lower conversion rates, the analysis would require some adjustment. For accounts of how algorithms determine the products and services that are offered to individual consumers, see Dreyfus, Chang, and Clausen (2020, 15–27), who found that Booking.com, Coles, Target, and other online sellers offered different suggested products to consumers on the basis of algorithmic consideration of the consumer's age, sex, search history, language, and other factors. For accounts of how algorithm-driven targeted advertising is based on consumers' browsing habits, current location, or predicted interests and behaviors, see Milgrom and Tadelis (2018, 21), citing evidence that companies use algorithms to advertise more expensive products to consumers who own a Mac computer, because "owning a Mac is correlated with higher income"; FE Online (2021): "Google Pay users in India will soon get to see targeted advertising on their payment gateway based on their spending habits and traffic on their platform"; Thompson (2019) shows that "digital ads are powered by vast, hidden datasets that allow advertisers to make eerily accurate guesses about who you are, where you've been, how you feel and what you might do next"; Facebook tells advertisers that Facebook's use of algorithmic data collection allows merchants to advertise to people based on "Location," "Demographics," "Interests," "Behavior," "Connections," "App Users," and more criteria. Already in 2014, the Federal Trade Commission (2014, 117) named lists traded between data brokers and suppliers that included categories such as "Diabetes Interest," "Cholesterol Focus," and "Urban Scramble." For more reports of how e-commerce sites actively use algorithms to

steer consumers toward particular products, see Mikians et al. (2012, 84); Hannak et al. (2014, 317); Ipsos, London Economics, and Deloitte Consortium (2018).

63. See Hacker (2021). See also Calo (2014), arguing that mass data collection will make firms increasingly "able to trigger irrationality or vulnerability in consumers" (996). "For instance, advertisers who understand that willpower is finite and could measure a consumer's emotional state could exploit their vulnerability to sell products" (999). Also, drawing from the behavioral economics research, Calo reasons that data-powered targeted advertising allows advertisers to target consumer vulnerability (1031–1032). Hauser et al. (2009, 203) develop an algorithm that uses clickstream data to infer an online customer's "cognitive style," for example, "impulsive (makes decisions quickly) versus deliberative (explores options in depth before making a decision), visual (prefers images) versus verbal (prefers text and numbers), or analytic (wants all details) versus holistic (just the bottom line)," and adjusts the "look and feel" of the seller's website accordingly, for example, "by changing the ratio of graphs and pictures to text, by reducing a display to just a few options . . . or by carefully selecting the amount of information presented about each [product]. A website might also morph by adding or deleting functional characteristics such as column headings, links, tools, persona, and dialogue boxes." Nadler and McGuigan (2018) describe the "Behavioral Emotion Moments" approach to advertising that uses big data to identify a consumer's emotional state and send targeted offers based on this emotional state. Matz et al. (2017) conducted three experiments delivering targeted ads tailored to users' particular personality traits to induce them to purchase various online products. The authors concluded that advertisements tailored to users' levels of "extroversion" and "openness"—estimated using their Facebook likes—substantially increased their likelihood to purchase the goods. Hui et al. (2013, 3) describe hundreds of "iPhone apps (e.g., Grocery Gadget) that allow users to build a grocery shopping list," so "brand managers and retailers can then [use that list to] provide targeted coupon offers for *unplanned* categories to consumers via a mobile app" (emphasis added). Dowling et al. (2019, 466) describe how big data enables "precise measurement of consumer states" and location, such that sellers can target consumers "at the right time and place [to] induce unplanned spending." Paterson et al. (2021, 8) write, "[B]ehavioural advertising . . . seek[s] to link advertising to consumers' predicted interests or behaviours in order to promote products that are unlikely to benefit them. For example, rich foods or expensive cosmetics might be advertised at particular times of day when consumers are predicted to be feeling tired or stressed or people exhibiting low self-esteem might be targeted with advertisements for diet products, or cosmetic surgery." Rosen (2013) criticizes marketing firms' recommendation to algorithmically advertise beauty products to women during "prime vulnerability moments," that is, at times "when women feel the most insecure about their bodies and overall appearance."

64. See EyeQ (n.d.). See also Wagner and Eidenmüller (2019, 593-94): "Facial recognition algorithms will detect when customers are down and weak. Just think of subscription offers from dating platforms to depressed singles that arrive during the Christmas holidays. All this might be further intensified through immersive virtual reality experiences."

65. Facebook responded that it "does not offer tools to target people based on their emotional state" and promised that the research on younger users "was never used to target ads." The leaked document was obtained by an Australian newspaper (Davidson 2017). On the leaked document and Facebook's response, see Tiku (2017) and Levin (2017). According to a related earlier story, Facebook allowed advertisers to target users based on recent changes to their relationship status (Entis 2014). Facebook gives advertisers a way to target by relationship status (Adams 2024).

66. The idea is that, with positive search costs, the product that is offered or prioritized by the seller is more likely to be purchased by the consumer, even if the consumer could potentially find an alternative—not offered or not prioritized—product. Paterson et al. (2021) and Wagner and Eidenmüller (2019) provide accounts of how algorithms help to match consumers with relevant product offerings. Similarly, Acemoglu et al. (forthcoming) argue that targeting based on big data can help consumers. The basic point is that AI-powered algorithms reduce the cost of targeting and product differentiation, and this can help consumers in S markets.

67. A formal analysis of algorithmic targeting in U markets is provided in the Appendix. We further develop and extend this analysis in Bar-Gill and Sunstein (forthcoming). We acknowledge that our assumption about pricing—that the perceived surplus is divided equally between Seller

and Buyer—is quite restrictive, and that the generalization, in the Appendix, which allows for unequal division is still restrictive. Our main results should hold for other assumptions about pricing, as long as both Seller's profits and the consumer surplus are a function of the perceived benefit from the product. Like us, Acemoglu et al. (forthcoming) show that targeting based on big data harms consumers in U markets. Acemoglu et al. assume a deviation from perfect rationality that is similar to our overestimation. They do not consider underestimation. Also, they do not consider the possibility that targeting or differentiation could help consumers in the overestimation case.

68. To focus on situations where the overestimation bias is potentially most troubling, we assume that the overestimated benefit from P2 exceeds the accurately perceived benefit from P1, that is, that the bias flips the relative desirability of the two products. Contrast this example with the car example that we used in Section A. There the larger car was optimal for one group of consumers (suburban families), and the smaller car was optimal for another group of consumers (city dwellers). Here, the larger car is optimal for all consumers—perhaps because the relevant market comprises only suburban families—and the only reason why someone would purchase the smaller car is the overestimation bias. Finally, we set aside the issue of externalities by assuming that both cars (P1 and P2) pollute the environment at similar levels.
69. We compare the option of offering only the larger vehicle or offering only the smaller vehicle. But there is another possibility: if sellers cannot discriminate, they might offer a third product design (i.e., not one of the two product designs described in the text).
70. Seller will never offer P2 at a price that will attract all consumers. Intuitively, in order to sell the smaller car to all consumers, Seller would have to reduce the price to a level that even unbiased consumers would be willing to pay. But if such a low price is needed to capture the entire market with the smaller car, it is more profitable for Seller to capture the entire market with the larger car that can fetch a higher price.
71. To focus on situations where the underestimation bias is potentially most troubling, we assume that the underestimated benefit from P1 is lower than the accurately perceived benefit from P2, that is, that the bias flips the relative desirability of the two products.
72. Seller will never offer P1 at a price that will attract all consumers. Intuitively, in order to sell the hybrid car to all consumers, Seller would have to reduce the price to a level that even biased consumers would be willing to pay. But if such a low price is needed to capture the entire market with the hybrid car, it is more profitable for Seller to capture the entire market with the gas guzzler that can fetch a higher price.
73. For example, Camerer et al. (2003) explain how extended warranties capitalize on people's tendencies to overact to salient but rare events. And in Vokes v. Arthur Murray, Inc., 212 So.2d 906 (Fla. Dist. Ct. App. 1968), a 51-year-old widow was induced to purchase 2,302 hours of dancing lessons despite lacking dance aptitude.
74. See also Wagner and Eidenmüller (2019), suggesting that, based on an initial interest that a consumer expresses, in hiking, for example, the algorithm might reinforce and develop this preference by offering hiking-related guidebooks and gear, while effectively preventing the consumer from exploring preferences for other activities.
75. There is another problem: an algorithm might seek to shape preferences so as to maximize a seller's profits. Advertisers try, of course, to do this every day. With large data sets and personalized information, algorithms might have an unprecedented capacity to learn about what works to shape tastes, and whose tastes can be shaped in what ways (Ashton & Franklin 2022). We bracket that question here.
76. In a more general model, we would not assume a single benefit for each product, but rather two demand curves—one for each product.
77. Alternatively, we could assume that the price leaves consumers with a share γ of the overall (perceived) surplus, for example, $\gamma(b_2 - c)$.
78. To see why Seller will offer P1 to the unbiased consumers, observe that Seller sets $p_1 = \gamma b_1$ for P1. Seller would set $p_2 = \gamma b_2$ for P2. Since $p_1 > p_2$, Seller offers P1 to unbiased consumers. In terms of consumer surplus, consumers who buy P1 get $b_1 - p_1 = (1 - \gamma) b_1$, and consumers who buy P2 get $b_2 - p_2 = (1 - \gamma) b_2$. Since $b_1 > b_2$, unbiased consumers prefer P1. This assumes that Seller can distinguish between biased and unbiased consumers and set a lower P2 price for unbiased consumers. If Seller sets a higher P2 price, based on the WTP of the biased consumers, that is, $p_{2B} = \gamma\delta b_2$, then P2 becomes even less attractive to the unbiased consumers. For similar reasons, biased consumers buy P2.

79. We compare the option of offering only the larger vehicle or offering only the smaller vehicle. But there is another possibility: if sellers cannot discriminate, they might offer a third product design (i.e., not one of the two product designs described in the text). In this case, algorithmic targeting might help some consumers while harming others.
80. If we relax the equal-cost assumption ($C_1 = C_2 \equiv C$.), then the answer will also depend on the relative manufacturing costs of the two car models.
81. To see this, observe that $CS_{2B}^{PA}(\hat{\alpha}_B) < CS_1^{PA}$ for $c = 0$ and that $\frac{d\hat{\alpha}_B}{dc} < 0$.
82. The result that $CS_{2B}^{PA}(\alpha_B = 1) < (1 - \gamma)\, b_1 = CS_1^{PA}$ follows from our assumption that $b_2 < b_1 < \delta b_2$.
83. These results follow from the expression $CS^A = \alpha_U (1 - \gamma)\, b_1 + \alpha_B (1 - \delta\gamma)\, b_2$, which we derived above.
84. To see why Seller will offer P1 to the unbiased consumers, observe that Seller sets $p_1 = \gamma b_1$ for P1. Seller would set $p_2 = \gamma b_2$ for P2. Since $p_1 > p_2$, Seller offers P1 to unbiased consumers. In terms of consumer surplus, consumers who buy P1 get $b_1 - p_1 = (1 - \gamma)\, b_1$, and consumers who buy P2 get $b_2 - p_2 = (1 - \gamma)\, b_2$. Since $b_1 > b_2$, unbiased consumers prefer P1. To see why Seller will offer P2 to the biased consumers, observe that Seller sets $p_2 = \gamma b_2$ for P2. Seller would set $p_{1B} = \gamma\delta b_1$ for P1. Since $p_2 > p_{1B}$, Seller offers P2 to biased consumers. In terms of consumer surplus, consumers who buy P2 get $b_2 - p_2 = (1 - \gamma)\, b_2$, and biased consumers who buy P1 think that they get $\delta b_1 - p_{1B} = (1 - \gamma)\, \delta b_1$. Since $b_2 > \delta b_1$, biased consumers prefer P2.
85. If we relax the equal-cost assumption ($c_1 = c_2 \equiv c$), then the answer will also depend on the relative manufacturing costs of the two models.

Chapter 4

86. In some cases the line between creating misperceptions and exploiting existing misperceptions is blurry. Such is the case with algorithms that foster addiction. For example, online shopping websites use "micro-cliffhangers" to prolong online shopping sessions and ensure that customers keep coming back. See Alter (2017), who gives the example of the shopping website Gilt: "In 2007, a team of entrepreneurs introduced a remarkably addictive online shopping experience called Gilt. Gilt's website and app promote flash sales that last between one and two days each. . . . New sales arrive without warning, so members constantly refresh their pages. Each newly loaded page produces a micro-cliffhanger. For many of Gilt's members, the site offers a low-grade thrill amid their otherwise predictable lives. You can see this in the spike of lunchtime traffic between noon and one every afternoon, during which the site sometimes draws in more than a million dollars in revenue" (204). Alter describes a casino algorithm that "senses [a slot machine player's] pain points" (e.g., from strings of losses), and artificially creates wins—to keep the player at the slot machine (where he will lose more money over time) (135). Similarly, the algorithms that power video games are designed to make these games addictive: game designers use big data to discover and then implement tactics that get gamers hooked, for example, giving the gamer a quick reward, such as a level-up or a new skill, at the beginning of the game, and then increasing the intervals between these rewards. And then, once the person is hooked, "the underlying algorithm changes so that [you] cannot win unless extra resources, abilities, or game currency are paid for" (162). See also Berthon, Pitt, and Campbell (2019); Choi and Kim (2004).
87. See Newitz (2015, 2016). According to this account, only 5% of Ashley Madison users were female, which explains the "need" to use fembots. According to McPhate (2016), 15% of users were women; now the ratio of men to women is 5 to 1. We are grateful to Nimrod Kozlovski for bringing the Ashley Madison fembot affair to our attention.
88. Stipulated Order for Permanent Injunction and Other Equitable Relief, Fed. Trade Comm'n v. Ruby Corp., No. 1:16-cv-02438 (D.D.C. Dec. 14, 2016).
89. See, for example, Park et al. (2023). The recent Executive Order on Safe, Secure, and Trustworthy Artificial Intelligence directs the U.S. Department of Commerce to develop guidance for content authentication and watermarking to clearly label AI-generated content. "Executive Order 14110 of October 30, 2023, Safe, Secure, and Trustworthy Development and Use of Artificial Intelligence," *Code of Federal Regulations*, title 3 (2023): 75191–75226, https://www.govinfo.gov/content/pkg/FR-2023-11-01/pdf/2023-24283.pdf.
90. Celebrities have been suing AI companies for using their voice (and other characteristics). See, for example, Complaint, Lehrman v. Lovo, Inc., No. 1:24-cv-03770 (S.D.N.Y. May 16, 2024); Complaint, Main Sequence, Ltd. v. Dudesy, No. 2:24-cv-00711 (C.D. Cal. Jan. 25, 2024);

Cho (2024) discusses a class action suit by voice actors including Scarlett Johansson, Ariana Grande, and Conan O'Brien against an AI start-up that replicated celebrity voices for advertisements; Lawlor (2024) describes a suit by George Carlin's estate against a podcast that used AI to create a comedy special based on Carlin's work; Young v. NeoCortext, Inc., No. 2:23-cv-02496, 2023 WL 616975 (C.D. Cal. 2023); Poritz (2023) discusses a right of publicity claim by a reality TV star against a face swap app; Kastrenakes (2024). Several bills would require disclosure when content is generated by AI. See, for example, AI Disclosure Act of 2023, H.R. 3831, 118th Cong. (2023); AI Labeling Act of 2023, S. 2691, 118th Cong. (2023); Advisory for AI-Generated Content Act, S. 2765, 118th Cong. (2023).

91. "The priority of information . . . derives from any aspect of how information is presented that increases the likelihood of buyers reviewing it ahead of other, deprioritized information. In a rational choice framework, information gets priority when the relative cost of acquiring it is reduced. Under imperfect rationality, information's priority depends on its salience in terms of mode, place, time, or context of presentation. Sellers control the factors that affect the cost of acquiring information about their products and the factors that affect the salience of certain information, and the law sometimes regulates these factors" (Bar-Gill & Ben-Shahar 2023, 307).
92. Chatbots have already learned to express emotion and humor, and these traits seem to correlate with a higher customer satisfaction (Lim et al. 2022; Schanke, Burtch, & Ray 2021; Seeger, Pfeiffer, & Heinzl 2021; Ahmad, Siemon, & Robra-Bissantz 2021; Shedletzky et al. 2023).
93. Some forms of algorithmic manipulation straddle the line between creating misperceptions and reenforcing preferences (while muting other preferences). See Wagner and Eidenmüller (2019), suggesting that, based on an initial interest that a consumer expresses, in hiking, for example, the algorithm might reinforce and develop this preference by offering hiking-related guidebooks and gear, while effectively preventing the consumer from exploring preferences for other activities.
94. Cf. Salvi et al. (2024), showing that LLMs can be more persuasive than humans, especially when they have access to sociodemographic information about the party they need to persuade and can thus personalize their messages.

Chapter 5

95. See Sherman Antitrust Act, 15 U.S.C. §§1–7 (1890): "Every contract, combination in the form of trust or otherwise, or conspiracy, in restraint of trade or commerce among the several States, or with foreign nations, is declared to be illegal."
96. Lawsuits filed against hotel companies allege that these companies collude by using algorithms that help determine room rates. See Kaye, Hirsch, and McCabe (2024). On algorithmic-facilitated coordination, see generally Ezrachi and Stucke (2016b); Gal (2017, 2019).
97. For policymakers, see Assad et al. (2021, 461), observing that "[t]he OECD, the EU Commissioner for Competition, Margrethe Vestager, the Federal Trade Commission (FTC) in the US, the Competition Market Authority (CMA) in the UK, and the French, German, and Canadian competition authorities all raised concerns about this risk and the need for additional information and monitoring," and specifically referencing Digital Competition Expert Panel (2019) and Competition & Markets Authority (2021). The latter report stated, "[C]ollusion appears an increasingly significant risk if the use of more complex pricing algorithms becomes widespread." Kahn (2023) notes that "the A.I. tools that firms use to set prices for everything from laundry detergent to bowling lane reservations can facilitate collusive behavior that unfairly inflates prices—as well as forms of precisely targeted price discrimination." For legal scholars, see Ezrachi and Stucke (2017a, 1781): "Computer algorithms may be used to optimize behavioral advertisements, individualized promotions, and targeted, discriminatory pricing." Ezrachi and Stucke (2016a) write, "[B]y increasing the speed at which price changes are communicated, detecting any cheating or deviations, and punishing those deviations, algorithms can foster new forms of collusion." See also Ezrachi and Stucke (2017b); Gal (2017, 2019); Mehra (2016), cited in Assad et al. (2024).
98. See Vogel (2022). RealPage has been sued by the Justice Department, a suit joined by North Carolina, California, Colorado, Connecticut, Minnesota, Oregon, Tennessee, and Washington, and is also facing multiple class action lawsuits and lawsuits by several state AGs (Parker 2024; Kaye, Hirsch, & McCabe 2024). In a related case, the FTC and Department of Justice argued that landlords violate Section 1 of the Sherman Act when they "jointly delegate key

aspects of their pricing to a common algorithm." See Statement of Interest of the United States at 3, Duffy v. Yardi Systems, Inc., No. 2:23-cv-01391 (W.D. Wash. Mar. 1, 2024).

99. See Assad et al. (2021, 462), describing the study by Calvano et al. (2020): "[R]elatively simple pricing algorithms systematically learn to play collusive strategies. The algorithms typically coordinate on prices that are somewhat below the monopoly level but substantially above the static Bertrand equilibrium." A similar simulation study, Klein (2021), is discussed in Assad et al. (2024, 728): "[W]hen the number of discrete prices is limited, competing Q-learning algorithms indeed often coordinate on collusive equilibria."

100. See Assad et al. (2024, 728–730), summarizing the literature; Asker, Fershtman, and Pakes (2022, 455–56) write, "[A]synchronous updating [by the AI pricing algorithms] leads to supra-competitive ('high') prices. . . . [But w]hen asynchronous algorithms are imbued with some limited economic sophistication . . . the supracompetitive prices that asynchronous algorithms generate are substantially mitigated. . . . [A]n understanding of the competitive impacts of algorithmic pricing games requires knowledge of how the algorithms learns." Asker, Fershtman, and Pakes (2021, 2–3) write, "When both [algorithms] employ synchronous learning, they converge to Nash pricing quickly. By contrast, when both [algorithms] employ asynchronous learning they converge to prices that are substantially above marginal costs." Den Boer, Meylahn, and Schinkel (2022) write, "We do not believe that, on the basis of the presented simulations, it can be concluded that Q-learning autonomously and systematically learns to collude." Other simulation studies focus on online platforms, like eBay and Amazon, and study how the rules implemented by these online marketplaces influence the likelihood of collusion. For example, Johnson, Rhodes, and Wildenbeest (2023, 1842) show that a platform's choice of how to prioritize sellers' products—how many products to display, whether to prioritize by price, and so on—can make collusion harder: "[S]ubtle [rules]—which condition on past behavior and treat sellers asymmetrically—may be required when there is a risk of collusion. . . . [The authors] focus on the power of an intermediary to design rules that shape competition, both to its own advantage and that of consumers, including when there is a risk of collusion." But this research also suggests that platforms might not have sufficient incentives to adopt collusion-preventing rules on their own (i.e., without regulatory intervention). See Assad et al. (2021, 463), discussing Johnson, Rhodes, and Wildenbeest (2023).

101. See Stigler (1964). Competition law prohibits coordinated conduct arising out of an agreement among coordinating parties. It does not assign liability for tacit collusion, where parallel conduct occurs without explicit human design. This latter type of coordination is most likely to arise in the algorithm-facilitated market (Gal 2017, 5–6). Whether arising out of tacit collusion or an explicit agreement, economic theory recognizes four conditions necessary for coordination to take place: (1) reaching an understanding on trade conditions profitable to all colluding parties; (2) detection of deviations; (3) creating a credible threat of retaliation against deviators; and (4) high barriers to market entry. Algorithms make it easier to meet each condition. (1) Algorithms' data collection and analysis capabilities make it easier for sellers to reach an understanding on conditions profitable to them all. (2) Algorithms make data on supplier offers available digitally, making detection of deviations by colluding sellers easier and faster. (3) Algorithms can be designed to react immediately upon detecting a deviation, increasing the credibility of the threat of retaliation for deviations. And (4) algorithms increase barriers to market entry by scaring off potential new entrants who know that algorithms will detect and retaliate against better offers (2–3).

102. See Calvano et al. (2020, 3268): "The algorithms typically coordinate on prices . . . crucially involve punishments." Also see Klein (2021, 548): "[T]he algorithms managed to coordinate on a joint-profit maximizing Nash equilibrium . . . [and] indeed learn strategies that have the effect of reward-punishment."

103. It is clear that an agreement to use the same algorithm is illegal (Garden-Monheit & Meber 2024; Statement of Interest of the United States at 5, Duffy v. Yardi Systems, Inc., No. 2:23-cv-01391 (W.D. Wash. Mar. 1, 2024)).

104. See Ezrachi and Stucke (2016b, 56–58, 65–68); Schwalbe (2019); see also OECD (2018).

105. See Gal (2019); Gal and Elkin-Koren (2017, 345).

106. Moreover, separate from an agreement to fix prices being illegal, it is also illegal to agree to a "facilitating practice," and pricing via algorithm may count as such a "facilitating practice." We thank Louis Kaplow for these suggestions.

107. See, for example, Assad et al. (2024, 461): "In Germany, advertisements show that at least one company offers its software to multiple stations and brands in the retail gas market." This is very similar to the clearly illegal case, where the vendor "sells" suggested prices (rather than an algorithm that suggests prices).
108. See generally Gal and Rubinfeld (2024). See also Abada and Lambin (2023), showing that algorithms can learn to engage in predatory pricing.

Chapter 6

109. See FTC (2016, 17–21); Jackson (2021); West, Whittaker, and Crawford (2019). There is a vast computer science literature on algorithmic bias that has focused on race- and sex-based discrimination, even though the technical analysis applies to discrimination between any two (pre-identified) groups. For introductions to or surveys of this literature, see Barocas and Selbst (2016), Chouldechova and Roth (2020), and Cowgill and Tucker (2019).
110. The idea that algorithms can reduce discrimination is implied in Kleinberg and Mullainathan (2019), who show that simple, interpretable algorithms increase discrimination relative to more complex algorithms.
111. See, for example, Washington v. Davis, 426 U.S. 229, 238 (1976); Personnel Adm'r of Mass. v. Feeney, 442 U.S. 256, 281 (1979). The Constitution is understood to forbid disparate treatment along a variety of specified grounds, including race and sex. In extreme cases, the existence of disparate treatment is obvious because a facially discriminatory practice or rule can be shown to be in place. In other cases, no such practice or rule can be identified, and the question is whether a facially neutral practice or rule was motivated by a discriminatory purpose.
112. See *Washington*, 426 U.S. at 238.
113. See, for example, Griggs v. Duke Power Co., 401 U.S. 424, 434–435 (1971) (interpreting Title VII of the 1964 Civil Rights Act).
114. See Griggs, 401 U.S. at 436.
115. 42 U.S.C. §§2000e-2(k)(1)(A)–(B). This and other doctrinal requirements make it quite challenging to prove disparate impact.
116. More precisely, algorithms should not use sex as a single or dominant proxy. Kleinberg, Ludwig, Mullainathan, and Rambachan (2018) show that algorithms should use both the neutral data and the data on sex, as this would achieve superior accuracy *and* less sex-based discrimination. The reason is that if sex is excluded as an input, the algorithm will mis-rank women among themselves (formally, because various features, such as age, when interacted with sex, have different effects on outcome prediction, such that excluding sex forces the algorithm to use the same measure of the effect of age for both sexes, mis-ranking within each of the groups). Gillis (2022, 1184) shows that outcome disparities decrease when the algorithm is given direct information about the protected characteristic.
117. Bartlett et al. (2022) find a lower rate of discrimination against Black and Latinx borrowers by algorithm-based fintech lenders as compared to non-fintech lenders, for some loans. And Avery, Leibbrandt, and Vecci (2023) find a lower rate of discrimination against women when algorithms are involved in the hiring process in the technology sector.
118. Slaughter (2021) discusses the problem of biased training data, using the example of an Amazon hiring algorithm that discriminated against women because it was trained on a male-heavy set of résumés from Amazon's existing applicant pool. See also Dastin (2018).
119. In the computer science literature, proxy bias is often described as label bias.
120. See Langenbucher (2022, 28–29): when AI-powered algorithms set prices for consumer credit or determine eligibility for certain credit products, there is a risk that the algorithm might learn of correlations between seemingly neutral characteristics and protected categories and treat borrowers differently on the basis of these characteristics.

Chapter 7

121. See Hasan et al. (2023). For a disturbing set of findings, see Chen at al. (2023).
122. See, for example, Schleich et al. (2019); Werthschulte and Loschel (2021); Kuchler and Pagel (2018); O'Donoghue and Rabin (2015); Benhabib, Bisin, and Schotter (2010): Wang and Sloan (2018). Importantly, Wang and Sloan find strong evidence of present bias in connection with health-related decisions.

123. There are plausible evolutionary explanations for present bias. If you are running from a tiger, you ought not to spend much time thinking about your retirement savings. But under modern circumstances, present bias can get you into a great deal of trouble.
124. It might, though. See Chen et al. (2023).
125. See Ayres and Curtis (2023). We could imagine a Keep It Simple version of a choice engine, offering only a little information and a few options to consumers. We could imagine a Tell Me Everything version of a choice engine, living up to its name. Consumers might be asked to choose what kind of choice engine they want. Alternatively, they might be defaulted into Keep It Simple or Tell Me Everything, depending on what AI thinks they would choose if they were to make an informed choice, free from behavioral biases.
126. Policymakers can help produce more effective consumer-side algorithms by requiring that sellers share information with these consumer-side algorithms. See Bar-Gill (2012); Van Loo (2015).
127. See, for example, Ferrara (2024); Mehrabi et al. (2021).
128. See, for example, Chen et al. (2023); Cheng, Durmus, and Jurafsky (2023, 1504): "The persistence of social bias and stereotypes in large language models (LLMs) is well-documented"; Yang et al. (2024, 4): "We find that GPT-3.5-turbo, when generating medical reports, tends to include biased and fabricated patient histories for patients of certain races, as well as generate racially skewed diagnoses"; Hofmann et al. (2024), showing that LLMs exhibit prejudice against those who interact with the algorithm using African American English; Koo et al. (2023), who design a framework and test kit to evaluate cognitive biases in common LLMs; Opedal et al. (2024), who find cognitive biases in commonly used LLMs mirroring those observed in children.
129. For Alexa, see OneSpace (n.d.); Amazon (n.d.). For Google Assistant, see Wang and Adams (2017). See also Shchory and Gal (2022, 131).

Part II

130. The call for algorithmic transparency is not new (Slaughter 2021). Indeed, legislation and regulation, in the United States and beyond, already impose certain transparency requirements. In the United States, under the Fair Credit Reporting Act of 1970 lenders must be able to disclose up to four key factors that adversely affected the credit score of a rejected consumer. The European Union's General Data Protection Regulation (2018) created a right to explanation, whereby a user may ask for an explanation of an algorithmic decision that was made about them (Council Regulation 2016/679, 2016 O.J. (L 119) 1; Goodman & Flaxman 2017, 50; Hacker & Passoth 2021). Our contribution is in explaining how algorithmic transparency can be implemented and, specifically, how this policy solution can be implemented to mitigate the algorithmic harms identified in Part I.
131. Cf. Yang, Muller, and Liang (2021), showing that transparency about greenhouse gas emissions has been effective in changing firm behavior.
132. While we do not explicitly discuss litigation, several of the legal reforms that we develop in this part involve, or can involve, a litigation component. For example, the proposed algorithmic transparency reforms may provide information that could trigger litigation. Also, our expanded disparate impact doctrine can be used in litigation. We note a concern that algorithmic differentiation might make it more difficult to successfully bring class action lawsuits (because of the "common issue" requirement).
133. Indeed, regulators are already using algorithms. For example, the British Competition and Markets Authority uses algorithms for different regulatory tasks. See Competition & Markets Authority (2021, 35–41). See also Gal and Rubinfeld (2024, 727–738). More generally on algorithms as valuable policy tools, see Ludwig, Mullainathan, and Rambachan (2024).

Chapter 8

134. See 21 C.F.R. 1141 (2021) (imposing labeling requirements for cigarette packages and advertisements).
135. Efforts to counteract "dark patterns" have particular importance because algorithms might promote actions that fall squarely in that category (such as default terms and hidden fees). See Luguri and Strahilevitz (2021, 44, 47, 61).
136. Cf. Bar-Gill (2012, 32–43, 105–112, 240–246), advocating for information-sharing mandates in a related context.

137. See Consumer Financial Protection Bureau (n.d.).
138. We thank Steve Shavell for suggesting this "public option." Of course, government-provided solutions suffer from their own challenges. See, for example, Van Loo (2017, 1272–73): "Publicly run alternatives face their own accountability flaws. Although agencies lack the same incentives to manipulate consumers for profit..." Public-private partnerships can be an attractive way to combine government resources and private-sector expertise and incentives (Freeman 2000). For example, a private company could develop the algorithms that will be hosted on a government website.
139. FTC (2012) calls on companies to "build in privacy at every stage of product development," "give consumers the ability to make decisions about their data," and "make information collection and use practices transparent." In the recent Executive Order on Safe, Secure and Trustworthy Artificial Intelligence, the president called on Congress to pass data privacy legislation. See "Executive Order 14110 of October 30, 2023, Safe, Secure, and Trustworthy Development and Use of Artificial Intelligence," *Code of Federal Regulations*, title 3 (2023): 75191–74226, https://www.govinfo.gov/content/pkg/FR-2023-11-01/pdf/2023-24283.pdf. Singer (2016) describes the Obama administration's blueprint Consumer Privacy Bill of Rights, which failed to pass as legislation. Regulation (EU) 2016/679 of the European Parliament and of the Council of 27 April 2016 on the Protection of Natural Persons with Regard to the Processing of Personal Data and on the Free Movement of Such Data adopts data privacy regulations for the European Union (Burton et al. 2016; Singer 2013). The Do Not Track initiative also holds some promise as a means for stemming the flow of data to sellers who wish to engage in price and quality discrimination (Electronic Frontier Foundation n.d.). See also Vladeck (2014, 160–161). While the United States has not made any substantive changes to data privacy laws on the federal level, some states have passed such laws. See, for example, Virginia Consumer Data Protection Act, VA. CODE ANN. §§59.1-575–59.1-584 (2021); Colorado Privacy Act, COLO. REV. STAT. §6-1-13 (2021); California Consumer Privacy Act, CAL. CIV. CODE §1798.100 (West 2018). The European Union has also established data protection obligations for EU institutions to adhere to when processing personal data and developing new policies. See Regulation 2018/1725 of the European Parliament and of the Council of 23 October 2018 on the Protection of Natural Persons with Regard to the Processing of Personal Data by the Union Institutions, Bodies, Offices and Agencies and on the Free Movement of Such Data, and Repealing Regulation 45/2001/EC, 2018 O.J. (L 295).
140. See, for example, Cabral (2002, 215): "The greater the degree of product differentiation, the greater the degree of market power"; Tirole (1988, 286): "Product differentiation is meant to relax price competition."
141. Calvano et al. (2020, 3268) write, "With three agents, prices are typically pretty close to the static Bertrand-Nash equilibrium, and with four agents or more they may even be lower. In this respect, Q-learning algorithms would appear to be different. In simulations with three firms, the average profit gain Δ decreases from 85% to 64%. With four agents, the profit gain is still a substantial 56%. . . . [T]he fact that it decreases so slowly seems to be a peculiar and somewhat worrying property."

Chapter 9

142. 14 C.F.R. Part 399. See also Council Regulation 2016/679, 2016 O.J. (L 119) 1, arts. 13–15 (mandating that "meaningful information about the logic" of automated systems be made available to data subjects).
143. For example, the Centers for Medicare & Medicaid Services (2024) have attempted to increase hospital price transparency, with the goal of enabling consumers to shop and compare prices across hospitals and estimate the cost of care before going to the hospital. And the Department of Transportation has issued a number of rules designed to increase price transparency to enable consumers to have more clarity about what they are buying or not buying and to discourage certain kinds of fees (Transparency of Airline Ancillary Service Fees, 82 Fed. Reg. 13572 (Mar. 14, 2017)).
144. The FTC enforces laws that require explainability, for example, explain why credit was denied or what factors affect your credit score (Smith 2020). See also Colo. Rev. Stat. Ann. §10-3-1104.9; Cal. Civ. Code §1798.145; Conn. Pub. Act. 22-15 ("An Act Concerning Personal Data Privacy and Online Monitoring," effective July 1, 2023). In Canada, Parliament is considering

the Artificial Intelligence and Data Act, which would impose transparency requirements on a class of "high-risk" algorithmic activities. See Law Commission of Ontario (2023, 8).

145. It is not clear that a high level of borrowing and a low level of savings necessarily implies myopia or present bias. It could also imply exponential discounting with a high discount rate; that is, it could imply a preference rather than a bias. In that case, low introductory prices and high long-term prices can be welfare increasing.
146. Under the Fair Credit Reporting Act (FCRA), 15 U.S.C. §§1681–1681x, when a company denies a customer credit or charges the customer a higher price for credit based on a credit report, the company must comply with certain disclosure requirements. There is a growing trend in which companies utilize big data and predictive analytics to make such credit eligibility determinations (FTC 2016, 15–16). Perhaps FCRA can be used to trigger the type of transparency requirements that we propose. Also, in many states, insurance companies that use algorithms are subject to some transparency requirements. See, for example, Colo. Rev. Stat. Ann. §10-3-1104.9; Cal. Civ. Code §1798.145; Conn. Pub. Act. 22-15 ("An Act Concerning Personal Data Privacy and Online Monitoring," effective July 1, 2023). More generally, several bills would create or enhance transparency requirements. For example, the Digital Platform Commission Act of 2023, S. 1671, 118th Cong. (2023), would empower the Commission to propose "voluntary or enforceable behavioral codes, technical standards, or other policies . . . with respect to transparency and accountability for algorithmic processes" (Section 8 of the bill). See also Algorithmic Justice and Online Platform Transparency Act, H.R. 4624, 118th Cong. (2023); Algorithmic Justice and Online Platform Transparency Act, S. 2325, 118th Cong. (2023).
147. We assume that a myopic, or present-biased, consumer would make a mistake by purchasing a gas guzzler. We acknowledge the possibility that such a purchase could be driven by intertemporal preferences with a high discount rate rather than by a bias. Will an algorithm be able to distinguish between the two? Will a transparency protocol, searching for key decision drivers, be able to distinguish between the two? The answer is unclear.
148. The AI Disclosure Act of 2023, H.R. 3831l, 118th Cong. (2023); the AI Labeling Act of 2023, S. 2691, 118th Cong. (2023); and the Advisory for AI-Generated Content Act, S. 2765, 118th Cong. (2023).
149. Relying on market forces and public pressure is not without risk. For example, as noted above (Chapter 6, Section C), in some situations, accounting for race or sex, or for variables that correlate with race or sex, can help historically disadvantaged groups. And yet public opinion might not reflect a nuanced understanding of when accounting for race or sex is harmful versus helpful.
150. In the policing context, the National Institute of Standards and Technology (NIST) has been testing face-recognition algorithms for accuracy. NIST does not formally certify these algorithms. But it issues public reports with vendor-specific performance data, and it publishes on its website a dynamic "leaderboard" ranking algorithm performance (NIST 2024). These evaluations and rankings provide incentives for vendors to design better algorithms, as evidenced by vendors' frequent citation to their NIST standings in press and sales materials (Friedman et al. 2022; Dooley, Goldstein, & Dickerson 2021; Kaye 2019). Friedman et al. have called for a formal certification, or pre-approval, requirement for algorithms and other technology used by police forces.
151. And there are commercial tools that purport to promote AI transparency. For example, Fiddler (n.d.) and Arthur (n.d.).
152. The growing use of black-box algorithms may be attributed to their greater effectiveness. It may also be attributed to the advantage they offer in terms of avoiding liability. The legal reforms discussed in this chapter are designed to minimize this advantage. (Compare: in the product liability context, it is understood that an optimally designed liability regime will provide incentives for sellers to investigate product risks [Friehe & Schulte 2017].) While we focus on AI-powered black-box algorithms, it should be acknowledged that some firms still use white-box algorithms, namely, algorithms that implement a set of instructions specified by the firm—by the seller or by the firm that wrote the algorithm. In this case, a standard transparency requirement—that firms share information about their algorithms that they already have—would be sufficient.
153. Arguably, the FTC already has authority to demand information about a firm's algorithms. Section 6(b) of the Federal Trade Commission Act empowers the Commission to require an

entity to file "annual or special . . . reports or answers in writing to specific questions" to provide information about the entity's "organization, business, conduct, practices, management, and relation to other corporations, partnerships, and individuals." Slaughter (2021) suggests that this authority can be used to demand information on the firm's use of algorithms (see also Van Loo 2019b, 1617–1624). Firms and algorithm designers have sometimes claimed that intellectual property rights allow them to resist demands for information about their algorithms. Such claims should be rejected.

154. If the algorithm is considering race or sex, it can be rebuilt so as to be blind to any such characteristics, although such blinding might end up harming the protected group (Gillis & Spiess 2019; Gillis 2022).

155. Blattner and Spiess (2022) applied several different "model diagnostic tools," what we called "transparency protocols," to evaluate lenders' machine-learning algorithms, and found that different tools performed equally well (in identifying important variables), but that these tools often identified different sets of important variables. Davis et al. (2022) implemented different explainability protocols in the consumer credit context, specifically, home-equity lines of credit, for example, Local Interpretable Model-Agnostic Explanations (LIME) and SHapley Additive exPlanations (SHAP), and found that the different protocols produce different sets of important, decision-affecting variables; even the same protocol applied multiple times can produce different sets of important, decision-affecting variables.

156. Another concern is that some of the protocols can be manipulated to hide biases (Slack et al. 2020).

157. Another response is to use transparency protocols tailored to explore the importance of a specific variable, the variable that is of interest to the regulator (Blattner, Nelson, & Spiess 2021). Fisher, Rudin, and Dominici (2019, 2) define the concept of "model class reliance" as the "highest and lowest degree to which any well-performing model within a given class may rely on a variable of interest for prediction accuracy"; they analyze variable importance across *classes* of models.

158. As noted above, it is not clear that a high level of borrowing and a low level of savings necessarily implies myopia or present bias; it could also imply exponential discounting with a high discount rate; that is, it could imply a (rational) preference rather than a bias. But a rational consumer with such a high discount rate would not get a gym subscription.

159. There is a question of whether the regulator should announce in advance what factors would be considered suspicious. In any event, over time firms will learn what characteristics are more likely to trigger scrutiny. If firms know that a variable will trigger scrutiny, they may exclude this variable from the data that is fed into the algorithm. The algorithm would then find another variable that is correlated with the excluded variable. This other variable would likely be equally suspicious. The transparency approach may thus lead to the gradual removal of variables that are likely to trigger consumer harm.

160. Baillon et al. (2022) show that while overestimation of risk pushes up the WTP, the risk-loving feature of the Prospect Theory utility function pushes it down, with the latter effect dominating.

161. Meier and Sprenger (2010) showed that biased consumers buy different products and use these products differently than unbiased consumers. We realize that incentivized choice experiments are more than simple surveys, such that the relevant evidence can be more difficult to obtain.

162. Compare: the sophisticated investor test in the securities context. See, for example, Terra Sec. ASA Konkursbo v. Citigroup, Inc., 820 F. Supp. 2d 541, 545–546 (S.D.N.Y. 2011).

163. This "identifiable characteristic" approach to algorithmic transparency can also be applied in the context of algorithmic behavior-based pricing. Past purchasing behavior can be thought of as akin to a "protected characteristic." Such past behavior should be relatively easy to detect, in the sense that a previous decision by the consumer—to buy or not to buy the product at an offered price—is identifiable and measurable. Accordingly, it should be relatively easy to learn, and to inform the market, that a seller's algorithm sets different prices to consumers based on their past purchasing behavior. Recall that behavior-based pricing is harmful especially when consumers are not aware of this pricing strategy. By informing consumers about the seller's pricing strategy, the transparency requirement directly targets, and potentially eliminates, a precondition for consumer harm. Indeed, as noted in Chapter 2, Section C, when consumers know about the BBP (and react strategically), sellers lose from BBP and would like to commit not to utilize BBP. The transparency reforms would facilitate such a commitment.

164. This suggestion follows recent proposals to utilize personalized disclosure mandates (Porat & Strahilevitz 2014; Ben-Shahar & Porat 2021).
165. For similar reasons, in order to change the decision of a machine-learning algorithm it is usually not enough to change a small number of variables (because the algorithm will just use correlates); you need to change a larger set of variables, including variables that are correlated with the initially identified important variables (Blattner & Spiess, 2022).
166. See Rudin (2019). See also Stratyfy (n.d.), a commercial product that relies on interpretable models.
167. The protocols described below do not exhaust the range of model-agnostic, post hoc protocols that have been developed by computer scientists. Molnar (2022) provides a comprehensive survey. See also Adadi and Berrada (2018); Blattner and Spiess (2022); Blattner, Nelson, and Spiess (2021). The literature also considers model-specific and intrinsic methods.
168. Biggs, Sun, and Ettl (2021) develop a method of translating a complex non-parametric prediction model into a simple pricing policy based on a decision tree. The leaves contain (user, item) pairs with similar optimal prices. In follow-up work, Subramanian et al. (2022) allow constraints, such as (i) requiring that all consumers are charged the same price except for loyalty-card holders, who are charged a lower price; or (ii) requiring that one item (say, an economy ticket) is priced at least X dollars less than another (a business class ticket). The general approach, called "knowledge distillation," was developed by Hinton, Vinyals, and Dean (2015).
169. There are additional protocols for sensitivity analysis, that is, protocols that measure the effects of changes in variable values on model performance, especially in neural networks. An example is layerwise relevance propagation (Bach et al. 2015; Lapuschkin et al. 2019).
170. How does the protocol identify "similar" consumers? The protocol views each consumer as a vector of variables or characteristics (e.g., income, education). It then uses mathematical formulas that measure the distance between two vectors. A similar consumer is closer to the original consumer, as measured by these distance formulas. It should be acknowledged, however, that there are different possible distance formulas, and that choosing the right formula—and thus the right set of similar consumers—may require a judgment call. Also note that the process of approximation may give greater weight to consumers who are more similar to the original consumer, namely, it would be more important for the interpretable model to provide better approximations for these more similar consumers.
171. The linear model would be derived in a manner that is similar to the one described above for the LIME protocol. The difference is that in this first step of the LIME protocol, the linear model is used to approximate a "local" set of decisions, whereas in the LIME protocol the linear model was used to approximate all decisions.
172. The LIME method was developed by Ribeiro, Singh, and Guestrin (2016). A downside of the LIME protocol is its instability. For example, the local analysis of two "close" decisions can yield very different variables as key decision drivers.
173. One advantage of SHAP is that the interactions between variables are incorporated into the measures of variable importance. A disadvantage of Shapley values is that they can quickly become computationally intractable, and thus the Shapley values will often need to be approximated. The SHAP protocol includes approximation methods that have been shown to work well.

Chapter 10

174. We could imagine a type of output-based transparency, in contrast to the input-based transparency of Chapter 9. If it is made public that a seller's algorithm produces discriminatory outputs, market scrutiny could follow.
175. There are commercial tools that test whether a model creates disparate impact and help train new models that do not create disparate impact. See, for example, SolasAI (n.d.). Proposed legislation seeks to implement the disparate impact analysis in the context of algorithmic decision-making. See, for example, the Algorithmic Accountability Act of 2023, H.R. 5628, 118th Cong. (2023), which "[d]irects the Federal Trade Commission to require impact assessments of automated decision systems and augmented critical decision processes"; California's Assembly Bill 2930, 2023–2024 Leg., Reg. Sess (Cal. 2024), which would ban algorithms that contribute to unjustified differential treatment or impacts disfavoring people based on protected categories.

176. Bhutta, Fuster, and Hizmo (2024) show that less sophisticated borrowers pay higher interest rates on mortgage loans.
177. Gillis and Spiess (2019) argue for disparate-impact-type analysis of outcomes and note the challenge of defining "similarly situated" consumers. See also Gillis (2022).
178. In the consumer credit context these variables will include standard underwriting variables, such as FICO score, loan-to-value ratio, debt-to-income ratio, loan amount, type of loan, and so on. Ayres, Klein, and West (2017) analyze In re Wells Fargo Mortgage Lending Discrimination Litigation, No. 08–MD–01930, 2011 WL 8960474 (N.D. Cal. Sept. 6, 2011), in which plaintiffs used regression analysis—including models with fewer controls and models with many controls—to prove unjustified disparate impacts. See also Ayres (2007), who distinguishes between charging higher prices to consumers who impose higher costs on the seller (justified) and charging higher prices to consumers without such a cost-based justification (not justified).
179. If a control variable is closely correlated with the protected-characteristic variable, then we might run into a multi-collinearity problem. Note that the way we propose to use the linear model here is different from the way it was used in Chapter 9, where the linear model was one of the available transparency protocols (described in the Appendix to Chapter 9). In the "suspicious characteristics" approach, regulators did not have a measurable protected-characteristic variable, and the goal was to identify characteristics that have a large effect on the algorithm's decisions and scrutinize the suspicious ones. In the "protected characteristic as a key decision driver" approach, regulators had a measurable, protected-characteristic variable, and the goal was to see if this variable emerges from the transparency protocol as a main decision driver. Here, regulators have a measurable protected-characteristic variable, and the goal is to assess the effect of this variable on "similarly situated" consumers (where "similarly situated" is defined by the control variables).
180. See Fairplay's (n.d.) Fairness Optimizer.
181. See, for example, Sharkey (2022, 2024); Buiten, de Streel, and Peitz (2023).
182. Our discussion about regulating the design and implementation of algorithms distinguishes between different stages of algorithm construction and implementation. This distinction (loosely) follows the framework in Rambachan et al. (2021): "We model a supervised machine learning algorithm as consisting of two components: a 'predictive algorithm,' which takes in training data consisting of outcomes and observed characteristics for a set of individuals and returns a prediction function, and a 'decision rule,' which uses the constructed prediction function to make decisions. A policymaker therefore has two distinct tools available: influencing the design of the predictive algorithm and influencing how the decision rule uses the predictions."
183. See also the EU Artificial Intelligence Act (2024) (summarizing the functions of Articles 8–25).
184. See Kleinberg, Ludwig, Mullainathan, and Rambachan (2018, 22); Rambachan et al. (2021): "in most existing work, fairness is often defined as a property of the algorithm" and policy proposals are generally limited to "constraining the algorithm itself." See also Dwork et al. (2012), who conclude that, given a "similarity metric" that can identify "similarly situated" individuals, it is possible to impose fairness constraints to ensure that these similarly situated individuals are treated similarly. See also the proposed Algorithmic Justice and Online Platform Transparency Act, H.R. 4624, 118th Cong. (2023) and Algorithmic Justice and Online Platform Transparency Act, S. 2325, 118th Cong. (2023), which would police algorithmic discrimination on the basis of protected categories.
185. As discussed above, it may be justified to set higher prices for consumers with protected characteristics, if these characteristics are correlated with other relevant (and not protected) characteristics. For example, race may be correlated with income, or gender may be correlated with preferences. Therefore, the fairness constraint needs to be defined thus: "similarly situated" consumers must be treated similarly, where "similarly situated" is operationalized as discussed in Section A above.
186. The FTC has warned firms that use algorithms to avoid disparate impact (Smith 2020). A standard defense against a disparate-impact antidiscrimination claim is "business necessity." Computer scientists have quantified the cost, in terms of lost profits, of imposing different fairness constraints on the algorithm. Such analysis should inform any assessment of "business necessity." Specifically, if a nondiscrimination constraint reduces profits by a relatively small amount, then the "business necessity" defense should be rejected.

187. Slaughter (2021, 38–41) discuss the potential use of the FTC's §5 powers to police certain types of algorithmic harms. Paterson et al. (2021, 12–16) discuss bans, and consider the use of something like the FTC's §5 powers to police algorithms; they also argue that "more subtle forms of manipulation through advertising that targets behavioral biases or emotional traits in order to produce sales" should be prohibited as unfair trade practices. Willis (2020, 176) argues that courts should treat conduct that exploits consumers' "pre-existing false beliefs as unfair." Van Loo (2015, 1370–1374) argues that the FTC can apply its unfair practices authority to algorithmic and big data-informed pricing practices that prey on consumers' biases. Selbst and Borocas (2023) argue that the FTC should apply its unfair practices authority to police race- and sex-based discrimination. In Canada, Parliament is considering the Artificial Intelligence and Data Act, which would ban AI systems that cause "serious harm" to individuals and impose regulatory requirements on a class of "high risk" algorithmic activities (Law Commission of Ontario 2023, 8).
188. In theory, price caps (and similar restrictions) can be personalized. If firms and their algorithms set personalized prices, regulators may eventually have sufficient information to set personalized price caps (Bar-Gill 2019; Ben-Shahar & Porat 2021).
189. A general tax on profits won't work. As long as profits are not taxed at a 100% rate, the monopolist will still price-discriminate and exploit consumers. The tax would have to target the extra profits made through algorithmic pricing. Going one step further, if policymakers have sufficient information, they could design personalized taxes (for individual firms), and also personalized subsidies to facilitate welfare-enhancing transactions that otherwise might not occur. This suggestion is similar to the personalized price cap suggestion discussed in note 188.

Chapter 11

190. 12 U.S.C. § 5531 (empowering the Consumer Financial Protection Bureau to take selected actions to prevent unfair, deceptive, or abusive acts or practices in connection with transactions or offers for consumer financial products or services).
191. Indeed, such reforms are already underway. See, for example, Require the Exposure of AI-Led Political Advertisements Act, S. 1865, 118th Cong. (2023), proposing a bill requiring political advertisements to disclose the use of AI-generated images or videos; AI Disclosure Act of 2023, H.R. 3831, 118th Cong. (2023), proposing a bill declaring the failure to disclose AI-generated output an unfair and deceptive act; AI Labeling Act of 2023, S. 2691, 118th Cong. (2023), proposing a bill requiring, among other things, disclosure for AI-generated content. Tenn. Code. Ann. §47-25-1105 creates civil and criminal liability for publication or performance of an individual's "voice or likeness," knowing that the use was unauthorized, for purposes of (among others) advertising, fundraising, or solicitation. California's recently enacted AB 2839: Elections: Deceptive Media in Advertisements prohibits knowingly sharing deceptive election-related deepfakes. AB 2355: Political Reform Act of 1974: Political Advertisements: Artificial Intelligence requires labeling of AI-generated deceptive audio, video, or images in political advertisements. AB 2655: Defending Democracy from Deepfake Deception Act of 2024 requires social media platforms to label or remove AI deepfakes within 72 hours after receiving a complaint.
192. In its antitrust lawsuit against RealPage, the government commissioned computer scientists to analyze RealPage's algorithm. See Kaye, Hirsch, and McCabe (2024).
193. Assad et al. (2021, 477) write, "One intriguing possibility is that regulators could gain access to the underlying algorithms and training data. Such access might allow regulators to gain insights into the design decisions behind specific algorithms, and to experiment to see how they behave in various settings." As noted in Chapter 5, Section A, economists and computer scientists have developed methods to run such simulations (Calvano et al. 2020).
194. Lawmakers have already begun to address the risk of algorithmic discrimination. See, for example, Colo. Rev. Stat. §6-1-1702: a developer of a "high-risk artificial intelligence system" must use "reasonable care to protect consumers from any known or reasonably foreseeable risks of algorithmic discrimination" arising from it.

Chapter 12

195. Employers use algorithms to predict whether workers will quit, become pregnant, or try to organize a union, which can affect hiring and promotion decisions. See Holton and Allen

(2019), who describe an algorithm calculating a "turnover propensity index" score trained on a litany of organizational data, including Glassdoor ratings, "stock price variation, news articles . . . regulatory or legal actions . . . number of past jobs, employment anniversary, tenure, skills, education, gender, and geography." Hao (2020) describes PredictiveHire's use of a machine learning-powered personality test using open-ended questions "meant to tease out traits that studies have previously shown to correlate strongly with job-hopping tendencies, such as being more open to experience, less practical, and less down to earth." Zarya (2016) describes Castlight, an algorithm that processes employee "medical claims, pharmacy claims, and search queries" and notifies employers of the percentage of its workforce trying to have children; Kessler (2020) describes models that use survey responses from employees and internal company sources to score companies along a "union vulnerability index." Aspan (2020) explains that the company HireVue provides employers with software that scores job applicants based on their tone of voice, word choice, and facial expressions during video interviews or in recorded answers to automated questions.

196. On algorithmic wage discrimination, see generally Dubal (2023); Teachout (2023). Teachout surfaces how employers like Uber "use behavioral science and massive information asymmetries to nudge drivers to make choices" (441). For instance, Uber loads fare opportunities before a last ride is over, exploiting a technique "where occasional rewards for doing a repeat practice can strongly incentivize behavior," motivating them to work harder (441). Additionally, Teachout highlights the equality concerns raised by algorithmic wage discrimination (445). See also Rieke and Bogen (2018), reporting that tools like Oracle Recruiting Cloud help employers predict the likelihood that a candidate will accept an offer and let employers "adjust salary, bonus, stock options, and other benefits to see in real time how the prediction changes."
197. Akerlof and Dickens (1982, 307–319) study a model where cognitive dissonance leads workers to underestimate the risk associated with their work.
198. Another cost-based consideration that affects hiring and promotion decisions is the likelihood that the employee will leave after a short period of time. Employers use algorithms to predict this likelihood (Liu 2019; Hao 2020). Yet another cost-based consideration, which may be illegal to consider, is the likelihood that the employee will try to organize a union. Employers use algorithms to predict this likelihood (Kessler 2020).
199. Employers use algorithms to predict whether workers will become pregnant (Zarya 2016).
200. See, for example, Unfair or Deceptive Fees Trade Regulation Rule Commission Matter No. R207011, 87 Fed. Reg. 67413 (proposed November 8, 2022); FTC (2021).
201. On the concern about algorithmic discrimination based on race, sex, and other protected characteristics, see Bernhardt, Kresge, and Suleiman (2021, 24); Kim (2017); Rieke and Bogen (2018), who argue that hiring algorithms might be biased and provide the following examples: (i) tools like HireVue that grade responses using such factors as facial expression and eye contact, vocal indications, and so on can perform poorly for women with darker skin; (ii) the distance between the employer's address and the worker's home—a factor strongly correlated with race—predicts worker attrition.
202. In the computer science literature, "proxy bias" is referred to as "label bias."
203. Some of these responses can fit under the general umbrella articulated by the recent Executive Order on Safe, Secure and Trustworthy Artificial Intelligence, which directs the development of principles and best practices to prevent employers from undercompensating workers, evaluating job applications unfairly, or impinging on workers' ability to organize (White House 2023).
204. Cf. Bernhardt, Kresge, and Suleiman (2021), arguing that employers should disclose their use of algorithms. New York City passed a law requiring companies to disclose how algorithms influence their hiring, promotion, and wage-setting decisions. See N.Y.C., N.Y. Local Law 2021/144 §1; N.Y.C., N.Y. ADMIN. CODE §20-871 (2021), requiring "automated employment decision tools" used in New York City to first be subject to a "bias audit" where a "summary of the results of the most recent bias audit . . . has been made publicly available." A "bias audit" entails an "impartial evaluation by an independent auditor" for "the tool's disparate impact" on persons of selected protected categories as defined under 42 U.S.C. §2000e-8. N.Y. ADMIN. CODE §20-870. See also Weber (2024).
205. New York Assembly Bill 9314 requires an "annual disparate impact" analysis for any algorithmic tool used by employers. N.Y. State Assembly Bill No. A9314, 2021–2022 Legislative

Session (introduced February 28, 2024). New York Assembly Bill 9315 prevents employers from using algorithms unless they have been the subject of a bias audit and the results of such audit have been made public. N.Y. State Assembly Bill No. A9315A, 2023–2024 Legislative Session (introduced February 28, 2024). The bill also requires notice to employment candidates that algorithms are being used. New York City's AI Hiring Law requires employers to audit their algorithms—those algorithms that significantly influence hiring, promotion, and wage-setting decisions—for potential race and gender bias, and then publish the results on their websites. See N.Y.C., N.Y. Local Law 2021/144 §1; N.Y.C., N.Y. ADMIN. CODE §20-871 (2021), requiring "automated employment decision tools" used in New York City to first be subject to a "bias audit" where a "summary of the results of the most recent bias audit . . . has been made publicly available." A "bias audit" entails an "impartial evaluation by an independent auditor" for "the tool's disparate impact" on persons of selected protected categories as defined under 42 U.S.C. §2000e-8. N.Y. ADMIN. CODE §20-870. The New York City law is a disclosure law. But the disclosure may trigger enforcement actions if it reveals significant bias in the algorithm's decisions. See also Weber (2024); Bernhardt, Kresge, and Suleiman (2021), arguing for "impact assessments"; Rieke and Bogen (2018), arguing that vendors and employers must be "dramatically more transparent about the predictive tools they build and use, and must allow independent auditing of those tools"; Kim (2017), arguing for a more muscular disparate impact doctrine.

206. A more extreme position would bar employers from using algorithms for making consequential decisions like hiring, firing, and promotion. See Bernhardt, Kresge, and Suleiman (2021, 23).

Chapter 13

207. See, for example, Denham (2020); Seitz-Wald (2024); Verma and Zakrzewski (2024), documenting a pattern of political deepfakes in elections in India, Taiwan, Moldova, and Bangladesh.
208. In the TV series *House of Cards*, season 4, episode 7, Frank Underwood, the U.S. president, discusses the data and algorithms that his Republican contender, Conway, brings to the race for the White House: "Conway has a powerful gun, a search engine. And it's powerful because with it he can tell what you think, what you want, where you are and who you are. He can turn all those searches into votes" (circa minute 17) (Shankland 2016). Later in the episode, Underwood's chief of staff and campaign manager talk to a leading data scientist about using NSA data. The data scientist asks, "You get what? Voter data? So you know who to target?" The campaign manager responds, "And how to target them, to influence them." The data scientist adds, "To brainwash them?" (circa minute 20) (Shankland 2016).
209. Several bills aim to prevent impersonation-by-AI. See, for example, the Require the Exposure of AI-Led Political Advertisements Act, S. 1596, 118th Cong. (2023), which amends the FECA to require disclosure for AI-generated content used in political advertising, given the "potential for their use in exacerbating and spreading misinformation and disinformation at scale." The Candidate Voice Fraud Prohibition Act, H.R. 4611, 118th Cong. (2023) bars distributing deceptive AI-generated audio impersonating the voice of a political candidate. The Protect Elections from Deceptive AI Act, S. 2770, 118th Cong. (2023) bars distributing deceptive AI-generated video that impersonates a political candidate. The Administration of Elections and AI Risks Act, S. 3897, 118th Cong. (2024) requires the Election Assistance Commission to study "how information generated and distributed by artificial intelligence technologies can affect the sharing of accurate election information and how election offices should respond."
210. United States v. Alvarez, 567 U.S. 709, 714 (2012).
211. United States v. Alvarez, 567 U.S. 709, 723 (citing Orwell 1949).

Bibliography

Abada, Ibrahim, & Xavier Lambin. 2023. "Unleashing the Predators: Autonomous Predation and Manipulation through Algorithms." ADEME Investment for the Future Program Working Paper. https://ssrn.com/abstract=4575100.

Acemoglu, Daron, Ali Makhdoumi, Azarakhsh Malekian, & Asuman Ozdaglar. Forthcoming. "When Big Data Enables Behavioral Manipulation." *American Economic Review: Insights.*

Adadi, Amina, & Mohammed Berrada. 2018. "Peeking Inside the Black-Box: A Survey on Explainable Artificial Intelligence (XAI)." *IEEE Access*, 6: 52138–52160.

Adams, R. L. 2024. "A Step-by-Step Guide on How to Make Money with Facebook Ads, According to Experts." *Entrepreneur*, April 17. https://www.entrepreneur.com/growing-a-business/how-to-make-money-with-facebook-ads/305380.

Agarwal, Sumit, Souphala Chomsisengphet, Neale Mahoney, & Johannes Stroebel. 2014. "A Simple Framework for Estimating Consumer Benefits from Regulating Hidden Fees." *Journal of Legal Studies*, 43(S2): S239–S252.

Agarwal, Sumit, Souphala Chomsisengphet, Neale Mahoney, & Johannes Stroebel. 2015. "Regulating Consumer Financial Products: Evidence from Credit Cards." *Quarterly Journal of Economics*, 130(1): 111–164.

Aguirre, Iñaki, Simon Cowan, & John Vickers. 2010. "Monopoly Price Discrimination and Demand Curvature." *American Economic Review*, 100(4): 1601–1615.

Ahmad, Rangina, Dominik Siemon, & Susanne Robra-Bissantz. 2021. "Communicating with Machines: Conversational Agents with Personality and the Role of Extraversion." In *Proceedings of the 54th Hawaii International Conference on System Sciences (ed. Bui, Tung, Conference Chair)*, Kauai, Hawaii, January 4-8 4043–4052. https://pdfs.semanticscholar.org/0b73/17668026ebb345237f3c52cdd82278fe49f3.pdf.

Akerlof, George, & William T. Dickens. 1982. "The Economic Consequences of Cognitive Dissonance." *American Economic Review*, 72(3): 307–319.

Akerlof, George A., & Robert J. Shiller. 2015. *Phishing for Phools: The Economics of Manipulation and Deception.* Princeton, NJ: Princeton University Press.

Alter, Adam. 2017. *Irresistible: The Rise of Addictive Technology and the Business of Keeping Us Hooked.* New York: Penguin Press.

Amazon. n.d. "Do More with Alexa." Accessed June 16, 2024. https://www.amazon.com/alexa-voice-shopping/b?ie=UTF8&node=14552177011.

Arthur. n.d. "The AI Delivery Engine." Accessed June 17, 2024. https://www.arthur.ai.

Ashley Madison. n.d. "Ashley Madison." Accessed June 14, 2024. https://www.ashleymadison.com.

Ashton, Hal, & Matija Franklin. 2022. "Solutions to Preference Manipulation in Recommender Systems Require Knowledge of Meta-Preferences." arXiv, September 14. https://arxiv.org/abs/2209.11801.

Asker, John, Chaim Fershtman, & Ariel Pakes. 2021. "Artificial Intelligence and Pricing: The Impact of AI-Algorithm Design." National Bureau of Economic Research Working Paper No. 28535. https://papers.ssrn.com/sol3/papers.cfm?abstract_id=3799826.

Asker, John, Chaim Fershtman, & Ariel Pakes. 2022. "Artificial Intelligence, Algorithm Design and Pricing." *AEA Papers and Proceedings*, 112: 452–456.

Aspan, Maria. 2020. "A.I. Is Transforming the Job Interview—And Everything After." *Fortune*, January 20. https://fortune.com/longform/hr-technology-ai-hiring-recruitment/.

Assad, Stephanie, Emilio Calvano, Giacomo Calzolari, Robert Clark, Daniel Ershov, Justin Johnson, Sergio Pastorello, Andrew Rhodes, Lei Xu, et al. 2021. "Autonomous Algorithmic Collusion: Economic Research and Policy Implications." *Oxford Review of Economic Policy*, 37(3): 459–478.

Assad, Stephanie, Robert Clark, Daniel Ershov, & Lei Xu. 2024. "Algorithmic Pricing and Competition: Empirical Evidence from the German Retail Gasoline Market." *Journal of Political Economy*, 132(3): 723–771.

Ayres, Ian, & Quinn Curtis. 2023. *Retirement Guardrails*. Cambridge: Cambridge University Press.

Avery, Mallory, Andreas Leibbrandt, & Joseph Vecci. 2023. "Does Artificial Intelligence Help or Hurt Gender Diversity? Evidence from Two Field Experiments on Recruitment in Tech." Unpublished manuscript, May 11. https://ssrn.com/abstract=4370805.

Ayres, Ian. 2007. "Market Power and Inequality: A Competitive Conduct Standard for Assessing When Disparate Impacts Are Justified." *California Law Review*, 95: 669–720.

Ayres, Ian, Gary Klein, & Jeffrey West. 2017. "The Rise and (Potential) Fall of Disparate Impact Lending Litigation." In *Evidence in Innovation in Housing Law and Policy*, edited by Lee Anne Fennell & Benjamin J. Keys, 231–254. Cambridge: Cambridge University Press.

Ayres, Ian, & Peter Siegelman. 1996. "The Q-Word as Red Herring: Why Disparate Impact Liability Does Not Induce Hiring Quotas." *Texas Law Review*, 74(7): 1487–1526.

Babic, Boris, Sarah Gerke, Theodoros Evgeniou, & I. Glenn Cohen. 2021. "Beware Explanations from AI in Health Care." *Science*, 373(6552): 284–286.

Bach, Sebastian, Alexander Binder, Grégoire Montavon, Frederick Klauschen, Klaus-Robert Müller, & Wojciech Samek. 2015. "On Pixel-wise Explanations for Non-linear Classifier Decisions by Layer-wise Relevance Propagation." *PLoS One*, 10(7): 1–46.

Baillon, Aurélien, Aleli Kraft, Owen O'Donnell, & Kim van Wilgenburg. 2022. "A Behavioral Decomposition of Willingness to Pay for Health Insurance." *Journal of Risk and Uncertainty*, 64(10): 43–87.

Baraniuk, Chris. 2015. "Ashley Madison: 'Suicides' over Website Hack." BBC News, August 24. https://www.bbc.com/news/technology-34044506.

Bar-Gill, Oren. 2012. *Seduction by Contract: Law, Economics, and Psychology in Consumer Markets.* Oxford: Oxford University Press.

Bar-Gill, Oren. 2019. "Algorithmic Price Discrimination When Demand Is a Function of Both Preferences and (Mis)perceptions." *University of Michigan Law Review*, 86(2): 217–254.

Bar-Gill, Oren. 2020. "Consumer Misperceptions in a Hotelling Model: With and without Price Discrimination." *Journal of Institutional and Theoretical Economics*, 176(1): 180–203.

Bar-Gill, Oren. 2021. "Price Discrimination with Consumer Misperception." *Applied Economics Letters*, 28(10): 829–834.

Bar-Gill, Oren, & Omri Ben-Shahar. 2023. "Misprioritized Information: A Theory of Manipulation." *Journal of Legal Studies*, 52(2): 305–344.

Bar-Gill, Oren, & Cass R. Sunstein. Forthcoming. "Consumer Misperceptions and Product Differentiation." *Journal of Risk and Uncertainty.*

Bar-Gill, Oren, Cass R. Sunstein, & Inbal Talgam-Cohen. 2023. "Algorithmic Harm in Consumer Markets." *Journal of Legal Analysis*, 15(1): 1–47.

Barocas, Solon, & Andrew D. Selbst. 2016. "Big Data's Disparate Impact." *California Law Review*, 104(3): 671–732.

Bartlett, Robert, Adair Morse, Richard Stanton, & Nancy Wallace. 2022. "Consumer-Lending Discrimination in the FinTech Era." *Journal of Financial Economics*, 143(1): 30–56.

Belanger, Ashley. 2024. "Air Canada Must Honor Refund Policy Invented by Airline's Chatbot." *Ars Technica*, February 16. https://arstechnica.com/tech-policy/2024/02/air-canada-must-honor-refund-policy-invented-by-airlines-chatbot/.

Benhabib, Jess, Alberto Bisin, & Andrew Schotter. 2010. "Present Bias, Quasi-Hyperbolic Discounting, and Fixed Costs." *Games and Economic Behavior*, 69(2): 205–223.

Benkler, Yochai, Robert Faris, & Hal Roberts. 2018. *Network Propaganda: Manipulation, Disinformation, and Radicalization in American Politics.* New York: Oxford University Press.

Ben-Shahar, Omri, & Ariel Porat. 2021. *Personalized Law: Different Rules for Different People.* Oxford: Oxford University Press.

Ben-Shahar, Omri, & Carl Schneider. 2014. *More Than You Wanted to Know: The Failure of Mandated Disclosure.* Princeton, NJ: Princeton University Press.

Bernhardt, Annette, Linda Kresge, & Reem Suleiman. 2021. "Data and Algorithms at Work: The Case for Workers' Technology Rights." Berkeley Labor Center. https://laborcenter.berkeley.edu/wp-content/uploads/2021/11/Data-and-Algorithms-at-Work.pdf.

Bernheim, B. Douglas. 2016. "The Good, the Bad, and the Ugly: A Unified Approach to Behavioral Welfare Economics." *Journal of Benefit-Cost Analysis*, 7(1): 12–68.

Bernheim, B. Douglas, & Antonio Rangel. 2009. "Beyond Revealed Preference: Choice-Theoretic Foundations for Behavioral Welfare Economics." *Quarterly Journal of Economics*, 124(1): 51–104.

Berthon, Pierre, Leyland Pitt, & Colin Campbell. 2019. "Addictive De-vices: A Public Policy Analysis of Sources and Solutions to Digital Addiction." *Journal of Public Policy & Marketing*, 38(4): 451–468.

Bhutta, Neil, Andreas Fuster, & Aurel Hizmo. 2024. "Paying Too Much? Borrower Sophistication and Overpayment in the US Mortgage Market." FRB of Philadelphia, Working Paper No. 24-11, https://ssrn.com/abstract=4870253.

Biggs, Max, Wei Sun, & Markus Ettl. 2021. "Model Distillation for Revenue Optimization: Interpretable Personalized Pricing." In *Proceedings of 38th International Conference on Machine Learning*, Virtual, July, https://proceedings.mlr.press/v139/biggs21a.html, 1–11.

Björkegren, Daniel, Joshua E. Blumenstock, & Samsun Knight. 2020. "Manipulation-Proof Machine Learning." arXiv, April 9. https://arxiv.org/pdf/2004.03865.pdf.

Blattner, Laura, Scott Nelson, & Jann Spiess. 2021. "Unpacking the Black Box: Regulating Algorithmic Decisions." Unpublished manuscript.

Blattner, Laura, & Jann Spiess. 2022. "Machine Learning Explainability and Fairness: Insights from Consumer Lending." FinRegLab Empirical White Paper, https://finreglab.org/research/machine-learning-explainability-fairness-insights-from-consumer-lending/.

Breiman, Leo. 2001. "Random Forests." *Machine Learning*, 45: 5–32.

Buiten, Miriam, Alexandre de Streel, & Martin Peitz. 2023. "The Law and Economics of AI Liability." *Computer Law & Security Review*, 48: 1–20.

Burke, Robin, Alexander Felfernig, & Mehmet H. Göker. 2011. "Recommender Systems: An Overview." *AI Magazine*, June 6.

Burton, Cédric, Laura De Boel, Christopher Kuner, Anna Pateraki, Sarah Cadiot, & Sára G. Hoffman. 2016. "The Final European Union General Data Protection Regulation." BNA, January 25. http://www.bna.com/final-european-union-n57982067329.

Butaru, Florentin, Qingqing Chen, Brian Clark, Sanmay Das, Andrew W. Lo, & Akhtar Siddique. 2016. "Risk and Risk Management in the Credit Card Industry." *Journal of Banking and Finance*, 72: 218–239.

Cabral, Luís M. B. 2002. *Introduction to Industrial Organization*. Cambridge, MA: MIT Press.

Calo, Ryan. 2014. "Digital Market Manipulation." *George Washington Law Review*, 82(4): 995–1051.

Calvano, Emilio, Giacomo Calzolari, Vincenzo Denicolò, & Sergio Pastorello. 2020. "Artificial Intelligence, Algorithmic Pricing, and Collusion." *American Economic Review*, 110(10): 3267–3297.

Camerer, Colin, Samuel Issacharoff, George Loewenstein, & Ted O'Donoghue. 2003. "Regulation for Conservatives: Behavioral Economics and the Case for Asymmetric Paternalism." *University of Pennsylvania Law Review*, 151(3): 1211–1254.

Carle, Susan. 2011. "A New Look at the History of Title VII Disparate Impact Doctrine." *Florida Law Review*, 63(1): 251–300.

Centers for Medicare & Medicaid Services, 2024. "Hospital Price Transparency." CMS.gov (https://www.cms.gov/priorities/key-initiatives/hospital-price-transparency) (last visited: December 19, 2024).

Chen, Le, Alan Mislove, & Christo Wilson. 2016. "An Empirical Analysis of Algorithmic Pricing on Amazon Marketplace." In *Proceedings of International Conference on World Wide Web (eds. Bourdeau, Jacqueline et al., General Chairs)*, Montréal, Québec, April 11–15, 1339–1349.

Chen, Shuqing, Zhengfeng Guo, & Xinlei Zhao. 2021. "Predicting Mortgage Early Delinquency with Machine Learning Methods." *European Journal of Operational Research*, 290(1): 358–372.

Chen, Yang, Meena Andiappan, Tracey Jenkin, & Anton Ovchinnikov. 2023. "A Manager and an AI Walk into a Bar: Does ChatGPT Make Biased Decisions Like We Do?" Smith School of Business Working Paper, https://papers.ssrn.com/sol3/papers.cfm?abstract_id=4380365.

Cheng, Myra, Esin Durmus, & Dan Jurafsky. 2023. "Marked Personas: Using Natural Language Prompts to Measure Stereotypes in Language Models." *Proceedings of the 61st Annual Meeting of the Association for Computational Linguistics*, 1: 1504–1532.

Cho, Winston. 2024. "Actors Hit AI Startup with Class Action Lawsuit over Voice Theft." *Hollywood Reporter*, May 16. https://www.hollywoodreporter.com/business/business-news/actors-hit-ai-startup-with-class-action-lawsuit-over-voice-theft-1235900689/.

Choi, Dongseong, & Jinwoo Kim. 2004. "Why People Continue to Play Online Games: In Search of Critical Design Factors to Increase Customer Loyalty to Online Contents." *Cyberpsychology & Behavior: The Impact of the Internet, Multimedia and Virtual Reality on Behavior and Society*, 7(1): 11–24.

Chouldechova, Alexandra, & Aaron Roth. 2020. "A Snapshot of the Frontiers of Fairness in Machine Learning." *Communications of the ACM*, May 1. https://cacm.acm.org/research/a-snapshot-of-the-frontiers-of-fairness-in-machine-learning/.

CNNMoney. 2000. "Amazon Pricing Flap." September 28. https://money.cnn.com/2000/09/28/technology/amazon/.

Cohen, Maxime C., Adam N. Elmachtoub, & Xiao Lei. 2022. "Price Discrimination with Fairness Constraints." *Management Science*, 68(12): 8536–8552.

Colker, Ruth. 1986. "Anti-subordination above All: Sex, Race, and Equal Protection." *New York University Law Review*, 61(8): 1003–1066.

Competition & Markets Authority. 2021. "Algorithms: How They Can Reduce Competition and Harm Consumers." January 19. https://www.gov.uk/government/publications/algorithms-how-they-can-reduce-competition-and-harm-consumers/algorithms-how-they-can-reduce-competition-and-harm-consumers.

Consumer Financial Protection Bureau. n.d. "Explore Interest Rates." Accessed June 16, 2024. https://www.consumerfinance.gov/owning-a-home/explore-rates/.

Council of Economic Advisors. 2015. "Big Data and Differential Pricing." February. https://obamawhitehouse.archives.gov/sites/default/files/whitehouse_files/docs/Big_Data_Report_Nonembargo_v2.pdf.

Cowgill, Bo, & Catherine E. Tucker. 2019. "Economics, Fairness, and Algorithmic Bias." Columbia Business School Research Paper. https://papers.ssrn.com/sol3/papers.cfm?abstract_id=3361280.

Dastin, Jeffrey. 2018. "Amazon Scraps Secret AI Recruiting Tool That Showed Bias against Women." Reuters, October 11. https://www.reuters.com/article/us-amazon-com-jobs-automation-insight/amazonscraps-secret-ai-recruiting-tool-that-showed-bias-against-women-idUSKCN1MK08G.

Davidson, Darren. 2017. "Facebook Targets 'Insecure' Young People to Sell Ads." *Australian*, May 1. https://www.theaustralian.com.au/business/media/facebook-targets-insecure-young-people-to-sell-ads/news-story/a89949ad016eee7d7a61c3c30c909fa6.

Davis, Randall, Andrew W. Lo, Sudhanshu Mishra, Arash Nourian, Manish Singh, Nicholas Wu, & Ruixun Zhang. 2022. "Explainable Machine Learning Models of Consumer Credit Risk." MIT Laboratory for Financial Engineering Working Paper, https://papers.ssrn.com/sol3/papers.cfm?abstract_id=4006840.

Debuk. 2015. "The Fembots of Ashley Madison." *Language: A Feminist Guide* (blog), September 12. https://debuk.wordpress.com/2015/09/12/the-fembots-of-ashley-madison/.

Deepbrain AI. n.d. "Deepbrain AI." Accessed June 7, 2024. https://www.deepbrain.io/.

den Boer, Arnoud V., Janusz M. Meylahn, & Maarten Pieter Schinkel. 2022. "Artificial Collusion: Examining Supracompetitive Pricing by Q-Learning Algorithms." Amsterdam Law School Research Paper No. 2022-25. https://ssrn.com/abstract=4213600.

Denham, Hannah. 2020. "Another Fake Video of Pelosi Goes Viral on Facebook." *Washington Post*, August 3. https://www.washingtonpost.com/technology/2020/08/03/nancy-pelosi-fake-video-facebook/.

Department of Treasury, Board of Governors of the Federal Reserve System, Federal Deposit Insurance Corporation, Bureau of Consumer Financial Protection, and National Credit Union Administration. "Request for Information and Comment on Financial Institutions' Use of Artificial Intelligence, Including Machine Learning." *Federal Register* 86, no. 60 (March 31, 2021): 16837. https://www.govinfo.gov/content/pkg/FR-2021-03-31/pdf/2021-06607.pdf.

Digital Competition Expert Panel. 2019. *Unlocking Digital Competition: Report of the Digital Competition Expert Panel.* London: Crown.

Dolan, Paul. 2015. *Happiness by Design: Finding Pleasure and Purpose in Everyday Life.* London: Penguin.

Dooley, Samuel, Tom Goldstein, & John P. Dickerson. 2021. "Robustness Disparities in Commercial Face Detection." arXiv, August 27. https://arxiv.org/pdf/2108.12508.pdf.

Dowling, Katharina, Daniel Guhl, Daniel Klapper, Martin Spann, Lucas Stich, & Narine Yergoryan. 2019. "Behavioral Biases in Marketing." *Journal of the Academy of Marketing Science*, 48: 449–477.

Dreyfus, Suelette, Shanton Chang, & Andrew Clausen. 2020. "Drawing Back the Curtain: Consumer Choice Online in a Data Tracking World." University of Melbourne, December. https://cprc.org.au/wp-content/uploads/2021/11/Phase-2-UoM-Report-Consumer-choice-online-in-a-data-tracking-world-December-2020.pdf.

Dubal, Veena. 2023. "On Algorithmic Wage Discrimination." *Columbia Law Review*, 123(7): 1929–1992.

Dube, Jean-Pierre, & Sanjog Misra. 2023. "Personalized Pricing and Consumer Welfare." *Journal of Political Economy*, 131(1): 131–189.

Duhigg, Charles. 2013. *The Power of Habit.* London: Random House.

Dwork, Cynthia, Moritz Hardt, Toniann Pitassi, Omer Reingold, & Richard Zemel. 2012. "Fairness through Awareness." In *Proceedings of the 3rd Innovations in Theoretical Computer Science Conference (ITCS '12) (ed. Goldwasser, Shafi, Program Chair)*, New York, January, 214–226. https://dl.acm.org/doi/10.1145/2090236.2090255.

Eaton, Kit. 2024. "Google Just Teased a Crazy AI Video Generating Service. Start Thinking of What It Could Do for Your Business." *Inc.*, January 26. https://www.inc.com/kit-eaton/google-just-teased-a-crazy-ai-video-generating-service-start-thinking-of-what-it-could-do-for-your-business.html.

Electronic Frontier Foundation. n.d. "Do Not Track." Accessed June 16, 2024. https://www.eff.org/issues/do-not-track.

Entis, Laura. 2014. "Facebook Gives Advertisers a Way to Target by Relationship Status." NBC News, February 21. https://www.nbcnews.com/id/wbna54457871.

EU Artificial Intelligence Act. 2024. "High-Level Summary of the AI Act." February 27. https://artificialintelligenceact.eu/high-level-summary/.

European Centre for Algorithmic Transparency. n.d. "European Centre for Algorithmic Transparency." Accessed June 13, 2024. https://algorithmic-transparency.ec.europa.eu/index_en.

EyeQ. n.d. "Who We Are." Accessed June 14, 2024. https://eyeq.tech/.

Ezrachi, Ariel, & Maurice E. Stucke. 2016a. "How Pricing Bots Could Form Cartels and Make Things More Expensive." *Harvard Business Review*, October 27. https://hbr.org/2016/10/how-pricing-bots-could-form-cartels-and-make-things-more-expensive.

Ezrachi, Ariel, & Maurice E. Stucke. 2016b. *Virtual Competition: The Promise and Perils of the Algorithm-Driven Economy.* Cambridge, MA: Harvard University Press.

Ezrachi, Ariel, & Maurice E. Stucke. 2017a. "Artificial Intelligence and Collusion: When Computers Inhibit Competition." *University of Illinois Law Review*, 2017(5): 1775–1810.

Ezrachi, Ariel, & Maurice E. Stucke. 2017b. "Two Artificial Neural Networks Meet in an Online Hub and Change the Future (of Competition, Market Dynamics and Society)." Oxford Legal Studies Research Paper No. 24/2017. https://papers.ssrn.com/sol3/papers.cfm?abstract_id=2949434.

Fairplay. n.d. "Fairness Optimizer." Accessed June 17, 2024. https://fairplay.ai/fairness-tools/#fairness-optimizer.

FE Online. 2021. "Google Pay India Users to Start Getting Targeted Ads: Here Is How You Can Opt Out." *Financial Express*, March 12. https://www.financialexpress.com/industry/technology/google-pay-india-users-to-start-getting-targeted-adshere-is-how-you-can-opt-out/2211457/.

Federal Communications Commission. n.d. "Broadband Consumer Labels." Accessed June 17, 2024. https://www.fcc.gov/broadbandlabels.

Federal Trade Commission. 2012. "Protecting Consumer Privacy in an Era of Rapid Change." March. https://www.ftc.gov/reports/protecting-consumer-privacy-era-rapid-change-recommendations-businesses-policymakers.

Federal Trade Commission. 2014. "Data Brokers: A Call for Transparency and Accountability Report." https://www.ftc.gov/system/files/documents/reports/data-brokers-call-transparency-accountability-report-federal-trade-commission-may-2014/140527databrokerreport.pdf.

Federal Trade Commission. 2016. "Big Data: A Tool for Inclusion or Exclusion? Understanding the Issues." January. https://www.ftc.gov/system/files/documents/reports/big-data-tool-inclusion-or-exclusion-understanding-issues/160106big-data-rpt.pdf.

Federal Trade Commission. 2018. "FTC Hearing #7: The Competition and Consumer Protection Issues of Algorithms, Artificial Intelligence, and Predictive Analytics." November 13–14. https://www.ftc.gov/news-events/events/2018/11/ftc-hearing-7-competition-consumer-protection-issues-algorithms-artificial-intelligence-predictive.

Federal Trade Commission. 2021. "FTC to Ramp up Enforcement against Illegal Dark Patterns That Trick or Trap Consumers into Subscriptions." October 28. https://www.ftc.gov/news-events/news/press releases/2021/10/ftc-ramp-enforcement-against-illegal-dark-patterns-trick-or-trap-consumers-subscriptions.

Federal Trade Commission. 2024. "Press Release: FTC Issues Orders to Eight Companies Seeking Information on Surveillance Pricing." July 23. https://www.ftc.gov/news-events/news/press-releases/2024/07/ftc-issues-orders-eight-companies-seeking-information-surveillance-pricing.

Ferrara, Emilio. 2024. "Fairness and Bias in Artificial Intelligence: A Brief Survey of Sources, Impacts, and Mitigation Strategies." *Science*, 6(1): 1–15.

Fiddler. n.d. "Enterprise AI Observability." Accessed June 17, 2024. https://www.fiddler.ai.

Fidelity. n.d. "Fidelity Go." Accessed June 16, 2024. https://www.fidelity.com/managed-accounts/fidelity-go/overview.

Financial Conduct Authority. 2019. "General Insurance Pricing Practices: Interim Report." Financial Conduct Authority Market Study MS18/1.2. https://www.fca.org.uk/publication/market-studies/ms18-1-2-interim-report.pdf.

Fisher, A. J., C. Rudin, & F. Dominici. 2019. "All Models Are Wrong, but Many Are Useful: Learning a Variable's Importance by Studying an Entire Class of Prediction Models Simultaneously." *Journal of Machine Learning Research*, 20(177): 1–81.

Fiss, Owen. 1976. "Groups and the Equal Protection Clause." *Philosophy & Public Affairs*, 5(2): 107–177.

Freeman, Jody. 2000. "The Private Role in Public Governance." *New York University Law Review*, 75(3): 543–675.

Friedman, Barry, Farhang Heydari, Max Isaacs, & Katie Kinsey. 2022. "Policing Police Tech: A Soft Law Solution." *Berkeley Technology Law Journal*, 37(2): 701–756.

Friehe, Tim, & Elisabeth Schulte. 2017. "Uncertain Product Risk, Information Acquisition, and Product Liability." *Economics Letters*, 159: 92–95.

Fung, Archon, & Dara O'Rourke. 2000. "Reinventing Environmental Regulation from the Grassroots Up: Explaining and Expanding the Success of the Toxics Release Inventory." *Environment Management*, 25(2): 115–127.

Gal, Michal S. 2017. "Algorithmic-Facilitated Coordination: Market and Legal Solutions." *CPI Antitrust Chronicles*, May. https://www.competitionpolicyinternational.com/wp-content/uploads/2017/05/CPI-Gal.pdf.

Gal, Michal S. 2019. "Algorithms as Illegal Agreements." *Berkeley Technology Law Journal*, 34(1): 67–118.

Gal, Michal, & Niva Elkin-Corren. 2017. "Algorithmic Consumers." *Harvard Journal of Law & Technology*, 30(2): 309–353.

Gal, Michal, & Daniel L. Rubinfeld. 2024. "Algorithms, AI and Mergers." *Antitrust Law Journal*, 85(3): 683–738.

Gao, Janet, Hanyi Yi, & David Zhang. 2023. "Algorithmic Underwriting in High Risk Mortgage Markets." Unpublished Manuscript, https://ssrn.com/abstract=4602411.

Garden-Monheit, Hannah, & Ken Merber. 2024. "Price Fixing by Algorithm Is Still Price Fixing." Federal Trade Commission. *Federal Trade Commission Business Blog*, March 1. https://www.ftc.gov/business-guidance/blog/2024/03/price-fixing-algorithm-still-price-fixing.

Gillis, Talia. 2022. "The Input Fallacy." *Minnesota Law Review*, 106(3): 1175–1263.

Gillis, Talia. 2024. "'Price Discrimination' Discrimination." Columbia Law School Working Paper, https://papers.ssrn.com/sol3/papers.cfm?abstract_id=4883262.

Gillis, Talia, Vitaly Meursault, & Berk Ustun. 2024. "Operationalizing the Search for Less Discriminatory Alternatives in Fair Lending." Paper presented at ACM Conference on Fairness, Accountability, and Transparency (ACM FAccT '24), Rio de Janeiro, June 3–6.

Gillis, Talia B., & Jann L. Spiess. 2019. "Big Data and Discrimination." *University of Chicago Law Review*, 86(2): 459–488.

Goldin, Jacob. 2015. "Which Way to Nudge? Uncovering Preferences in the Behavioral Age." *Yale Law Journal*, 125(1): 226–270.

Goodman, Bryce, & Seth Flaxman. 2017. "EU Regulations on Algorithmic Decision-Making and a 'Right to Explanation.'" *AI Magazine*, 38(3): 50–57.

Graham, Lindsey, & Elizabeth Warren. 2023. "When It Comes to Big Tech, Enough Is Enough." *New York Times*, July 27. https://www.nytimes.com/2023/07/27/opinion/lindsey-graham-elizabeth-warren-big-tech-regulation.html.

Hacker, Philipp. 2021. "Manipulation by Algorithms: Exploring the Triangle of Unfair Commercial Practice, Data Protection, and Privacy Law." *European Law Journal*, 29(1–2): 142–175.

Hacker, Philipp, & Jan-Hendrik Passoth. 2021. "Varieties of AI Explanations under the Law: From the GDPR to the AIA, and Beyond." In *xxAI—Beyond Explainable AI*, edited by Randy Goebel, Wolfgang Wahlster, & Zhi-Hua Zhou, 343–373. Vienna: Springer.

Hamilton, James T. 2005. *Regulation through Revelation: The Origin, Politics, and Impacts of the Toxics Release Inventory Program*. Cambridge: Cambridge University Press.

Hannak, Aniko, Gary Soeller, David Lazer, Alan Mislove, & Christo Wilson. 2014. "Measuring Price Discrimination and Steering on e-Commerce Web Sites." *IMC '14: Proceedings of the 2014 Conference on Internet Measurement Conference*, 14: 305–318.

Hao, Karen. 2020. "An AI Hiring Firm Says It Can Predict Job Hopping Based on Your Interviews." *MIT Technology Review*, July 24. https://www.technologyreview.com/2020/07/24/1005602/ai-hiring-promises-bias-free-job-hopping-prediction/.

Hardesty, Larry. 2019. "The History of Amazon's Recommendation Algorithm." *Amazon Science* (blog), November 22. https://www.amazon.science/the-history-of-amazons-recommendation-algorithm.

Hasan, Zahid, Daicy Vaz, Vidya S. Athota, Sop Sop Maturin Désiré, & Vijay Pereira. 2023. "Can Artificial Intelligence (AI) Manage Behavioural Biases among Financial Planners?" *Journal of Global Information Management*, 31(2): 1–18.

Hauser, John R., Glen L. Urban, Guilherme Liberali, & Michael Braun. 2009. "Website Morphing." *Marketing Science*, 28(2): 202–223.

Hershfield, Hal. 2011. "Future Self-Continuity: How Conceptions of the Future Self Transform Intertemporal Choice." *Decision Making over the Life Span*, 1235(1): 30–43.

Hinton, Geoffrey, Oriol Vinyals, & Jeff Dean. 2015. "Distilling the Knowledge in a Neural N Network." arXiv, March 9. https://arxiv.org/abs/1503.02531.

Hofmann, Valentin, Pratyusha Ria Kalluri, Dan Jurafsky, & Sharese King. 2024. "Dialect Prejudice Predicts AI Decisions about People's Character, Employability, and Criminality." arXiv, March 1. https://arxiv.org/pdf/2403.00742.pdf.

Hogan, Kevin. 2018. "Consumer Experience in the Retail Renaissance: How Leading Brands Build a Bedrock with Data." *Deloitte Digital*, June 6. https://web.archive.org/web/20220901050739/ https://www.deloittedigital.com/us/en/blog-list/2018/consumer-experience-in-the-retail-renaissance%97how-leading-brand.html.

Holton, Brooks, & David Allen. 2019. "Better Ways to Predict Who's Going to Quit." *Harvard Business Review*, August 16. https://hbr.org/2019/08/better-ways-to-predict-whos-going-to-quit.

Hui, Sam K., J. Jeffrey Inman, Yanliu Huang, & Jacob A. Suher. 2013. "The Effect of In-Store Travel Distance on Unplanned Spending: Applications to Mobile Promotion Strategies." *Journal of Marketing*, 77(2): 1–16.

Humphries, Megan. 2019. "ATPCO Reduces Barrier to Entry for Airlines to Adopt Dynamic Pricing." ATPCO Press Release, October 1. https://perma.cc/AY7G-WPAY.

Huq, Aziz. 2019. "Racial Equity in Algorithmic Criminal Justice." *Duke Law Journal*, 68(6): 1043–1134.

Ipsos, London Economics, & Deloitte Consortium. 2018. "Consumer Market Study on Online Market Segmentation through Personalised Pricing/Offers in the European Union." Request for Specific Services 2016 85 02 for the Implementation of Framework Contract EAHC/2013/CP/04 European Commission Report. Brussels: European Union.

Jackson, Maya C. 2021. "Artificial Intelligence and Algorithmic Bias: The Issues with Technology Reflecting History and Humans." *Journal of Business and Technology Law*, 16(2): 299–316.

Jäger, Simon, Christopher Roth, Nina Roussille, & Benjamin Schoefer. 2023. "Worker Beliefs about Outside Options." National Bureau of Economic Research Working Paper No. 29623. https://www.nber.org/papers/w29623.

Jäger, Simon, Christopher Roth, Nina Roussille, & Benjamin Schoefer. 2024. "Worker Beliefs about Outside Options." *Quarterly Journal of Economics*, no. qjae001 (January): 1–52.

Jin, Yilun, Wenyu Zhang, Xin Wu, Yanan Liu, & Zeqian Hu. 2021. "A Novel Multi-stage Ensemble Model with a Hybrid Genetic Algorithm for Credit Scoring on Imbalanced Data." *IEEE Access*, 9: 143593–143607.

Johnson, Justin P., Andrew Rhodes, & Matthijs Wildenbeest. 2023. "Platform Design When Sellers Use Pricing Algorithms." *Econometrica*, 91(5): 1841–1879.

Kahn, Lina M. 2023. "We Must Regulate A.I.: Here's How." *New York Times*, May 3. https://www.nytimes.com/2023/05/03/opinion/ai-lina-khan-ftc-technology.html.

Kahn-Lang, Jenya. 2022. "Competing for (In)attention: Price Discrimination in Residential Electricity Markets." Energy Institute Working Paper No. 333. https://haas.berkeley.edu/wp-content/uploads/WP333.pdf.

Kamenica, Emir, Sendhil Mullainathan, & Richard Thaler. 2011. "Helping Consumers Know Themselves." *American Economic Review*, 101(3): 417–422.

Kaplow, Louis. 2011. "On the Meaning of Horizontal Agreements in Competition Law." *California Law Review*, 99(3): 683–818.

Kastrenakes, Jacob. 2024. "Scarlett Johansson Told OpenAI Not to Use Her Voice—and She's Not Happy They Might Have Anyway." *Verge*, May 20. https://www.theverge.com/2024/5/20/24161253/scarlett-johansson-openai-altman-legal-action.

Kaye, Danielle, Lauren Hirsch, and David McCabe. 2024. "U.S. Accuses Software Maker RealPage of Enabling Collusion on Rents." *New York Times*, August 23.

Kaye, Kate. 2019. "This Little-Known Facial-Recognition Accuracy Tests Has Big Influence." *IAPP*, January 7. https://iapp.org/news/a/this-little-known-facial-recognition-accuracy-test-has-big-influence.

Kessler, Sarah. 2020. "Companies Are Using Employee Survey Data to Predict—and Squash—Union Organizing." *OneZero* (blog), July 30. https://onezero.medium.com/companies-are-using-employee-survey-data-to-predict-and-squash-union-organizing-a7e28a8c2158.

Keynes, John Maynard. 1921. *A Treatise on Probability*. London: Macmillan.

Kim, Pauline T. 2017. "Data-Driven Discrimination at Work." *William and Mary Law Review*, 58(3): 857–936.

Klein, Timo. 2021. "Autonomous Algorithmic Collusion: Q-Learning under Sequential Pricing." *The RAND Journal of Economics*, 52(3): 538–558.

Kleinberg, Jon, Jens Ludwig, Sendhil Mullainathan, & Cass R. Sunstein. 2018. "Discrimination in the Age of Algorithms." *Journal of Legal Analysis*, 10: 113–174.

Kleinberg, Jon, & Sendhil Mullainathan. 2019. "Simplicity Creates Inequity: Implications for Fairness, Stereotypes, and Interpretability." National Bureau of Economic Research Working Paper No. 25854. https://ideas.repec.org/p/nbr/nberwo/25854.html.

Knight, Frank H. 1933. Risk, Uncertainty and Profit. 1921; London: London School of Economics.

Koo, Ryan, Minhwa Lee, Vipul Raheja, Jong Inn Park, Zae Myung Kim, & Dongyeop Kang. 2023. "Benchmarking Cognitive Biases in Large Language Models as Evaluators." arXiv, September 29. https://minnesotanlp.github.io/cobbler-project-page/.

Kuchler, Theresa, & Michaela Pagel. 2018. "Sticking to Your Plan: The Role of Present Bias for Credit Card Paydown." National Bureau of Economic Research Working Paper No. 24881. https://www.nber.org/system/files/working_papers/w24881/w24881.pdf.

Kvamme, Håvard, Nikolai Sellereite, Kjersti Aas, & Steffen Sjursen. 2018. "Predicting Mortgage Default Using Convolutional Neural Networks." *Expert Systems with Applications*, 102: 207–217.

Langenbucher, Katja C. 2022. "Consumer Credit in the Age of AI—Beyond Anti-discrimination Law." European Corporate Governance Institute—Law Working Paper No. 663/2022, LawFin Working Paper No. 42. https://ssrn.com/abstract=4275723.

Lapuschkin, Sebastian, Stephan Wäldchen, Alexander Binder, Grégoire Montavon, Wojciech Samek, & Klaus-Robert Müller. 2019. "Unmasking Clever Hans Predictors and Assessing What Machines Really Learn." *Nature Communications*, 10(1): 1–10.

Law Commission of Ontario. 2023. "Consumer Protection in the Digital Marketplace: Consultation Paper." Toronto, June. https://www.lco-cdo.org/en/our-current-projects/consumer-protection-in-the-digital-marketplace/.

Lawlor, Mason. 2024. "George Carlin–AI 'Deepfake' Lawsuit Could Set New Standards for Celebrities' Rights of Publicity, Industry Veteran Says." *Law.com*, February 9. https://www.law.com/2024/02/09/george-carlin-ai-deepfake-lawsuit-could-set-new-standards-for-celebrities-rights-of-publicity-industry-veteran-says/.

Lessmann, Stefan, Bart Baesens, Hsin-Vonn Seow, & Lyn C. Thomas. 2015. "Benchmarking State-of-the-Art Classification Algorithms for Credit Scoring: An Update of Research." *European Journal of Operation Research*, 247(1): 124–136.

Levin, Sam. 2017. "Facebook Told Advertisers It Can Identify Teens Feeling 'Insecure' and 'Worthless.'" *Guardian*, May 1. https://www.theguardian.com/technology/2017/may/01/facebook-advertising-data-insecure-teens.

Lim, Weng Marc, Satish Kumar, Sanjeev Verma, & Rijul Chaturvedi. 2022. "Alexa, What Do We Know about Conversational Commerce? Insights from a Systematic Literature Review." *Psychology & Marketing*, 39(6): 1129–1155.

Lippi, Marco, Giuseppe Contissa, Agnieszka Jablonowska, Francesca Lagioia, Hans-Wolfgang Micklitz, Przemyslaw Palka, Giovanni Sartor, & Paolo Torroni. 2020. "The Force Awakens: Artificial Intelligence for Consumer Law." *Journal of Artificial Intelligence Research*, 67: 169–190.

Liu, Jennifer. 2019. "This Algorithm Can Predict When Workers Are About to Quit—Here's How." *CNBC MakeIt*, September 10. https://www.cnbc.com/2019/09/10/this-algorithm-can-predict-when-workers-are-about-to-quitheres-how.html.

Ludwig, Jens, Sendhil Mullainathan, & Ashesh Rambachan. 2024. "The Unreasonable Effectiveness of Algorithms." National Bureau of Economic Research Working Paper No. 32125. http://www.nber.org/papers/w32125.

Luguri, Jamie, & Lior Jacob Strahilevitz. 2021. "Shining a Light on Dark Patterns." *Journal of Legal Analysis*, 13(1): 43–109.

Lundberg, Scott, & Su-In Lee. 2017. "A Unified Approach to Interpreting Model Predictions." *Advances in Neural Information Processing Systems*, 30: 1–10.

Ma, Xiaojun, Jinaln Sha, Dehua Wang, Yuanbo Yu, Qian Yang, & Xueqi Niu. 2018. "Study on a Prediction of p2p Network Loan Default Based on the Machine Learning Lightgbm and Xgboost Algorithms according to Different High Dimensional Data Cleaning." *Electronic Commerce Research and Applications*, 31: 24–39.

Mahdawi, Arwa. 2018. "Is Your Friend Getting a Cheaper Uber Fare Than You Are?" *Guardian*, April 13. https://www.theguardian.com/commentisfree/2018/apr/13/uber-lyft-prices-personalized-data.

MarketsandMarkets. 2024. "Conversational AI Market by Component (Platform and Services), Type (IVA and Chatbots), Technology, Application (Customer Support, Personal Assistant, and Customer Engagement and Retention), Deployment Mode, Vertical, and Region: Global Forecast to 2024." April. https://www.marketsandmarkets.com/Market-Reports/conversational-ai-market49043506.html.

Martin, Kirsten. 2016. "Data Aggregators, Consumer Data, and Responsibility Online: Who Is Tracking Consumers Online and Should They Stop?" *Information Society*, 32(1): 51–63.

Mas-Colell, Andreu, Michael D. Whinston, & Jerry R. Green. 2012. *Microeconomic Theory*. 4th edition. Oxford: Oxford University Press.

Matz, S. C., M. Kosinski, G. Nave, & D. J. Stillwell. 2017. "Psychological Targeting as an Effective Approach to Digital Mass Persuasion." *Proceedings of the National Academy of Sciences*, 114(48): 12714–12719.

Mauring, Eeva. 2022. "Search and Price Discrimination Online." CEPR Discussion Paper No. 15729. Paris: CEPR Press.

Mayson, Sandra G. 2019. "Bias In, Bias Out." *Yale Law Journal*, 128(8): 2218–2300.

McCarthy, Paul X. 2019. "Conversational AI—A New Wave of Voice-Enabled Computing." *Forbes*, December 19. https://www.forbes.com/sites/paulxmccarthy/2019/12/17/conversationalai—a-new-wave-of-voice-enabled-computing/#f90e51b1a109.

McPhate, Mike. 2016. "Ashley Madison Faces F.T.C. Inquiry amid Rebranding." *New York Times*, July 5. https://www.nytimes.com/2016/07/06/business/ashley-madison-ftc-rebranding.html.

Mehra, Salil K. 2016. "Antitrust and the Robo-Seller: Competition in the Time of Algorithms." *Minnesota Law Review*, 100(4): 1323–1375.

Mehrabi, Ninareh, Fred Morstatter, Nripsuta Saxena, Kristina Lerman, & Aram Galstyan. 2021. "A Survey on Bias and Fairness in Machine Learning." *ACM Computing Surveys*, 54(6): 1–35.

Meier, Stephan, & Charles Sprenger. 2010. "Present-Biased Preferences and Credit Card Borrowing." *American Economic Journal: Applied Economics*, 2(1): 193–210.

Mikians, Jakub, László Gyarmati, Vijay Erramilli, & Nikolaos Laoutaris. 2012. "Detecting Price and Search Discrimination on the Internet." *Proceedings of ACM Workshop on Hot Topics in Networks*, 11: 79–84.

Milgrom, Paul R., & Steven Tadelis. 2018. "How Artificial Intelligence and Machine Learning Can Impact Market Design." National Bureau of Economic Research Working Paper No. 24282. https://www.nber.org/system/files/working_papers/w24282/w24282.pdf.

Miller, Tim. 2019. "Explanation in Artificial Intelligence: Insights from the Social Sciences." *Artificial Intelligence*, 267: 1–38.

Miller, Tim. 2021. "Contrastive Explanation: A Structural-Model Approach." *Knowledge Engineering Review*, 36: 1–22.

Molnar, Christoph. 2024. "Interpretable Machine Learning: A Guide for Making Black Box Models Explainable." Independently published, May 26. https://christophm.github.io/interpretable-ml-book/.

Mundt, Andreas. 2020. "Algorithms and Competition in a Digitalized World." *Competition Policy International*, July 13. https://www.competitionpolicyinternational.com/algorithms-and-competition-in-a-digitalized-world/.

Nadler, Anthony, & Lee McGuigan. 2018. "An Impulse to Exploit: The Behavioral Turn in Data-Driven Marketing." *Critical Studies in Media Communication*, 35(2): 151–165.

Nalebuff, Barry. 2009. "Price Discrimination and Welfare." *Competition Policy International*, 5(2): 221–241.

National Institute of Standards and Technology. 2024. "Face Recognition Technology Evaluation (FRTE) 1:N Identification." May 30. https://pages.nist.gov/frvt/html/frvt1N.html.

Netflix Research. n.d. "Recommendations." Accessed June 13, 2024. https://research.netflix.com/research-area/recommendations.

Newitz, Annalee. 2015. "How Ashley Madison Hid Its Fembot Con from Users and Investigators." *Gizmodo*, September 8. https://gizmodo.com/how-ashley-madison-hid-its-fembot-con-from-users-and-in-1728410265.

Newitz, Annalee. 2016. "Ashley Madison Admits Using Fembots to Lure Men into Spending Money." *Ars Technica*, July 8. https://arstechnica.com/tech-policy/2016/07/ashley-madison-admits-using-fembots-to-lure-men-into-spending-money/.

Obermeyer, Ziad, Brian Powers, Christine Vogeli, & Sendhil Mullainathan. 2019. "Dissecting Racial Bias in an Algorithm Used to Manage the Health of Populations." *Science*, 366(6464): 447–453.

Occupational Safety and Health Administration. n.d. "Hazard Communication." Accessed June 17, 2024. https://www.osha.gov/hazcom.

O'Donoghue, Ted, & Matthew Rabin. 2015. "Present Bias: Lessons Learned and to Be Learned." *American Economic Review*, 105(5): 273–279.

OECD Directorate for Financial and Enterprise Affairs Competition Committee. 2018. "Personalised Pricing in the Digital Era—Note by the United States." https://www.ftc.gov/system/files/attachments/us-submissions-oecd-2010-present-other-international-competition-fora/personalized_pricing_note_by_the_united_states.pdf.

Office of Management and Budget. 2022. "Memorandum for the Heads of Executive Departments and Agencies: Guidance for Regulation of Artificial Intelligence Applications." November 16. https://www.whitehouse.gov/wp-content/uploads/2020/11/M-21-06.pdf.

Oishi, Shigehiro, & Erin C. Westgate. 2022. "A Psychologically Rich Life: Beyond Happiness and Meaning." *Psychological Review* 129: 790–811.

OneSpace. n.d. "Alexa Voice Shopping and Amazon Content: A Primer for Brands." Accessed August 15, 2022. https://perma.cc/7AXE-92XL.

Opedal, Andreas, Alessandro Stolfo, Haruki Shirakami, Ying Jiao, Ryan Cotterel, Bernhard Schölkopf, Abulhair Saparov, & Mrinmaya Sachan. 2024. "Do Language Models Exhibit the Same Cognitive Biases in Problem Solving as Human Learners?" arXiv, June 17. https://arxiv.org/abs/2401.18070.

OpenAI. n.d. "Creating Video from Text." Accessed June 7, 2024. https://openai.com/index/sora/.

Organisation for Economic Co-operation and Development. 2017. "Algorithms and Collusion: Competition Policy in the Digital Age." https://web-archive.oecd.org/2019-02-17/449397-Algorithms-and-colllusion-competition-policy-in-the-digital-age.pdf.

Orwell, George. 1949. *1984*. London: Penguin.

Park, Joon Sung, Joseph C. O'Brien, Carrie J. Cai, Meredith Ringel Morris, Percy Liang, & Michael S. Bernstein. 2023. "Generative Agents: Interactive Simulacra of Human Behavior." arXiv, April 7. https://arxiv.org/abs/2304.03442.

Parker, Will. 2024. "Alleged Rent-Fixing of Apartments Nationwide Draws More Legal Scrutiny." *Wall Street Journal*, April 15. https://www.wsj.com/us-news/law/apartment-rent-fixing-drawing-nationwide-legal-scrutiny-8b2867ab.

Paterson, Jeannie Marie, Shanton Chang, Marc Cheong, & Chris Culnane. 2021. "The Hidden Harms of Targeted Advertising." *International Journal of Consumer Law and Practice*, 9: 1–17.

Perry, Pamela. 1991. "The Two Faces of Disparate Impact Discrimination." *Fordham Law Review*, 59(4): 523–595.

Peterson, Barbara. 2019. "Airline Dynamic Pricing Getting Closer to Reality, Says ATPCO." *Travel Market Report*, October 1. https://www.travelmarketreport.com/articles/Airline-Dynamic-Pricing-Getting-Closer-to-Reality-Says-ATPCO.

Porat, Ariel, & Lior J. Strahilevitz. 2014. "Personalizing Default Rules and Disclosure with Big Data." *Michigan Law Review*, 112(8): 1417–1478.

Porat, Haggai. 2022. "Consumer Protection and Disclosure Rules in the Age of Algorithmic Behavior-Based Pricing." Unpublished manuscript. On file with author.

Poritz, Isaiah. 2023. "AI Face Swap App Fails to Escape TV Celebrity's Publicity Suit." *Bloomberg Law*, September 6. https://news.bloomberglaw.com/ip-law/ai-face-swap-app-fails-to-escape-tv-celebritys-publicity-suit.

Posner, Nathaniel, Andrey Simonov, Kellen Mrkva, & Eric J. Johnson. 2023. "Dark Defaults: How Choice Architecture Steers Political Campaign Donations." *Proceedings of the National Academy of Sciences*, 120(40): 1–6.

Purina. n.d. "Welcome to the Purina Dog Breed Selector." Accessed June 16, 2024. https://www.purina.co.uk/find-a-pet/dog-breeds/breed-selector.

Rambachan, Ashesh, Jon Kleinberg, Sendhil Mullainathan, & Jens Ludwig. 2021. "An Economic Approach to Regulating Algorithms." National Bureau of Economic Research Working Paper No. 27111. https://www.nber.org/papers/w27111.

Rathi, Shubham. 2019. "Generating Counterfactual and Contrastive Explanations Using SHAP." Paper presented at 2nd Workshop on Humanizing AI (HAI) at IJCAI'19, Macao, China, August 10–12. https://arxiv.org/abs/1906.09293.

Reimers, Imke, & Benjamin R. Shiller. 2019. "The Impacts of Telematics on Competition and Consumer Behavior in Insurance." *Journal of Law & Economics*, 62(4): 613–632.

Rhodes, Andrew, & Jidong Zhou. 2024. "Personalized Pricing and Competition." *American Economic Review*, 114(7): 2141–2170. https://ssrn.com/abstract=4103763.

Ribeiro, Marco Tulio, Sameer Singh, & Carlos Guestrin. 2016. "Why Should I Trust You? Explaining the Predictions of Any Classifier." Paper presented at Proceedings of the 22nd ACM SIG KDD International Conference on Knowledge Discovery and Data Mining, San Francisco, CA, August 13–17, 1135–1144.

Rieke, Aaron, & Miranda Bogen. 2018. "Help Wanted: An Examination of Hiring Algorithms, Equity, and Bias." UpTurn, December. https://www.upturn.org/static/reports/2018/hiring-algorithms/files/Upturn%20—%20Help%20Wanted%20-%20An%20Exploration%20of%20Hiring%20Algorithms,%20Equity%20and%20Bias.pdf.

Rosen, Rebecca J. 2013. "Is This the Grossest Advertising Strategy of All Time?" *Atlantic*, October 3. https://www.theatlantic.com/technology/archive/2013/10/is-this-the-grossest-advertising-strategy-of-all-time/280242/.

Rossi, Peter, Robert E. McCulloch, & Greg M. Allenby 1996. "The Value of Purchase History Data in Target Marketing." *Marketing Science*, 15(4): 321–340.

Rudin, Cynthia. 2019. "Stop Explaining Black Box Machine Learning Models for High Stakes Decisions and Use Interpretable Models Instead." *Nature Machine Intelligence*, 1(5): 206–215.

Rutherglen, George. 2006. "Disparate Impact, Discrimination, and the Essentially Contested Concept of Equality." *Fordham Law Review*, 74(4): 2313–2338.

Salvi, Francesco, Manoel Horta Ribeiro, Riccardo Gallotti, & Robert West. 2024. "On the Conversational Persuasiveness of Large Language Models: A Randomized Controlled Trial." Unpublished Manuscript, https://www.researchgate.net/publication/381186642_On_the_Conversational_Persuasiveness_of_Large_Language_Models_A_Randomized_Controlled_Trial.

Sarin, Natasha. 2019. "Making Consumer Finance Work." *Columbia Law Review*, 119(6): 1519–1596.

Schanke, Scott, Gordon Burtch, & Gautam Ray. 2021. "Estimating the Impact of 'Humanizing' Customer Service Chatbots." *Information Systems Research*, 32(3): 736–751.

Schleich, Joachim, Xavier Gassmann, Thomas Meissner, & Corinne Faure. 2019. "A Large Scale Test of the Effects of Time Discounting, Risk Aversion, Loss Aversion, and Present Bias on Household Adoption of Energy-Efficient Technologies." *Energy Economics*, 80: 377–393.

Schwalbe, Ulrich. 2019. "Algorithms, Machine Learning, and Collusion." *Journal of Competition Law &* Economics, 14(4): 568–607.

Seeger, Anna-Maria, Jella Pfeiffer, & Armin Heinzl. 2021. "Texting with Humanlike Conversational Agents: Designing for Anthropomorphism." *Journal of the Association for Information Systems*, 22(4): 931–967.

Seitz-Wald, Alex. 2024. "Political Consultant Who Admitted Deepfaking Biden's Voice Is Indicted, Fined $6 Million." NBC News, May 22. https://www.nbcnews.com/politics/politics-news/steve-kramer-admitted-deepfaking-bidens-voice-new-hampshire-primary-rcna153626.

Selbst, Andrew, & Solon Borocas. 2023. "Unfair Artificial Intelligence: How FTC Intervention Can Overcome the Limitations of Discrimination Law." *University of Pennsylvania Law Review*, 171(4): 1023–1093.

Shankland, Tom, director. 2016. *House of Cards.* Season 4, Episode 7, "Chapter 46." Writing credits to Michael Dobbs, Andrew Davies, Beau Willimon, Bill Kennedy, & Laura Eason, featuring Kevin Spacey, Robin Wright, & Constance Zimmer. Aired March 4, 2016. Netflix.

Sharkey, Catherine M. 2022. "Products Liability in the Digital Age: Online Platforms as 'Cheapest Cost Avoiders.'" *Hastings Law Journal*, 73(5): 1327–1352.

Sharkey, Catherine M. 2024. "A Products Liability Framework for AI." *Columbia Science and Technology Law Review*, 25(2): 21–41.

Shchory, Noga Blickstein, & Michal S. Gal. 2022. "Voice Shoppers: From Information Gaps to Choice Gaps in Consumer Markets." *Brooklyn Law Review*, 88(3): 111–162.

Shedletzky, Chen Elyashar, Inbal Yahav, & Sagit Bar-Gill. 2023. "Should a Chatbot Show It Cares? Toward Optimal Design of Chatbot Personality via Emotion Recognition and Sentiment Analysis." Tel Aviv University Working Paper. https://ssrn.com/abstract=4487314.

Shiller, Benjamin R. 2020. "Approximating Purchase Propensities and Reservation Prices from Broad Consumer Tracking." *International Economy Review*, 61(2): 847–870.

Singer, Natasha. 2013. "Data Protection Laws, an Ocean Apart." *New York Times*, February 3. http://www.nytimes.com/2013/02/03/technology/consumer-data-protection-laws-an-ocean-apart.html.

Singer, Natasha. 2016. "Why a Push for Online Privacy Is Bogged Down in Washington." *New York Times*, February 29. https://www.nytimes.com/2016/02/29/technology/obamas-effort-on-consumer-privacy-falls-short-critics-say.html.

Skrovan, Sandy. 2017. "Kroger's Analytics and Personalized Pricing Keep It a Step Ahead of Its Competitors." *Grocery Dive*, July 10. https://www.grocerydive.com/news/grocery—krogers-analytics-and-personalized-pricing-keep-it-a-step-ahead-of-its-comp/534926/.

Slack, Dylan, Sophie Hilgard, Emily Jia, Sameer Singh, & Himabindu Lakkaraju. 2020. "Fooling LIME and SHAP: Adversarial Attacks on Post Hoc Explanation Methods." Paper presented at Proceedings of the AAAI/ACM Conference on AI, Ethics, and Society, New York, February, 180–186.

Slaughter, Rebecca Kelly. 2021. "Algorithms and Economic Justice: A Taxonomy of Harms and a Path Forward for the Federal Trade Commission." *Yale Journal of Law and Technology*, 23(S1): 1–59.

Smith, Andrew. 2020. "Using Artificial Intelligence and Algorithms: Federal Trade Commission." *Federal Trade Commission Business Blog*, April 8. https://www.ftc.gov/business-guidance/blog/2020/04/using-artificial-intelligence-algorithms.

SolasAI. n.d. "SolasAI." Accessed June 17, 2024. https://solas.ai.

Spherical Insights LLP. 2024. "Global Chatbot Market Size to Exceed USD 42.83 Billion by 2033: CAGR of 23.03%." *GlobeNewswire*, March 13. https://www.globenewswire.com/news-release/2024/03/13/2845189/0/en/Global-Chatbot-Market-Size-To-Exceed-USD-42-83-Billion-By-2033-CAGR-of-23-03.html.

Steele, Chandra. 2022. "The Best Price-Comparison Apps for Shopping." *PC Magazine*, November 12. https://www.pcmag.com/picks/best-price-comparison-apps-for-shopping.

Stigler, George J. 1964. "Theory of Oligopoly." *Journal of Political Economy*, 72(1): 44–61.

Stole, Lars A. 2007. "Price Discrimination and Competition." In *Handbook of Industrial Organization*, edited by Mark Armstrong & Robert H. Porter, 2221–2299. Amsterdam: North Holland Publishing.

Stratyfy. n.d. "Our Mission." Accessed June 17, 2024. https://stratyfy.com/credit-risk-assessment/.

Strauss, David A. 1989. "Discriminatory Intent and the Taming of Brown." *University of Chicago Law Review*, 56(3): 935–1015.

Stucke, Maurice, & Ariel Ezrachi. 2017. "How Digital Assistants Can Harm Our Economy, Privacy, and Democracy." *Berkeley Technology Law Journal*, 32(3): 1239–1299.

Subramanian, Shivaram, Wei Sun, Youssef Drissi, & Markus Ettl. 2022. "Constrained Prescriptive Trees via Column Generation." Paper presented at Proceedings of the 36th AAAI Conference on Artificial Intelligence, Palo Alto, CA, February–March, 4602–4610.

Sunstein, Cass R. 1993. "The Anticaste Principle." *Michigan Law Review*, 92(z8): 2414–2455.

Sunstein, Cass R. 2020. *Too Much Information*. Cambridge, MA: MIT Press.

Sunstein, Cass R. 2024. "Choice Engines and Paternalistic AI." *Humanities and Social Sciences Communications*, 11: 888–891.

Sunstein, Cass R., & Richard H. Thaler. 2008. *Nudge: Improving Decisions about Health, Wealth, and Happiness*. New York: Penguin Books.

Teachout, Zephyr. 2023. "Algorithmic Personalized Wages." *Politics & Society*, 51(3): 436–458.

Thisse, Jacques-Francois, & Xavier Vives. 1988. "On the Strategic Choice of Spatial Price Policy." *American Economic Review*, 78(1): 122–137.

Thomas, Lyn C. 2009. *Consumer Credit Models: Pricing, Profit and Portfolios*. Oxford: Oxford University Press.

Thomas, Sal. 2014. "Does Dynamic Pricing Risk Turning Personalisation into Discrimination?" *Campaign*, October 22. https://www.campaignlive.co.uk/article/does-dynamic-pricing-risk-turning-personalisation-discrimination/1317995.

Thompson, Stuart. 2019. "These Ads Think They Know You." *New York Times*, April 30. https://www.nytimes.com/interactive/2019/04/30/opinion/privacy-targetedadvertising.html.

Tiku, Nitasha. 2017. "Get Ready for the Next Big Privacy Backlash against Facebook." *Wired*, May 1. https://www.wired.com/2017/05/welcome-next-phase-facebook-backlash/.

Tirole, Jean. 1988. *Theory of Industrial Organization*. Cambridge, MA: MIT Press.

Tobin, Meaghan. 2023. "China Announces Rules to Keep AI Bound by 'Core Socialist Values.'" *Washington Post*, July 14. https://www.washingtonpost.com/world/2023/07/14/china-ai-regulations-chatgpt-socialist/.

U.S. Department of Transportation. 2019. "Press Release: EPA, Dot Unveil the Next Generation of Fuel Economy Labels." August 1. https://www.transportation.gov/briefing-room/epa-dot-unveil-next-generation-fuel-economy-labels.

U.S. Food and Drug Administration. n.d. "The Nutrition Facts Label." Accessed June 17, 2024. https://www.fda.gov/food/nutrition-education-resources-materials/nutrition-facts-label.

Valentino-DeVries, Jennifer, Jeremy Singer-Vine, & Ashkan Soltani. 2012. "Websites Vary Prices, Deals Based on Users' Information." *Wall Street Journal*, December 24. https://www.wsj.com/articles/SB10001424127887323777204578189391813881534.

Van Loo, Rory. 2015. "Helping Buyers Beware: The Need for Supervision of Big Retail." *University of Pennsylvania Law Review*, 163(5): 1311–1392.

Van Loo, Rory. 2017. "Rise of the Digital Regulator." *Duke Law Journal*, 66(2): 1267–1329.

Van Loo, Rory. 2019a. "Digital Market Perfection." *Michigan Law Review*, 117(5): 815–883.

Van Loo, Rory. 2019b. "The Missing Regulatory State: Monitoring Businesses in an Age of Surveillance." *Vanderbilt Law Review*, 72(5) 1563–1631.

Varian, Hal R. 2010. *Intermediate Microeconomics: A Modern Approach*. 8th edition. New York: W. W. Norton.

Verma, Pranshu, & Cat Zakrzewski. 2024. "AI Deepfakes Threaten to Upend Global Elections. No One Can Stop Them." *Washington Post*, April 23. https://www.washingtonpost.com/technology/2024/04/23/ai-deepfake-election-2024-us-india/.

Vladeck, David C. 2014. "Digital Marketing, Consumer Protection, and the First Amendment: A Brief Reply to Professor Ryan Calo." *George Washington University Law Review*, 82: 159–173.

Vogel, Heather. 2022. "Rent Going Up? One Company's Algorithm Could Be Why." *ProPublica*, October 15. https://www.propublica.org/article/yieldstar-rent-increase-realpage-rent.

Wachter, Sandra, Brent Mittelstadt, & Chris Russell. 2018. "Counterfactual Explanations without Opening the Black Box: Automated Decisions and the GDPR." *Harvard Journal of Law & Technology*, 31(2): 841–888.

Wagner, Gerhard, & Horst Eidenmüller. 2019. "Down by Algorithms? Siphoning Rents, Exploiting Biases, and Shaping Preferences: Regulating the Dark Side of Personalized Transactions." *University of Chicago Law Review*, 86(2): 581–609.

Wallheimer, Brian. 2018. "Are You Ready for Personalized Pricing? Companies Are Figuring Out What Individual Customers Will Pay—and Charging Accordingly." *Chicago Booth Review*, February 26. https://www.chicagobooth.edu/review/are-you-ready-personalized-pricing.

Wang, David, & Larry Adams. 2017. "Start Shopping with the Google Assistant on Google Home." *Google: The Keyword* (blog), February 16. https://blog.google/products/home/start-shopping-google-assistant-google-home/.

Wang, Yang, & Frank Sloan. 2018. "Present Bias and Health." *Journal of Risk and Uncertainty*, 57(2): 177–198.

Weber, Lauren. 2024. "New York City Passed an AI Hiring Law. So Far, Few Companies Are Following It." *Wall Street Journal*, January 22. https://www.wsj.com/business/new-york-city-passed-an-ai-hiring-law-so-far-few-companies-are-following-it-7e31a5b7.

Werthschulte, Madeline, & Andreas Loschel. 2021. "On the Role of Present Bias and Biased Price Beliefs in Household Energy Consumption." *Journal of Environmental Economics and Management* 109: 1–17.

West, Sarah Myers, Meredith Whittaker, & Kate Crawford. 2019. "Discriminating Systems: Gender, Race and Power in AI." AI Now Institute, April 1. https://ainowinstitute.org/publication/discriminating-systems-gender-race-and-power-in-ai-2.

White House. 2023. "Fact Sheet: President Biden Issues Executive Order on Safe, Secure, and Trustworthy Artificial Intelligence." October 30. https://www.whitehouse.gov/briefing-room/statements-releases/2023/10/30/fact-sheet-president-biden-issues-executive-order-on-safe-secure-and-trustworthy-artificial-intelligence/.

Willis, Lauren E. 2020. "Deception by Design." *Harvard Journal of Law and Technology*, 34(1): 115–190.

Wisser, Leah. 2019. "Pandora's Algorithmic Black Box: The Challenges of Using Algorithmic Risk Assessments in Sentencing." *American Criminal Law Review*, 56(4): 1811–1832.

Yang, Kai Hao. 2022. "Selling Consumer Data for Profit: Optimal Market-Segmentation Design and Its Consequences." *American Economic Review*, 112(4): 1364–1393.

Yang, Lavender, Nicholas Z. Muller, & Pierre Jinghong Liang. 2021. "The Real Effects of Mandatory CSR Disclosure on Emissions: Evidence from the Greenhouse Gas Reporting Program." National Bureau of Economic Research Working Paper No. 28984. https://www.nber.org/system/files/working_papers/w28984/w28984.pdf.

Yang, Yifan, Xiaoyu Liu, Qiao Jin, Furong Huang, & Zhiyong Lu. 2024. "Unmasking and Quantifying Racial Bias of Large Language Models in Medical Report Generation." arXiv, January 25. https://arxiv.org/abs/2401.13867.

Yap, Bee Wah, Seng-Huat Ong, & Nor Huselina Mohamed Husain. 2011. "Using Data Mining to Improve Assessment of Credit Worthiness via Credit Scoring Models." *Expert System with Applications*, 38(10): 13274–13283.

Zarya, Valentina. 2016. "Employers Are Quietly Using Big Data to Track Employee Pregnancies." *Fortune*, February 18. https://fortune.com/2016/02/17/castlight-pregnancy-data/.

Index

For the benefit of digital users, indexed terms that span two pages (e.g., 52–53) may, on occasion, appear on only one of those pages.